Rick Steves'
LONDON
2000

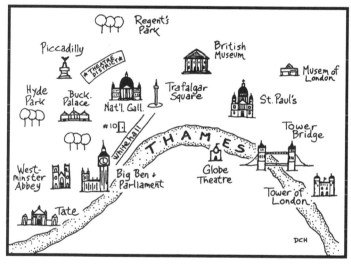

by Rick Steves
and Gene Openshaw

John Muir Publications
Santa Fe, New Mexico

Other JMP travel guidebooks by Rick Steves
Europe 101: History and Art for the Traveler (with Gene Openshaw)
Rick Steves' Europe Through the Back Door
Rick Steves' Mona Winks (with Gene Openshaw)
Rick Steves' Best of Europe
Rick Steves' France, Belgium & the Netherlands (with Steve Smith)
Rick Steves' Germany, Austria & Switzerland
Rick Steves' Great Britain & Ireland
Rick Steves' Italy
Rick Steves' Paris (with Steve Smith and Gene Openshaw)
Rick Steves' Postcards from Europe
Rick Steves' Rome (with Gene Openshaw)
Rick Steves' Scandinavia
Rick Steves' Spain & Portugal
Asia Through the Back Door (with Bob Effertz)
Rick Steves' Phrase Books: German, Italian, French, Spanish/Portuguese, and
    French/Italian/German

John Muir Publications, P.O. Box 613, Santa Fe, NM 87504
Copyright © 2000, 1999 by Europe Through the Back Door, Inc.
Cover copyright © 2000, 1999 by John Muir Publications
All rights reserved.

Printed in the United States of America. Second printing May 2000.

Portions of this book were originally published in *Rick Steves' Mona Winks* © 1998,
1996, 1993, 1988 by Rick Steves and Gene Openshaw and in *Rick Steves' France,
Belgium & the Netherlands* © 2000, 1999, 1998, 1997, 1996 by Rick Steves and
Steve Smith.

ISBN 1-56261-523-8
ISSN 1522-3280

For the latest on Rick's lectures, books, tours, and television series, contact Europe
Through the Back Door, Box 2009, Edmonds, WA 98020, tel. 425/771-8303, fax
425/771-0833, www.ricksteves.com, or e-mail: rick@ricksteves.com.

Europe Through the Back Door Editor: Risa Laib
John Muir Publications Editors: Laurel Gladden Gillespie, Krista Lyons-Gould,
    Chris Hayhurst
Production & Typesetting: Kathleen Sparkes, White Hart Design
Cover and Interior Design: Janine Lehmann
Maps: David C. Hoerlein
Photography: p. 26: Leo de Wys Inc./Steve Vidler; p. 51: Leo de Wys Inc./
    Sylvain Grandadam; p. 171: Leo de Wys Inc./TPL; all others: Rick Steves
Printer: Publishers Press
Cover Photo: Big Ben; London, England; Leo de Wys Inc./Dave & Les Jacobs

Paris chapter coauthored with Steve Smith, excerpted from *Rick Steves' France,
Belgium & the Netherlands 2000*.

Distributed to the book trade by Publishers Group West, Berkeley, California

CONTENTS
london

INTRODUCTION

Blow through the city on the open deck of a double-decker orientation tour bus and take a pinch-me-I'm-in-Britain walk through the West End. Ogle the crown jewels at the Tower of London, hear the chimes of Big Ben, and see the Houses of Parliament in action. Hobnob with the tombstones in Westminster Abbey, duck WWII bombs in Churchill's underground Cabinet War Rooms, and stand in awe over the original Magna Carta at the British Library. Overfeed the pigeons at Trafalgar Square. Cruise the Thames River. Visit with Leonardo, Botticelli, and Rembrandt in the National Gallery. Whisper across the dome of St. Paul's Cathedral and rummage through our civilization's attic at the British Museum. And sip your tea with pinky raised and clotted cream all over your scone. With Greenwich just downstream and millennium activities everywhere, London is a great getaway in 2000.

You'll enjoy some of Europe's best people watching at Covent Garden and snap to at Buckingham Palace's Changing of the Guard. Just sit in Victoria Station, Piccadilly Circus, or a major tube station and observe. Spend one evening at a theater and the others catching your breath.

London is more than its museums and landmarks. It's a living, breathing, thriving organism... a coral reef of humanity. The city has changed dramatically in recent years, and many visitors are surprised to find how "un-English" it is. Whites are now a minority in major parts of the city that once symbolized white imperialism. Arabs have nearly bought out the area north of Hyde Park. Chinese take-outs outnumber fish-and-chips shops. Many hotels are run by people with foreign accents (who hire English chambermaids), while outlying suburbs are home to huge communities of Indians and Pakistanis. London is learning—sometimes fitfully—to live as a microcosm of its formerly vast empire. With the English Channel Tunnel complete and union with Europe inevitable, many locals see even more holes in their bastion of Britishness.

This Information Is Accurate and Up-to-Date

This book is updated every year. Most publishers of guidebooks that cover a city from top to bottom can afford an update only every two or three years. Since this book is selective, covering only the places I think make the top week or so in and around London, I can update it each summer. Even with an annual update, things change. But if you're traveling with the current edition of this book, I guarantee you're using the most up-to-date information available. This book will help you have an inexpensive, hassle-free trip. Use this year's edition. Saving a few bucks by traveling on old information is not smart. If you're packing an old book, you'll learn the seriousness of your mistake ... in London. Your trip costs at least $10 per waking hour. Your time is valuable. This guidebook saves you lots of time.

Welcome to My London City Guide

This book is organized the following way:

London Orientation includes tourist information and public transportation. The "Planning Your Time" section offers a suggested schedule with thoughts on how to best use your limited time.

Sights provides a succinct overview of London's most important sights, arranged by neighborhood, with ratings: ▲▲▲—Don't miss; ▲▲—Try hard to see; ▲—Worthwhile if you can make it; No rating—Worth knowing about.

The **Westminster Walk** takes you on a personal tour through downtown London, from Big Ben to Trafalgar Square.

The **Self-Guided Museum Tours** lead you through the British Museum, National Gallery, Tate Gallery, British Library, Westminster Abbey, St. Paul's, and the Tower of London.

Day Trips chapters recommend nearby sights: Greenwich, Cambridge, Bath, and even Paris.

Sleeping is a guide to my favorite budget hotels, mainly in four pleasant London neighborhoods.

Eating offers good-value restaurants ranging from inexpensive eateries to splurges, with an emphasis on good value.

London with Children includes my top recommendations to keep your kids (and you) happy in London.

Shopping offers tips on shopping painlessly and enjoyably, without letting it overwhelm your vacation or ruin your budget.

Entertainment is a guide to entertainment and evening fun, music, walks, and theater.

Transportation Connections covers connections by train (including the Eurostar to Paris) and by plane (with detailed information on London's two airports), laying the groundwork for your smooth arrival and departure.

The **Appendix** includes a London timeline, British history, TV tips, handy telephone numbers, a climate chart, and a British/Yankee dictionary.

Throughout this book, when you see a ✪ in a listing, it means that the sight is covered in much more depth in my self-guided walk or one of my museum tours—a page number will tell you just where to look to find more information.

Browse through this book and choose your favorite sights. Then have a great trip! You'll become your own guide with my self-guided walk and museum tours. Traveling like a temporary local, you'll get the absolute most out of every mile, minute, and dollar. You won't waste time on mediocre sights because, unlike other guidebooks, this one covers only the best. Since your major financial pitfall is lousy, expensive hotels, I've worked hard to assemble the best accommodations values.

Trip Costs

Five components make up your trip costs: airfare, surface transportation, room and board, sightseeing/entertainment, and shopping/miscellany.

Airfare: Don't try to sort through the mess. Find and use a good travel agent. A basic, round-trip, United States-to-London flight costs $500 to $1,000, depending on where you fly from and when.

Surface Transportation: For a typical one-week visit, allow about $30 for tube tickets (20 single rides or a one-week pass). The cost of round-trip trains to day-trip destinations ranges from $10 for Greenwich (cheaper by tube), $20 for Cambridge, $50 for Bath, to about $170 for Paris via Eurostar train. (Save money by taking buses instead of trains, and see the Transportation Connections chapter for tips on how to get the cheapest Eurostar tickets.) Add an additional $100 if you plan to take a couple of taxi rides between London's Heathrow airport and your hotel (or save money by taking the tube, train, or airport bus).

Room and Board: You can thrive in London on $90 a day per person for room and board. A $90-a-day budget allows $10 for lunch, $20 for dinner, and $60 for lodging (based on two people splitting the cost of a $120 double room that includes breakfast). That's doable. Students and tightwads do it on $50 a day ($30 per bed-and-breakfast, $20 for groceries). But budget sleeping and eating require the skills and information covered below (and in greater detail in my book, *Rick Steves' Europe Through the Back Door*).

Sightseeing and Entertainment: Some of the best sights in London are free (British Museum, National Gallery, Tate Gallery, British Library, and others). Figure on paying $7 to $15 for the major sights that charge admission (Westminster Abbey–$8, Tower of London–$17), $8 for guided walks, and $20 for bus tours and splurge experiences (plays range from $15 to $60). Given London's free museums, an overall average of $15 a day works for most. Don't skimp here. After all, this category directly powers most of the experiences all the other expenses are designed to make possible.

The British Heritage pass, which gets you into more than 500 British Heritage and National Trust properties, doesn't make sense for a London visit, but is worth considering if you'll be traveling extensively throughout Britain (£30 for seven days, £42 for 15 days, £56 for 30 days; sold at airport information desks and the British Travel Centre on Regent Street in London).

Shopping and Miscellany: Figure $1 per postcard, tea, or ice-cream cone, and $3 per beer. Shopping can vary in cost from nearly nothing to a small fortune. Good budget travelers find that this category has little to do with assembling a trip full of lifelong and wonderful memories.

Exchange Rate

I list prices in pounds (£) throughout this book.

---

1 British pound (£1) = about $1.70

The British pound sterling (£), also called a "quid," is broken into 100 pence (p). Pence means "cents." You'll find coins ranging from 1p to £2 and bills from £5 to £50. To roughly convert pounds to dollars, multiply British prices by two and then subtract 10 percent: £6 is about $10.50, £3 is about $5, and 80p is about $1.40.

Prices, Times, and Discounts

The prices in this book, as well as the hours and telephone numbers, are accurate as of late 1999. The economy is flat and inflation is low, so these prices should be pretty accurate in 2000. But Britain is always changing, and I know you'll understand that this, like any other guidebook, starts to yellow even before it's printed.

In Britain you'll be using the 24-hour clock. After 12:00 noon, keep going—13:00, 14:00.... For anything over 12, subtract 12 and add p.m. (14:00 is 2:00 p.m.).

This book lists year-around hours, but 2000 will bring lots of changes and it's wise to call to confirm times. While I don't list discounts (called "concessions" in Britain), nearly all British sights are discounted for seniors (loosely defined as anyone retired or willing to call themselves a "senior"), youths (ages 8 to 18), students, groups of 10 or more, and families.

When to Go

July and August are the peak-season months—my favorite time—with very long days, the best weather, and the busiest schedule of tourist fun. Prices and crowds don't go up as dramatically in Britain as they do in much of Europe. Still, travel during "shoulder season" (May, early June, September, and early October) is easier and a bit less expensive. Shoulder-season travelers get minimal crowds, decent weather, and the full range of sights and tourist fun spots. Winter travelers find absolutely no crowds and soft room prices, but shorter sightseeing hours. The weather can be cold and dreary, and nightfall draws the shades on sightseeing well before dinnertime. While England's rural charm falls with the leaves, London's sights are fine in the winter.

Plan for rain no matter when you go. Just keep going and take full advantage of "bright spells." Conditions can change several times in a day, but rarely is the weather extreme. Daily averages throughout the year range between 42 and 70 degrees Fahrenheit. Temperatures below 32 or over 80 degrees causes headlines (see the climate chart in the Appendix). July and August are not much better than shoulder months. May and June can be lovely. While sunshine may be rare, summer days are very long. The summer sun is up from 6:30 to 22:30 (10:30 p.m.). It's not uncommon to have a grey day, eat dinner, and enjoy hours of sunshine afterwards.

Red Tape and Taxes

You need a passport, but no visa or shots, to travel in Britain.

Sales Tax: Britain's sales tax, the "value added tax" or VAT (17.5 percent), is built into the price of nearly everything you buy. Tourists can get this VAT refunded on souvenirs they take out of the country. But unless you buy something worth at least $100, your refund won't be worth the trouble. Before you make a substantial purchase of merchandise, ask the store clerk if you will be able to get a VAT refund. You'll likely get a "Tax-Free Shopping Cheque" which is redeemable for cash or credit-card credit at virtually any European airport before you fly home.

Banking

Credit or debit cards are widely accepted in Britain (and are necessary for renting a car and handy for booking rooms, theater seats, and transportation tickets over the phone). For cash advances you'll find that Barclays, National Westminster, and places displaying an Access or Eurocard sign accept MasterCard. Visa is accepted at Barclays and Midland banks. In general Visa is far more widely accepted than American Express.

Many travelers also carry an ATM card. They get you a better exchange rate than traveler's checks and are as commonplace in Britain as they are in the United States. Be certain your PIN is only four numbers long.

Traveler's checks work fine in Britain. Many people traveling exclusively in Britain buy traveler's checks in pounds sterling. On the road, save time and money by changing plenty of money at a time. Banks commonly charge a commission fee from £2 to £4 and even more. American Express doesn't charge a fee but their exchange rates are mediocre at best.

Even in jolly olde England you should use a money belt. Thieves target tourists. A money belt (call 425/771-8303 for our free newsletter/catalog) provides peace of mind. You can carry lots of cash safely in a money belt—and, given the high bank fees, you should.

Bank holidays bring most businesses to a grinding halt on Christmas, December 26, New Year's Day, Good Friday, Easter Monday, the first and last Monday in May, and the last Monday in August.

Travel Smart

Reread this book as you travel. Buy a phone card and use it for reservations and confirmations. You speak the language; use it! Enjoy the friendliness of the local people. Ask questions. Most locals are eager to point you in their idea of the right direction. Pack along a pocket-size notebook to organize your thoughts, and practice the virtue of simplicity. Those who expect to travel smart, do. Plan ahead for banking, laundry, post office chores, and picnics. Every traveler needs slack days. Pace yourself. Assume you will return.

Really, this book can save you lots of time and money. But to have an "A" trip, you need to be an "A" student. Read the entire thing before your trip and take notes. For instance, if you like to save money, take photos, and free up your busy days, Westminster Abbey is open and empty Wednesday evenings—for half price. It also happens to be the only time they allow cameras. Some activities are better on Sunday, others are worse. The City (London's old center) is lively during the day on weekdays, dead at night and on weekends. The two-hour orientation bus tour is best on Sunday morning (when some sights are closed). The theater district is relatively lifeless on Sunday when there are no plays. A smart trip is a puzzle—a fun, doable, and worthwhile challenge.

If you're planning to stay in Bath as well as London, consider a gentler small-town start in Bath (the ideal jet-lag pillow), and visit London afterward when you're rested and accustomed to travel in Britain. Heathrow Airport has direct connections to Bath and other cities.

Consider making these travel arrangements and reservations before your trip:

• Reserve a room for London. For my recommended hotels, see the Sleeping chapter.

• If you want to book a play, you can call from the United States as easily as from London, using your credit-card number to pay for your tickets. For the current schedule and phone numbers, photocopy your hometown library's London newspaper theater section or visit www.officiallondontheatre.co.uk. For simplicity, I book plays while in London. For more information, see Entertainment.

• If you want to attend the pageantry-filled changing of the keys in the Tower of London, write for tickets (details under Sights, East London).

• Gather tourist information before you depart. Britain's national tourist office in the United States is responsive to individual needs and offers a wealth of meaty material. Before your trip, request any information you may want, such as city maps and schedules of upcoming festivals. Their London and Britain maps are excellent and free (sold for £1.40 each at TIs in Britain). Contact the **British Tourist Authority** (BTA) at 551 Fifth Ave., Seventh Floor, New York, NY 10176, tel. 800/462-2748 or 212/986-2200, fax 212/986-1188, www.visitbritain.com or www.londontown.com. For a listing of London's events, browse the Web: www.timeout.co.uk or www.thisislondon.com.

• If you'll be day-tripping to Paris via Eurostar train, consider ordering a ticket in advance (or buy in Britain); for details, see the Transportation Connections chapter.

Recommended Guidebooks
For most travelers, this book is all you need. But racks of fine London guidebooks are sold at bookstores throughout London. The Michelin Green Guide to London, which is somewhat scholarly, and the more readable Access guide for London are both well researched. *Let's Go London* is youth oriented with good coverage of nightlife, hosteling, and cheap transportation deals. Newsstands sell the excellent *Time Out London Visitors' Guide* (£4; concise and opinionated rundown on sightseeing, shopping, entertainment, eats, and sleeps; good maps). If you'll be traveling elsewhere in Britain, consider *Rick Steves' Great Britain & Ireland 2000*.

Rick Steves' Books and Videos

Rick Steves' Europe Through the Back Door 2000 (John Muir Publications) gives you budget-travel skills such as minimizing jet lag, packing light, planning your itinerary, traveling by car or train, finding beds without reservations, changing money, avoiding rip-offs, outsmarting thieves, hurdling the language barrier, staying healthy, taking great photographs, and much more. The book also includes chapters on 34 of my favorite "Back Doors," eight of which are in Great Britain and Ireland.

Rick Steves' Country Guides are a series of seven guidebooks covering the Best of Europe; Great Britain and Ireland; France, Belgium, and the Netherlands; Italy; Spain and Portugal; Germany, Switzerland, and Austria (with Prague); and Scandinavia. All are updated annually and come out in January.

Rick Steves' City Guides include this book, Paris, and Rome. With the sleek Eurostar train, Paris is now just three hours from London. Consider combining the two cities (and books) for a great visit.

Europe 101: History and Art for the Traveler (John Muir Publications, 1996, cowritten with Gene Openshaw) gives you the story of Europe's people, history, and art. Written for smart people who were sleeping in their history and art classes before they knew they were going to Europe, *101* really helps Europe's sights come alive. However, this book is more applicable to travel on the European continent than to travel in Britain.

Rick Steves' Mona Winks (also cowritten with Gene Openshaw, John Muir Publications, 1998) gives you fun, easy-to-follow self-guided tours of Europe's top 20 museums. All of the *Mona Winks* chapters on London are included in this London guidebook. But if you'd like similar coverage for the great museums in Paris, Amsterdam, Madrid, Venice, Florence, and Rome, *Mona*'s for you.

Of the 52 episodes in my television series, *Travels in Europe with Rick Steves*, eight shows feature Britain and Ireland. A new series of 13 shows, planned for 2000, will include shows on London and England. Episodes air nationally on public television and the Travel Channel. These are also available in information-packed home videos, along with my two-hour slide-show lecture on Britain (call 425/771-8303 for our free newsletter/catalog).

Rick Steves' Postcards from Europe (John Muir Publications, 1999), my autobiographical book, packs more than 25 years of travel anecdotes and insights into the ultimate 3,000-mile European adventure. Through my guidebooks, I share my favorite European discoveries with you. *Postcards* introduces you to my favorite European friends.

Maps

The maps in this book, designed and drawn by Dave Hoerlein, are concise and simple. Dave, who is well traveled in London and Britain, has designed the maps to help you orient quickly and get to where you want to go painlessly. In London, buy a detailed city map at the tourist information office and you're ready to travel. (Or get a free London map from the BTA in the United States; see "Tourist Information," above.)

Tours of Britain and Ireland

Your travel agent can tell you about all the normal tours. But they won't tell you about ours. At Europe Through the Back Door we offer 20-day Britain tours, 14-day Ireland tours, and one-week winter getaways to London featuring the all-stars covered in my guidebooks (call us at 425/771-8303 for details). And ETBD tour guide Roy Nicholls leads his own garden tours and south England tours in his spare time (call Roy in England at 44/1749/812-873, www.brittours.com).

Transportation

Transportation concerns within London are limited to the tube (subway), buses, and taxis, all of which are covered in the Orientation chapter. If you have a car, stow it. You don't want to drive in London. Transportation to day-trip destinations is covered in the Day Trips and Transportation Connections chapters.

For all the specifics on transportation throughout Great Britain by train or car, see *Rick Steves' Great Britain & Ireland 2000*.

Telephones and Mail

The British telephone system is great. Easy-to-find public phone booths take cards and coins. Buy a handy BT phone card (£3, £5, £10, or £20) at any newsstand, TI, or post office. (Some "credit card phones" have a slot that will take—but not accept—your BT phone card; stick with BT "phone card" booths.) For a cheaper alternative to BT cards, see PIN cards, under "Calling the United States," below.

Coin-op phones take coins from 10p to £1. A display shows how your money supply is doing. Only completely unused coins will be returned, so put in biggies with caution. (If money is left over, rather than hang up, push the "make another call" button and call someone.)

London is a big city. Use the telephone routinely to confirm tour times, book theater tickets, or make reservations at fancy restaurants. If you call before heading out, you'll travel more smoothly.

In London dial 999 for emergency help and 192 for directory

assistance (free from public phone booths, otherwise 35p). London's new area code is 020. Last year London's phone numbers were seven digits with a 0171 area code for downtown and a 0181 code for the suburbs. Now all 0171 and 0181 seven-digit numbers are 020 with eight digits. Old 0171 numbers now start with 7; 0181 numbers now start with 8. So, last year's 0171/321-4321 is now 020/7321-4321. Beware of area codes starting with 0839. These are toll numbers with recorded information—usually slow moving and very expensive.

Long distance within Britain: Calling long distance in Britain is most expensive from 8:00 to 13:00 and cheapest from 17:00 to 8:00. A short call across the country is quite inexpensive. Don't hesitate to call long distance. First dial the area code (which starts with zero), then dial the local number. Area codes are listed by city on phone booth walls or are available from directory assistance (free and happy to help—dial 192 in Britain).

International calls: To make an international call, dial the international access code (Britain's is 00), then the country code (for Canada and United States, it's 1), then the area code (drop the inital zero if the area code starts with zero) and the local number. For example, London's downtown area code is 020. To call one of my recommended London B&Bs from New York, I dial 011 (U.S. international access code), 44 (Britain's country code), 20 (London's area code without the zero), then 7730-8191 (the B&B's number). To call it from Britain's old York, dial 020/7730-8191.

To call my office from Britain, I dial 00 (Britain's international access code), 1 (U.S. country code), 425 (Edmonds' area code), then 771-8303. For a listing of international access codes and country codes, see the Appendix.

Calling the United States: You have a number of options. Simply dialing direct from any British phone booth costs less than a dollar a minute. New phone cards with PIN numbers give you about five minutes for a dollar. Cards are sold—for a minimum of £3—at minimarts, newsstands, and exchange bureaus; look for ads in the window displaying rates for many countries (ask for an "international calling card"). The cards, which list an access number and a secret personal-identification number, work great from phone booths and most hotel phones throughout Britain for any type of call: local, long-distance, or international.

USA Direct Services, such as AT&T, MCI, and Sprint, used to be a good value until direct-dialing rates dropped and PIN cards appeared. It's much cheaper to dial direct (but for your convenience, I'll list the numbers of calling card operators in Britain: AT&T: 0800-89-00-11; MCI: 0800-89-02-22; and Sprint: 0800-89-08-77).

Mail: To arrange for mail delivery, reserve a hotel in advance and give its address to friends, or use American Express Company's mail services (available to anyone who has at least one Amex traveler's check). Allow 10 days for a letter to arrive. Phoning is so easy that I've dispensed with mail stops all together.

Sleeping

In the interest of smart use of your time, I favor accommodations (and restaurants) handy to your sightseeing activities. Rather than list hotels scattered throughout London, I've chosen several favorite neighborhoods and recommend the best accommodations values for each.

I look for places that are friendly (enjoy Americans); located in a central, safe, quiet neighborhood; clean, with good beds; a good value; and not mentioned in other guidebooks (therefore, filled mostly by English travelers). I'm more impressed by a handy location and a fun-loving philosophy than hair dryers and shoe-shine machines.

I've described my recommended hotels and B&Bs with a standard code. Prices listed are for one-night stays in peak season, include a hearty breakfast, and assume you're going direct and not through a tourist information office. Prices may be soft for off-season and longer stays. "Twin" means two single beds, and "double" means one double bed. If you'll take either one, let them know or you might be needlessly turned away. Some hotels offer family deals (I note this within their listing), which means that parents with young children can easily get a room with an extra child's bed or a discount for larger rooms. Call to negotiate the price. Kids under five sleep almost free. Teenage kids are generally charged as adults.

B&Bs are not hotels. If you want to ruin your relationship with your host, treat him or her like a hotel clerk. Americans often assume they'll get new towels each day. The British don't, and neither will you. Hang them up to dry and reuse. Many places now offer nonsmoking rooms (listed in descriptions). Breakfast rooms are nearly always smoke-free.

Most places listed have three floors of rooms and steep stairs. Elevators are rare. If you're concerned about stairs, call and ask about ground-floor rooms or pay for a fancy place with a lift.

All rooms have sinks. Any room without a bathroom has access to a free bath or shower on the corridor. In Britain, rooms with private plumbing are called "en suite"; rooms that lack private plumbing are "standard." As more rooms go en suite, the hallway bathroom is shared with fewer standard rooms. If money's tight, request standard rooms.

Sleep Code

To give maximum information with a minimum of space, I use this code to describe accommodations listed in this book. Prices in this book are listed per room, not per person. Breakfast is included.

S = Single room, or price for one person in a double.

D = Double or twin room. (I specify double- and twin-bed rooms only if they are priced differently, or if a place has only one or the other. When reserving, you should specify.)

T = Three-person room (often a double bed with a single).

Q = Four-person room (adding an extra child's bed to a T is usually cheaper).

b = Private bathroom with toilet and shower or tub.

t = Private toilet only. (The shower is down the hall.)

s = Private shower or tub only. (The toilet is down the hall.)

CC = Accepts credit cards (**V** = Visa, **M** = MasterCard, **A** = American Express). If CC isn't mentioned, assume you'll need to pay cash.

According to this code, a couple staying at a "Db-£60, CC:VM" hotel would pay a total of £60 (about $100) per night for a room with a private toilet and shower (or tub). The hotel accepts Visa, MasterCard, or cash.

Making Reservations

Reserve your London room by phone or e-mail as soon as you can commit to a date. It's possible to visit London any time of year without reservations, but given the high stakes, erratic accommodations values, and the quality of the gems I've listed, I recommend calling ahead for a room.

A few national holidays jam things up (especially "bank holiday" Mondays) and merit reservations long in advance. Mark these dates in red on your travel calendar: Good Friday, Easter Monday, the first and last Monday in May, the last Monday in August, Christmas, December 26, and New Year's Day. Just like at home, Monday holidays are preceded by busy weekends; book the entire weekend in advance.

It's easy to reserve by phone. I've taken great pains to list telephone numbers with long-distance instructions (see "Telephones and Mail," above; also see the Appendix). Some places will trust you and hold a room until 16:00 without a deposit, although most places will ask you for a credit-card number. Honor (or cancel by phone) your reservations.

To reserve from home, call, fax, e-mail, or write the hotel. E-mail is preferred when possible. To fax, use the fax form in the Appendix (online at www.ricksteves.com/reservation). If you're writing, add the zip code and confirm the need and method for a deposit.

A two-night stay in August would be "2 nights, 16/8/00 to 18/8/00" (Europeans write the date day/month/year, and hotel jargon uses your day of departure). You'll often receive a letter back requesting one night's deposit. A credit card will usually work. If your credit card is the deposit, you can pay with your card or cash when you arrive. If you don't show up, you'll be billed for one night. Reconfirm your reservations a day in advance for safety. Also, don't just assume you can extend. Consider carefully—and well in advance—how long you'll stay.

Eating

I don't mind English food. But then, I liked dorm food. True, England isn't famous for its cuisine and probably never will be, but we tourists have to eat. If there's any good place to cut corners to stretch your budget, it's in eating. Here are a few tips on budget eating:

The traditional "fry" is famous as a hearty way to start the day. Also known as a "heart attack on a plate," the breakfast—cereal, toast, ham, eggs, tomatoes, juice, tea or coffee—is especially feasty if you've just come from the land of the skimpy continental breakfast across the Channel.

Many B&Bs don't serve breakfast until 8:00. If you need an early start, ask politely if it's possible. While they may not make you a cooked breakfast, they can usually put out cereal, toast, juice, and coffee.

Picnicking saves time and money. Set up a hotel-room pantry. Try boxes of orange juice (pure by the liter), fresh bread, tasty English cheese, meat, a tube of Colman's English mustard, local eatin' apples, bananas, small tomatoes, a small tub of yogurt (they're drinkable), rice crackers, gorp or nuts, plain "Digestive Biscuits" (the chocolate-covered ones melt), and any local specialties. At supermarkets you can get food in small quantities. (Three tomatoes and two bananas cost me 50p.) Decent sandwiches (£2) are sold everywhere. I often munch a simple picnic in a bus, boat, or subway to save time as well as money.

London's restaurants are fairly expensive, but cheap alternatives abound: fish-and-chips joints, Chinese and Indian takeouts, cafeterias, pubs (see below), and your typical, good old greasy-spoon cafés. At a sit-down place with table service, tip no more than 10 percent.

For fresh, fast, and cheap lunches, bakeries have meat pies (and microwaves), pastries, yogurt, and cartons of "semiskimmed" milk. The meat pies, called pasties, make a quick hot meal.

People of leisure punctuate their day with a "cream tea." You'll get a pot of tea, two homemade scones, jam, and thick, creamy-as-honey clotted cream. For maximum pinky-waving taste per calorie, slice your scone thin, like a miniloaf of bread.

Pub Grub and Beer

Pubs are a basic part of the British social scene, and whether you're a teetotaler or a beer guzzler they should be a part of your travel here. Pub is short for "public house." It's an extended living room where, if you don't mind the stickiness, you can feel the pulse of London. Unfortunately, many of London's pubs have been afflicted with an excess of brass, ferns, and video games. In any case, smart travelers use the pubs to eat, drink, get out of the rain, watch the latest sporting event, and make new friends.

Pub grub gets better each year. It's Britain's best eating value. For £6 you'll get a basic budget hot lunch or dinner in friendly surroundings. The *Good Pub Guide*, published annually by the British Consumers Union, is excellent. Pubs attached to restaurants often have fresher food and a chef who knows how to cook.

Pubs generally serve assorted meat pies such as steak and kidney pie or shepherd's pie, curried dishes, fish, quiche, vegetables, and (invariably) chips and peas. Better pubs let you substitute a "jacket potato" (stuffed baked potato) for your fries. Meals are usually served from 12:00 to 14:00 and from 18:00 to 20:00, not throughout the day. Servings are hearty, service is quick, and you'll rarely spend more than £7. Your beer or cider adds another couple pounds. (Free tap water is always available.) A "ploughman's lunch" is a modern "traditional English meal" that nearly every tourist tries ... once. Pubs that advertise their food and are crowded with locals are less likely to be the kinds that serve only lousy microwaved snacks.

In a pub you order your beer at the bar. Part of the experience is standing before a line of "hand pulls," or taps, and wondering which beer to choose. Most pubs will have lagers (cold, refreshing, American-style beer), ale (amber-colored, room-temperature beer), bitters (hop-flavored ales), and stouts (dark and somewhat bitter, like Guinness). The British take great pride in their beer. They think that drinking beer cold and carbonated, as Americans do, ruins the taste. At pubs, long hand pulls are used to pull the traditional rich-flavored "real ales" up from the cellar. These are the connoisseur's favorites: fermented naturally, varying from sweet to bitter, often with a hoppy or nutty flavor. Notice the fun names.

Short hand pulls at the bar mean colder, fizzier, mass-produced, and less interesting keg beers. Mild beers are sweeter with a creamy malt flavoring. Try the draft cider (sweet or dry)... carefully. Proper English ladies like a half-beer and half-lemonade "shandy." Teetotalers can order a soft drink.

Drinks are served by the pint or the half-pint. (It's almost feminine for a man to order just a half; I order mine with quiche.) There's no table service. Order drinks and meals at the bar. Pay as you order and don't tip.

Pub hours vary. The strict wartime hours (designed to keep the wartime working force sober and productive) finally ended a few years ago, and now pubs can serve beer from 11:00 to 23:00, and Sunday from noon to 22:30. Children are served food and soft drinks in pubs, but you must be 18 to order a beer. A cup of darts is free for the asking. People go to a "public house" to be social. They want to talk. Get vocal with a local. The pub is the next best thing to relatives in every town. Cheers!

Stranger in a Strange Land

We travel all the way to Europe to enjoy differences—to become temporary locals. You'll experience frustrations. There are certain truths that we find God-given and self-evident, such as cold beer, ice in drinks, bottomless coffee cups, "the customer's always right," easy shower faucets, and driving on the right side of the road. One of the benefits of travel is the eye-opening realization that there are logical, civil, and even better alternatives. A willingness to go local ensures that you'll enjoy a full dose of English hospitality.

Send Me a Postcard, Drop Me a Line

If you enjoy a successful trip with the help of this book and would like to share your discoveries, please fill out and send the survey at the end of this book to me at Europe Through the Back Door, Box 2009, Edmonds, WA 98020. I personally read and value all feedback. Thanks in advance—it helps a lot.

For our latest travel information, tap into our Web site: www.ricksteves.com. To check on any updates for this book, visit www.ricksteves.com/update. My e-mail address is rick@ricksteves .com. Anyone can request a free issue of our newsletter.

Judging from the happy postcards I receive from travelers, it's safe to assume you'll enjoy a great, affordable vacation—with the finesse of an experienced, independent traveler. Thanks, and happy travels!

BACK DOOR TRAVEL PHILOSOPHY
As Taught in *Rick Steves' Europe Through the Back Door*

Travel is intensified living—maximum thrills per minute and one of the last great sources of legal adventure. Travel is freedom. It's recess, and we need it.

Experiencing the real Europe requires catching it by surprise, going casual ... "Through the Back Door."

Affording travel is a matter of priorities. (Make do with the old car.) You can travel—simply, safely, and comfortably—in Europe for $70 a day plus transportation costs. In many ways, spending more money only builds a thicker wall between you and what you came to see. Europe is a cultural carnival, and time after time you'll find that its best acts are free and the best seats are the cheap ones.

A tight budget forces you to travel close to the ground, meeting and communicating with the people, not relying on service with a purchased smile. Never sacrifice sleep, nutrition, safety, or cleanliness in the name of budget. Simply enjoy the local-style alternatives to expensive hotels and restaurants.

Extroverts have more fun. If your trip is low on magic moments, kick yourself and make things happen. If you don't enjoy a place, maybe you don't know enough about it. Seek the truth. Recognize tourist traps. Give a culture the benefit of your open mind. See things as different but not better or worse. Any culture has much to share.

Of course, travel, like the world, is a series of hills and valleys. Be fanatically positive and militantly optimistic. If something's not to your liking, change your liking. Travel is addicting. It can make you a happier American, as well as a citizen of the world. Our Earth is home to nearly 6 billion equally important people. It's humbling to travel and find that people don't envy Americans. They like us, but with all due respect, they wouldn't trade passports.

Globetrotting destroys ethnocentricity. It helps you understand and appreciate different cultures. Travel changes people. It broadens perspectives and teaches new ways to measure quality of life. Many travelers toss aside their hometown blinders. Their prized souvenirs are the strands of different cultures they decide to knit into their own character. The world is a cultural yarn shop. And Back Door travelers are weaving the ultimate tapestry. Come on, join in!

ORIENTATION

London is more than 600 square miles of urban jungle. With 9 million struggling people—many of whom speak English—it's a world in itself and a barrage on all the senses. On my first visit, I felt extremely small.

To grasp London comfortably, see it as the old town in the city center without the modern, congested sprawl. Most of the visitor's London lies between the Tower of London and Hyde Park, about a three-mile walk. Mentally—maybe even physically—scissor down your map to include only the area between the Tower, King's Cross Station, Paddington Station, Victoria and Albert Museum, and Victoria Station. With this focus and a good orientation, you'll find London manageable and even fun. You'll get a good taste of the city's top sights, history, and cultural entertainment, as well as its ever-changing human face.

Planning Your Time

London's a great one-week getaway. Its sights can keep even the most fidgety traveler well entertained for a week. After considering London's major tourist sights, I've covered just my favorites. You won't be able to see all of these, so don't try. You'll keep coming back to London. After dozens of visits myself, I still enjoy a healthy list of excuses to return.

Here's a suggested schedule:

Day 1: 9:00–Tower of London (Beefeater tour, crown jewels), 12:30–Munch a sandwich on the Thames while cruising from Tower to Westminster Bridge, 14:00–Tour Westminster Abbey, coffee in the cloisters, 15:30–Visit the House of Commons if the line's not too long, 16:30–Follow the self-guided Westminster Walk, 18:00–Visit the National Tourist Information Centre (closes at 18:30) near Piccadilly.

LONDON

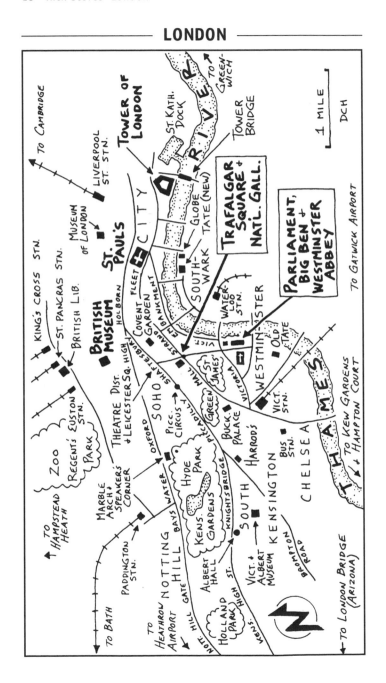

Day 2: 9:00–Take double-decker hop-on, hop-off London sight-seeing bus tour (start at Victoria Street and hop off for the Changing of the Guard—11:00 at Wellington Barracks, then 11:30 at Buckingham Palace; guards change daily May through June and every even-numbered day July through April), 13:00–Covent Garden for lunch, shopping, and people watching, 15:00–Tour British Museum. Have a pub dinner before a play, concert, or evening walking tour.

Day 3: Tour British Library, St. Paul's Cathedral, and Museum of London. See Shakespeare play at the Globe Theatre (14:00 or 19:30).

Day 4: 10:00–National Gallery, fun and lunch on or near Trafalgar Square, National Portrait Gallery, 14:00–Boat to Kew Gardens, tube back into town.

Day 5: Morning at an antique market and visit a famous London department store. Depending upon your personality, choose from Imperial War Museum, Tate Gallery of British Art, or Tate Gallery of Modern Art (opens May 2000). A play, guided walk, or concert tonight.

Day 6: Celebrate the millennium at the Greenwich Dome. Zip down by tube, ride the boat back to Westminster Pier. Cap the day with a ride on the Millennium Observation Wheel.

Day 7: For a one-week visit to London, I'd spend a day or two side-tripping. To keep an England focus, side-trip out to Bath and/or Cambridge for one day. For maximum travel thrills, consider a 36-hour Paris getaway. With the zippy English Channel train, Paris is only three hours away and can even be worth a long day trip. To pull this off, see the Day Trip: Paris chapter.

Arrival in London

By Train: London has eight train stations, all connected by the tube (subway), all with exchange offices and luggage storage. From any station, ride the tube or taxi to your hotel.

By Bus: The bus station is one block southwest of Victoria Station, which has a TI (tourist information center) and tube entrance.

By Plane: For detailed information on getting from London's airports to downtown London, see the Transportation Connections chapter.

Tourist Information

The **British Visitors Centre** is the best information service in town (Mon–Fri 9:00–18:30, Sat–Sun 10:00–16:00, just off Piccadilly Circus at 1 Lower Regent Street, tel. 020/8846-9000, www.visitbritain.com). It's great for London information. If traveling beyond London, take advantage of its well-equipped London/ England desk, Wales desk (tel. 020/7803-3838), Ireland desk (tel. 020/7493-3201), and Scotland desk. At the center's extensive book-shop, gather whatever information you'll need: guidebooks, youth hostel directory, and maps. If venturing beyond London, consider the Michelin Green Guide to London or Britain (£9), the Britain road atlas (£10), and Ordnance Survey maps for areas you'll be exploring by car. There's also a travel agency upstairs.

The **Scottish Tourist Centre** (19 Cockspur Street, tel. 020/7930-8661) and the slick new **French National Tourist Office** (Mon–Sat 9:00–17:30, 179 Piccadilly Street, tel. 0990-848-848) are nearby.

Unfortunately London's Tourist Information Centres are now owned by the big hotels and are simply businesses selling advertis-ing space to companies with fliers to distribute. They are not very helpful. Avoid their 50p-per-minute telephone information service (instead try the British Visitors Centre at 020/8846-9000). Loca-tions include: Heathrow Airport's Terminal 3 (daily 6:00–23:00, most convenient and least crowded); Heathrow Airport's Terminal 1 and 2 tube station (daily 8:00–18:00); Victoria Station (daily 8:00–18:00, shorter hours in winter, crowded and commercial); and Waterloo International Terminal Arrivals Hall (serving trains from Paris, daily 8:30–22:30).

Bring your itinerary and a checklist of questions to any of the TIs. Pick up these publications: *London Planner* (free monthly listing all the sights with latest hours and events), walking-tour schedule fliers, and a theater guide. Consider buying their fine £1.40 London map—it rivals the £4 maps sold in newsstands (free from British Tourist Authority in the United States: 551 Fifth Avenue, Seventh Floor, New York, NY 10176, tel. 800/462-2748 or 212/986-2200, www.visitbritain.com). The TIs sell BT phone cards, long-distance bus tickets and passes, British Heritage Passes (not worth it for a London-only trip), and tickets to plays (steep booking fee). They also book rooms (avoid their £5 booking fee by calling hotels direct).

Helpful Hints

Theft Alert: The artful dodger is alive and well—with lots of friends—in London. Be on guard, particularly when using public transportation and in places crowded with tourists. Tourists, con-sidered naive and rich, are targeted. Over 7,500 handbags are stolen annually at Covent Gardens alone. Thieves paw you so you don't feel the pickpocketing.

Changing Money: Standard transaction fees at banks are £2 to £4. American Express Offices change any brand of traveler's checks for no fee, but offer mediocre rates (Heathrow Terminal 4 tube station and at 6 Haymarket near Piccadilly, daily 9:00–18:00, tel. 020/7930-4411). Avoid changing money at exchange bureaus. Their latest scam: They advertise very good rates with a same-as-the-banks fee of 2 percent. But the fine print explains that the fee of 2 percent is for buying pounds. The fee for *selling* pounds is 9.5 percent. Ouch! ATMs are really the way to go.

What's Up: For the best listing of what's happening (plays, movies, restaurants, concerts, exhibitions, protests, walking tours, shopping, and children's activities) and a look at the trendy London scene, pick up a current copy of *Time Out* (£1.80, www .timeout.co.uk) or *What's On* at any newsstand. The TI's free monthly *London Planner* lists sights, plays, and events at least as well. For a fun Web site on London's entertainment, theater, restaurants, and news, go to www.thisislondon.com.

Free Sights: The British Museum, British Library, National Gallery, National Portrait Gallery, and both Tate Galleries are always free. The following museums are free from 16:30 to closing (17:30 or 18:00), saving you £5 or so: Imperial War Museum, Museum of London, Natural History Museum, and Victoria and Albert Museum. More museums will be free in the next few years.

Travel Bookstores: Stanfords Travel Bookstore is good and stocks current editions of my guidebooks near Victoria Station (52 Grosvenor Gardens), at Covent Garden (12 Long Acre, tel. 020/ 7836-1321), and at 156 Regent Street. Waterstones Bookstore, on the corner of Trafalgar Square, is also handy and has a fine travel selection next to the Coffee Republic Café (WC upstairs, tel. 020/7839-4411). The best London map I've seen is the Bensons Mapguide of London (£2, May 1999 edition even includes the Greenwich Dome).

Travel Agency: The student travel agency, USIT, across from Victoria Station, has great deals on flights for people of all ages (Mon–Fri 9:00–18:00, Sat–Sun 10:00–17:00, Buckingham Palace Road, tel. 0870/240-1010, www.usitcampus.co.uk). Also, look in the *Sunday Times* travel section for great deals on flights.

Getting around London

London's taxis, buses, and subway system make a private car unnecessary. To travel smart in a city this size, you must get comfortable with public transportation.

By Taxi: London is the best taxi town in Europe. Big, black, carefully regulated cabs are everywhere. I never met a crabby cabbie in London. They love to talk and know every nook and cranny in town. I ride one a day just to get my London questions answered. Rides start at £1.40 and cost about £1.50 per tube stop. Connecting downtown sights is quick and easy for about £4

LONDON TUBE

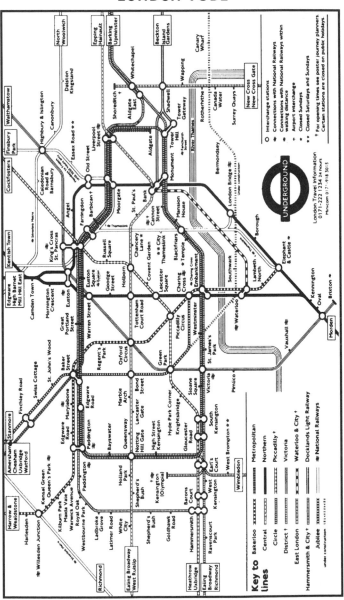

Copyright London Transport Executive

(e.g., St. Paul's to the Tower). For a short ride, three people in a cab travel at tube prices. Groups of four or five should taxi everywhere. If a cab's top light is on, just wave it down. (Drivers flash lights when they see you.) Wave in either direction. They have a tiny turning radius. If waving doesn't work, ask for a taxi stand. Stick with metered cabs. While telephoning a cab gets one in minutes, it's generally not necessary and adds to the cost. London is such a great wave-'em-down taxi town that most cabs don't even have a radio phone.

By Bus: London's extensive bus system is easy to follow. Just pick up a free map from a TI or tube station. Signs at stops list routes clearly. Conductors are terse but helpful. Ask to be reminded when it's your stop. Just hop on, tell the driver where you're going, pay what he says, grab a ticket, take a seat, and relax. (The best views are upstairs.) Rides start at 90p. If the driver is not taking money, hop in and grab a seat. The conductor will eventually sell you a ticket. If you have a transit pass, get in the habit of hopping buses for quick little straight shots (even just to get to a metro stop). During bump-and-grind rush hours (8:00–10:00 and 16:00–19:00), you'll go faster by tube.

By Tube: London's subway is one of this planet's great people movers and the fastest (and cheapest) long-distance transport in town. Any ride in the Central Zone (on or within the Circle Line, including virtually all my recommended sights and hotels) costs £1.40. Avoid ticket-window lines in tube stations by buying tickets from coin-op machines; practice on the punchboard to see how the system works (hit "adult single" and your destination). Again, nearly every ride will be £1.40. These tickets are valid only on the day of purchase. Beware: Overshooting your zone gets you a £10 fine.

Get a color-coded tube map (included in some city maps, free at any station window) and learn the system. Each line has a name (such as Circle Line, Central, or Bakerloo). Figure out which direction you'll need to travel on that line (north, south, east, or west; hint: all city maps have north on top). Once in the station, you'll have a choice of two platforms per line (such as East/West). Follow signs to your line and your direction (such as Central: East), and you'll end up at the right platform. These signs also clearly list all the stops along the way. If you need help, ask a local or an orange-vested staff person. The system can be confusing. Some tracks are shared by several lines, and electronic signboards announce which train is next and the minutes remaining until various arrivals. Each train has its final destination or line name above its windshield. Read the system notices clearly posted at the platform; they explain the tube's latest flood, construction, or bomb scare. Bring something to do to pass the waits productively. And always . . . mind the gap.

You can't leave the system without feeding your ticket to the turnstile. Save time by choosing the best street exit (look at the maps on the walls). "Subway" means pedestrian underpass in "English." For tube and bus information, call 020/7222-1234.

London Tube and Bus Passes: The "Travel Card," covering Zones 1 and 2, gives you unlimited travel for a day, starting after 9:30 and anytime on weekends, for £3.80. The all-zone version of this card costs £4.50 (and includes Heathrow airport). The "LT Card," a one-day, two-zone pass with no time restriction, costs £4.80. Families save with the one-day "Family Travel Card." The "Weekend Travel Card" covers Zones 1 and 2 for £5.70 and costs 25 percent less than two one-day cards. The "7 Day Travel Card" costs £18, covers Zone 1, and requires a passport-type photo (cut one out of any snapshot and bring it from home). All passes are available for more zones and are purchased as easily as a normal ticket at any station. If you figure you'll take three rides in a day, get a day pass.

If you want to travel a little each day or if you're part of a group, a £10 "carnet" is a great deal: You get 10 separate tickets for tube travel in Zone 1 (£1.00 each rather than £1.40). Wait for the machine to lay all 10 tickets.

Tours of London

▲▲▲**Hop-on Hop-off Double-Decker Bus Tours**—Two competitive companies ("Original" and "Big Bus") offer essentially the same tours with live (English-only) guides on board. This two-hour, once-over-lightly tour drives by all the most famous sights, providing a stressless way to get your bearings and at least see the biggies. You can sit back and enjoy the entire two-hour orientation tour (a good idea if you like the guide and the weather) or "hop on and hop off" at any of the 20-plus stops and catch a later bus. Buses run about every 10 minutes in summer, every 20 minutes in winter. It's an inexpensive form of transport as well as an informative tour. Buses run every day except Christmas (from about 9:00 in summer—9:30 in winter—until early evening from one block north of Victoria Station on Victoria Street, Marble Arch, Piccadilly Circus, Trafalgar Square, and so on). Each company offers a core two-hour overview tour and two other routes (buy ticket from driver, ticket good for 24 hours, bring a sweater and extra film). Note: If you start at Victoria at 9:30, you can hop off near the end of the two-hour loop at the Buckingham Palace stop (Bressenden Place), a five-minute walk from the Palace and the Changing of the Guard at 11:30. If you start from Victoria at 9:00, you'd also have time to catch the guard action at 11:00 at Wellington Barracks. Sunday morning, with light traffic and a number of museums closed, is a fine time for the tour.

Original London Sightseeing Bus Tour: Live guided buses

have a Union Jack flag and a yellow triangle on the front of the bus. If the front has many flags or a green triangle, it's a tape-recorded multilingual tour—avoid it unless you have kids who'd enjoy the more entertaining recorded kids' tour (£12.50; £3.50 off with this book—limit two discounts per book, they'll rip off the corner of this page; ticket good for 24 hours, tel. 020/8877-1722).

Big Bus London Tours: These are also good. For £15 you get the same basic tour plus coupons for four different one-hour London walks and the scenic and entertaining Thames boat ride (normally £4.60) between Westminster Pier and the Tower of London. The pass and extras are valid for 24 hours. While the price is steeper, Big Bus guides seem more dynamic than the Original guides and the Big Bus system is probably better organized (tel. 020/8944-7810, www.bigbus.co.uk).

▲▲**Walking Tours**—Many times a day top-notch local guides lead small groups through specific slices of London's past. Schedule fliers litter the desks of TIs, hotels, and pubs. *Time Out* lists many but not all scheduled walks. Simply show up at the announced location, pay £5, and enjoy two chatty hours of Dickens, the Plague, Shakespeare, Legal London, the Beatles, Jack the Ripper, or whatever is on the agenda. "Original London Walks" is the dominant company (at TIs and hotels; pick up their beefy, plain black-and-white newsletter listing their extensive daily schedule, or call 020/7624-3978, www.walks.com). They do private tours for £80.

Robina Brown, who winters in Seattle (a bizarre concept), leads tours on foot or with small groups in her Toyota Previa. Standard rates for London's registered guides: £83 for four hours, £125 for nine hours. For car and guiding she charges £145 for three hours and about £300 per day per group (tel. & fax 020/7228-2238, e-mail: robina.brown@which.net). Brit Lonsdale, an energetic mother of twins, is another registered London guide (tel. 020/7386-9907, fax 020/7386-9807). Chris Salaman does daylong specialty walks (his favorite: industrial tours) including lunch, a tube travel card, and museum admissions for £120 for up to six people (tel. 020/8871-9048). For other guides call 020/7403-2062 (www.touristguides.org.uk).

▲▲**Cruise the Thames**—Boat tours with an entertaining commentary sail regularly from Westminster Pier (base of Westminster Bridge under Big Ben). You can cruise to the Tower of London (£4.60, round-trip £5.80, included with Big Bus London tour, 3/hrly from 10:20–21:00 in peak season, until 18:00 in winter, 30-min cruise, tel. 020/7930-9033), Greenwich (£6, round-trip £7.30, 2/hrly from 10:00–17:00, 50 min, tel. 020/7930-4097), and Kew Gardens (£6, round-trip £10, 5/day, 90 min, tel. 020/7930-2062). For pleasure and efficiency, consider combining a one-way cruise with a tube ride back.

LONDON
SIGHTS

These sights are arranged by neighborhood for handy sight-seeing. When you see a ⭐ in a listing it means the sight is covered in much more depth in my self-guided walk or one of the museum tours. Students, families, and seniors should ask about "concessions" (discounts). Telephoning first to check hours and confirm plans—especially off-season when hours can shrink—is always smart.

From Westminster Abbey to Trafalgar Square

⭐ These sights are linked by the Westminster Walk on page 42.

▲▲▲**Westminster Abbey**—England's historic coronation church is a crowded collection of famous tombs of kings, poets, and politicians. Like a stony refugee camp huddled outside St. Peter's gates, this is an English hall of fame. Choose among tours (in this book—free, walkman—£2, or live—£3). Consider attending an evensong (weekdays except Wed at 17:00, Sat and Sun at 15:00) or the Sunday 17:45 organ recital. (£5 for abbey entry, tours extra, Mon–Fri 9:00–16:45, Sat 9:00–14:45, technically no visitors on Sun, also open for half-price on Wed 18:00–19:45—the only time photography is allowed, last admission 60 min before closing, lattes in the cloister, tube: Westminster, tel. 020/7222-7110.) For a free peek at the nave with no line, enter via Deans Yard (arch near west end of church) and go through the group entrance as if you're going to the museum. At the cloister, turn left and enter the nave. Since the church is often closed to the public for special services, it's wise to call first. Praying is free; use separate marked entrance. ⭐ See Westminster Abbey Tour on page 110.

▲▲**Houses of Parliament (Palace of Westminster)**—This neo-Gothic icon of London, the royal residence from 1042 to 1547, is now the meeting place of the legislative branch of government. If Parliament is in session—indicated by a flag flying atop the

CENTRAL LONDON

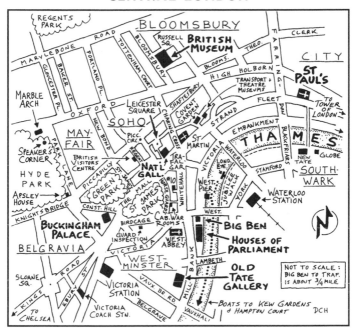

Victoria Tower—you can view debates in either the bickering House of Commons or the genteel House of Lords (Mon, Tue, and Thu 14:30–22:00, Wed 9:30–22:00, Fri 9:30–15:00, generally less action and no lines after 18:00, use St. Stephen's entrance, tube: Westminster, tel. 020/7219-4272 for schedule).

While it's not worth a long wait and the actual action is usually dull, it is a thrill to be inside and see the British government inaction. The House of Lords has more pageantry, shorter lines, and less-interesting debates (tel. 020/7219-3107 for schedule). If confronted with a too-long House of Commons line, see the House of Lords first. Once you've seen the Lords (hide your HOL flier), you can often slip directly to the Commons by joining the gang waiting in the lobby. If there's only one line outside, it's for the House of Commons. Go to the gate and tell the guard you want the Lords. You may pop right in. While other guidebooks tout the U.S. Embassy "entry cards," which get you directly in, they only give out four per day, and trying to land one is usually futile.

After passing security, slip to the left and study the big, dark, 11th-century Westminster Hall (a survivor of the 1834 fire). Its

Millennium London

London seems hell-bent on hosting the world's grandest millennium celebrations. The year 2000 brings London revamped museums, a huge Ferris wheel, and a giant dome at Greenwich.

Greenwich, site of the world's prime meridian and "the place from where time is measured," kicked off the millennium with gusto, playing host to Her Majesty and Prince Charles' big New Year's Eve 2000 bash in the Millennium Dome. This exhibition hall, 50 meters high and a kilometer around, is the biggest millennium project anywhere. Fourteen theme zones (such as Mind, Body, Spirit, Work, National Identity, Play, and a display of Princess Diana's dresses) surround a vast central stage. Expect lots of live entertainment, huge video screens, virtual-reality gimmicks, and enthusiastic interactivity. After 2000 the dome will be redeveloped as a theme park or exhibition center. In the town of Greenwich, the Queen's House hosts the new *Story of Time* exhibit (until September 24) and the Old Royal Naval College opens its Painted Hall and Chapel to the public. (For details, see Day Trips chapter "Greenwich.")

On London's South Bank, a grand Ferris wheel (at 450 feet high, the highest public viewpoint in London) spins opposite Big Ben. The new Tate Gallery of Modern Art, opening this May, will be linked to St. Paul's Cathedral by the new pedestrian Millennium Bridge. And the Globe Theater has expanded its exhibit on the history of the Globe to cover more on Shakespeare, his contempoaries and the beginnings of theater. (For details, see "South London," below.)

The British Museum opens its Great Court and elegant, round Reading Room (that Karl Marx liked so much) to the public this fall. The museum hosts a thought-provoking exhibit exploring the legacy of the Book of Revelations—The Apocalypse and the Shape of Things to Come. The exhibit traces ideas about the apocalypse from the 11th century to World War II (through April 24, 2000).

The "Arts 2000" movement plans to free art from its normal places all over Britain and hang it in unusual, everyday places from train stations to shopping malls.

Like nowhere else in Europe, London and Greenwich know how to throw a party. They make it easy to turn 2000.

famous self-supporting hammer-beam roof was added in 1397. The Houses of Parliament are located in what was once the Palace of Westminster, long the palace of England's medieval kings before it was largely destroyed by the fire of 1834. The palace was rebuilt in Victorian Gothic style (a move away from Neoclassicism back to England's Christian and medieval heritage, true to the Romantic age). Completed in 1860, only a few of its 1,000 rooms are open to the public.

The Jewel Tower, along with Westminster Hall, is about the only surviving part of the old Palace of Westminster. It contains a fine little exhibit on Parliament (first floor—history, second floor—parliament today) and includes a 30-minute video and lonely, picnic-friendly benches (£1.50, daily 10:00–18:00, closing at 16:00 or 17:00 off-season, across the street from St. Stephens Gate, tel. 020/7222-2219).

The clock tower (315 feet high) is named for its 13-ton bell, Ben. The light above the clock is lit when the House of Commons is sitting. For a hip HOP view, walk halfway over Westminster Bridge.

▲▲**Cabinet War Rooms**—This is a fascinating walk through the underground headquarters of the British government's fight against the Nazis in the darkest days of the Battle for Britain. The 21-room nerve center of the British war effort was used from 1939 to 1945. Churchill's room, the map room, and other rooms are left just as they were in 1945. To appreciate every drop of blood, sweat, toil, and tears, pick up a headset at the entry and follow the excellent 45-minute audioguide tour (£4.80, daily 9:30–18:00, last admission 17:15, on King Charles Street 200 yards off Whitehall, follow the signs, tube: Westminster, tel. 020/7930-6961).

Horse Guards—The Horse Guards change daily at 11:00 (10:00 on Sunday) with a colorful dismounting ceremony at 16:00. The rest of the day they just stand there (on Whitehall, between Trafalgar Square and #10 Downing Street, tube: Westminster). While Buckingham Palace pageantry is canceled when it rains, the horse guards change regardless of the weather.

▲**Banqueting House**—England's first Renaissance building was designed by Inigo Jones around 1620. It's one of the few London landmarks spared by the 1666 fire and the only surviving part of the original Palace of Whitehall. Don't miss its Rubens ceiling, which, at Charles I's request, drove home the doctrine of the legitimacy of the divine right of kings. In 1649, divine right ignored, Charles I was beheaded on the balcony of this building by a Cromwellian parliament. Admission includes a restful 15-minute audiovisual history that shows the place in banqueting action, a 30-minute tape-recorded tour interesting only to history buffs, and a look at a fancy banqueting hall (£3.80, Mon–Sat 10:00–17:00, last entry at 16:15, subject to closure for government functions, aristocratic WC, immediately across Whitehall from Horse Guards, tube: Westminster, tel. 020/7930-4179).

Just up the street is...

Trafalgar Square

▲▲**Trafalgar Square**—London's central square is a thrilling place to just hang out. Lord Nelson stands atop his 185-foot-tall fluted granite column, gazing out to Trafalgar, where he lost his life but defeated the French fleet. Part of this 1842 memorial is made from the melted-down cannons of his victims at Trafalgar. He's surrounded by giant lions, hordes of people, and even more pigeons. Buy a 25p cup of bird-pleasing seed. To make the birds explode into flight, simply toss a sweater into the air. (When bombed, resist the impulse to wipe immediately—it'll smear. Wait for it to dry and then flake it off gently.) This high-profile square is the climax of most marches and demonstrations (tube: Charing Cross).

▲▲▲**National Gallery**—Wonderfully renovated, displaying Britain's top collection of European paintings from 1250 to 1900 (works by Leonardo, Botticelli, Velázquez, Rembrandt, Turner, van Gogh, and the Impressionists), this is one of Europe's great galleries (free, daily 10:00–18:00, Wed until 21:00, free one-hour tours most weekdays at 11:30 and 14:30, on Trafalgar Square, tube: Charing Cross or Leicester Square, tel. 020/7839-3321, recorded information 020/7747-2885). The CD Walkman tours are the best I've used in Europe (£3 donation requested). ✪ See National Gallery Tour on page 71.

▲**National Portrait Gallery**—Put off by halls of 19th-century characters who meant nothing to me, I used to call this "as interesting as someone else's yearbook." But a select walk through this five-centuries-long Who's Who of British History is quick, free, and puts faces on the story of England. An added bonus is the chance to admire some great art by painters such as Holbein, Van Dyck, Hogarth, Reynolds, and Gainsborough. The collection is well described, not huge, and runs in historical sequence from the 16th century on the top floor to today's royal family on the bottom.

Highlights include: Henry VIII and wives; several fascinating portraits of the "Virgin Queen" Elizabeth I, Sir Francis Drake, and Sir Walter Raleigh; the only real-life portrait of Shakespeare; Charles I and Oliver Cromwell with their heads on; self-portraits and other portraits by Gainsborough and Reynolds; the Romantics (Blake, Byron, Wordsworth, and company); Queen Victoria and her era; and the present royal family including the late Princess Diana. For more information, follow the fine CD Walkman tours (£3 donation requested, tells more history than art, hear actual interviews of 20th-century subjects) or the 60p quick-overview guidebooklet. (Free, Mon–Sat 10:00–18:00, Sun 12:00–18:00, entry 100 yards off Trafalgar Square, around the corner from National Gallery, opposite Church of St. Martin-in-the-Fields, tel. 020/7306-0055.)

▲**St. Martin-in-the-Fields**—This church, built in the 1720s with a Gothic spire placed upon a Greek-type temple, is an oasis of peace on wild and noisy Trafalgar Square. St. Martin cared for the poor. "In the fields" was where the first church stood on this spot (in the 13th century), between Westminster and the City. Stepping inside, you still feel a compassion for the needs of the people in this community. The church is famous for its concerts. Consider a free lunchtime concert (most weekdays at 13:00) or an evening concert (Thu–Sat 19:30, £6–15, tel. 020/7930-0089). Downstairs you'll find a ticket office, a good shop, a brass rubbing center, and a budget support-the-church cafeteria (see Eating chapter).

More Top Squares: Piccadilly, Soho, and Covent Garden

For a "Food is Fun" dinner crawl from Covent Garden to Soho, see page 173.

▲▲**Piccadilly Circus**—London's touristy "Town Square" is surrounded by fascinating streets and swimming with youth on the rampage. The Rock Circus offers a commercial but serious history of rock music with Madame Tussaud wax stars. While overpriced, it's an entertaining hour under radio earphones for rock 'n' roll romantics (£8, daily 10:00–20:00, plenty of photo ops, many enter with a beer buzz and sing happily off-key under their headphones—nearly as entertaining as the exhibit itself, tube: Piccadilly Circus). For overstimulation, drop by the extremely trashy Pepsi Trocadero Center's "theme park of the future" for its Segaworld virtual-reality games, nine-screen cinema, and thundering new IMAX theater (admission to Trocadero is free; individual attractions cost £2–8; find a discounted ticket at brochure racks at TIs or hotels before paying full price for IMAX; between Coventry and Shaftesbury, just off Piccadilly). Chinatown, to the east, has swollen since Hong Kong lost its independence. Nearby Shaftesbury Avenue and Leicester Square teem with fun-seekers, theaters, Chinese restaurants, and street singers.

Soho—North of Piccadilly, seedy Soho is becoming trendy and is well worth a gawk. Soho is London's red-light district where "friendly models" wait in tiny rooms up dreary stairways and scantily clad con artists sell strip shows. While venturing up a stairway to check out a model is interesting, anyone who goes into any one of the shows will be ripped off. Every time. Even a

£3 show comes with a £100 cover or minimum (as it's printed on the drink menu) and a "security man." You may accidentally buy a £200 bottle of bubbly. And suddenly, the door has no handle. By the way, telephone sex is hard to avoid these days in London. Phone booths are littered with racy fliers of busty ladies "new in town." Some travelers gather six or eight phone booths' worth of fliers and take them home for kinky wallpaper.

▲▲Covent Garden—This boutique-ish shopping district is a people watcher's delight with cigarette-eaters, Punch-and-Judy acts, food that's good for you (but not your wallet), trendy crafts, sweet whiffs of pot, two-tone hair (neither natural), and faces that could set off a metal detector. Three small museums may give your Covent Garden visit a little focus:

Cabaret Mechanical Theatre is a tiny bit of push-button and wind-up fun in the market's lower court. A puppet stamps your ticket and you slip into a room with 30 or so modern and humble yet clever automated toys (£2, Mon–Sat 10:00–18:30, Sunday 11:00–18:30, www.cabaret.co.uk). Cabaret endeavors to remain a "haven of wit, intelligence, and individuality in an increasingly homogeneous and mass-produced world."

The Theatre Museum notes that while a painter's art lives on, an actor's art dies with him. This earnest museum is an attempt to change that as it traces the development of British theater from Shakespeare to today. It's probably only worthwhile for theater buffs (£4.50, Tue–Sun 10:00–18:00, closed Mon, a block east of the market down Russell Street, call about guided tours, makeup demos, and costume workshops, tel. 020/7836-7891).

The London Transport Museum is a wonderful museum and a delight for kids. Whether you're cursing or marveling at the buses and tube, the growth of Europe's biggest city has been made possible by its public transit system. Think about it: In 1900 London had 50,000 transport horses leaving 1,000 tons of dung on the streets every day. Trace the growth of the tube, then sit in the simulator to "drive" a train (£5, Sat–Thu 10:00–18:00, Fri 11:00–18:00, 30 yards southeast of the market, tel. 020/7836-8557).

For better Covent Garden lunch deals, walk a block or two away from the eye of this touristic tornado (check out the places along Neal and Endell Streets, a block north of the tube station; see Eating chapter; tube: Covent Garden).

North London

▲▲▲British Museum—Simply put, this is the greatest chronicle of our civilization ... anywhere. A visit here is like taking a long hike through Encyclopedia Britannica National Park (free, £2 donation requested, Mon–Sat 10:00–17:00, Sun 12:00–18:00, least crowded weekday late afternoons, guided 90-min £7 tours offered daily—4/day—call museum for times, free "eye-opener" 50-minute talks on particular subjects nearly hourly—schedule at entry, tube: Tottenham Court Road, tel. 020/7636-1555, www.british-museum.ac.uk). ✪ See British Museum Tour on page 51.

▲▲▲**British Library**—Wander through the manuscripts that have enlightened and brightened our lives for centuries in the new and impressive British Library (free, £4 tours, Mon–Fri 9:30–18:00, Tue until 20:00, Sat 9:30–17:00, Sun 11:00–17:00, tube to King's Cross/St. Pancras, leaving station, turn right and walk a block to 96 Euston Road, tel. 020/7412-7332, www.bl.uk). ✪ See British Library Tour on page 100.

▲**Madame Tussaud's Waxworks**—This is expensive but dang good. The original Madame Tussaud did wax casts of heads lopped off during the French Revolution (e.g., Marie Antoinnette). She took her show on the road and ended up in London. And now it's much easier to be featured. The gallery is one big Who's Who photo-op—a huge hit with the kind of travelers who skip the British Museum. Don't miss the "make a model" exhibit (showing Jerry Hall getting waxed) or the gallery of has-been heads that no longer merit a body (such as Sammy Davis Jr. and Nikita Khruschev). After looking a hundred famous people in the glassy eyes, and surviving a silly hall of horror, you'll board a Disney-type ride and cruise through a kid-pleasing "Spirit of London" time trip (£11, children £7, under five free, daily 9:00–18:00, closes at 17:00 in winter, last admission 30 min before closing, Marylebone Road, tube: Baker Street, tel. 020/7935-6861; combined ticket for Tussaud's and Planetarium is £13 for adults, £8.50 for kids). Avoid a wait by arriving late in the day—90 minutes is plenty of time for the exhibit.

Sir John Soane's Museum—Architects and fans of eclectic knick-knacks love this quirky place (free, Tue–Sat 10:00–17:00, closed Sun and Mon, 13 Lincoln's Inn Fields, five blocks east of British Museum, tube: Holborn, tel. 020/7405-2107).

Buckingham Palace

▲**Buckingham Palace**—This has been the royal residence since 1837. When the queen's at home, the royal standard flies; otherwise the Union Jack flaps in the wind. To pay for the restoration of the fire-damaged Windsor Castle, the royal family is opening its lavish home to the public through 2000 (£10 to see the state apartments and throne room, open Aug and Sept only, daily 9:30–16:30, only 8,000 visitors a day—come early to get an appointed visit time, or call 020/7321-2233 and reserve a ticket with your credit card, tube: Victoria).

▲▲**Changing of the Guard at Buckingham Palace**—The guards

change with much fanfare daily throughout May and June at 11:30, and generally every even-numbered day July through April (no band when wet, worth a phone call any day to confirm that they'll change, tel. 020/930-4832). Join the mob behind the palace (the front faces a huge and extremely private park). You'll need to be early or tall to see much of the actual changing of the guard, but for the pageantry in the street you can pop by at 11:30. Stake out the high ground on the circular Victoria Monument for the best general views. The marching troops and bands are colorful and even stirring, but the actual changing of the guard is a nonevent. It is interesting, however, to see nearly every tourist in London gathered in one place at the same time. Hop into a big black taxi and say, "Buck House, please." The show lasts about 30 minutes: three troops parade by, the guard changes with much shouting, the band plays a happy little concert, and then they march out. On a balmy day, it's a fun happening.

For all the color with none of the crowds, see the Inspection of the Guard Ceremony at 11:00 in front of the Wellington Barracks, 500 yards east of the palace on Birdcage Walk. Afterward, stroll through nearby St. James' Park. (tube: Victoria, St. James' Park, or Green Park).

West London: Hyde Park and Nearby

▲**Hyde Park and Speakers' Corner**—London's "Central Park"— originally Henry VIII's hunting ground—has more than 600 acres of lush greenery, a huge manmade lake, the royal Kensington Palace (not worth touring), and the ornate neo-Gothic Albert Memorial across from the Royal Albert Hall. Early afternoons on Sunday, Speaker's Corner offers soapbox oratory at its best (tube: Marble Arch). "The grass roots of democracy" is actually a holdover from when the gallows stood here and the criminal was allowed to say just about anything he wanted to before he swung. I dare you to raise your voice and gather a crowd—it's easy to do.

▲**Apsley House (Wellington Museum)**—After he beat Napoleon at Waterloo, the Duke of Wellington was the most famous man in Europe. He was given London's ultimate address, #1 London. His newly refurbished mansion offers one of London's best palace experiences. An 11-foot-tall marble statue of Napoleon (by Canova), clad only in a fig leaf, greets you. Downstairs is a small gallery of Wellington memorabilia (including a 30-minute video and a pair of Wellington boots). The lavish upstairs shows off the Duke's fine collection of paintings, including works by Velázquez and Jan Steen (well described by the included CD tour wand, £4.50, Tue–Sun 11:00–17:00, closed Mon, 20 yards from Hyde Park Corner tube station, tel. 020/7499-5676). Hyde Park's pleasant and picnic-wonderful rose garden is nearby.

▲▲**Victoria and Albert Museum**—The world's top collection of decorative arts is a gangly (150 rooms over 12 miles of corridors) but surprisingly interesting assortment of artistic stuff from the West as well as Asia and Islam. The V&A, which grew out of the Great Exhibition of 1851—that ultimate festival celebrating the industrial revolution and the greatness of Britain—was originally for manufactured art. But after much support from Queen Victoria and Prince Albert, it was renamed after the royal couple and its present building was opened in 1909. The idealistic Victorian notion that anyone can be continually improved by education and example remains the driving force behind this museum.

While just wandering works well here, consider catching one of the regular 60-minute orientation tours, buying the fine £5 *Hundred Highlights* guidebook, or walking through these ground-floor highlights: Medieval Treasury (room 43, well-described treasury of Middle Age European art), the finest collection of Indian decorative art outside India (room 41), the Dress Gallery (room 40, 400 years of English fashion corseted into 40 display cases), the Raphael Gallery (room 48a, seven huge watercolor "cartoons" painted as designs for tapestries to hang in the Sistine Chapel, among the greatest art treasures in Britain and the best works of the High Renaissance), reliefs by the Renaissance sculptor Donatello (room 16), a close-up look at medieval stained glass (room 28, much more upstairs), the fascinating Cast Courts (46a and 46b, two giant rooms filled with plaster copies of the greatest art of our civilization—such as Trajan's Column and Michelangelo's *David*—made for the benefit of 19th-century art students who couldn't afford a railpass), and the hall of "great" fakes and forgeries (room 46). Upstairs you can walk through the British Galleries for centuries of aristocratic living rooms. (£5, daily 10:00–18:00, usually Wed until 21:30 in summer, free after 16:30, the museum café is in the delightfully ornate Gamble Room from 1868—just off room 14, tube: South Kensington, a long tunnel leads directly from the tube station to the museum, tel. 020/7938-8500.)

▲**Natural History Museum**—Across the street from the Victoria and Albert Museum, this mammoth museum is housed in a giant and wonderful Victorian neo-Romanesque building. Built in the 1870s specifically to house the huge collection (50 million specimens), it presents itself in two halves: the Life Galleries (creepy-crawlies, human biology, origin of the species, "our place in evolution," and awesome dinosaurs) and the Earth Galleries (meteors, volcanoes, earthquakes, and so on). Exhibits are wonderfully explained with lots of creative interactive displays (£6.50, free for kids under 16, free for anyone after 16:30 on weekdays and after 17:00 on weekends—pop in if only for the wild collection of

dinosaurs, Mon–Sat 10:00–18:00, Sun 11:00–18:00, a long tunnel
leads directly from the South Kensington tube station to the
museum, tel. 020/7938-9123, www.nhm.ac.uk).

East London: "The City"

▲▲**The City of London**—When Londoners say "The City," they
mean the one-square-mile business, banking, and journalism center
that 2,000 years ago was Roman Londinium. The outline of the
Roman city walls can still be seen in the arc of roads from Blackfriars
Bridge to Tower Bridge. Within the City are 24 churches designed
by Christopher Wren. Today, while home to only 5,000 residents,
the City thrives with over 500,000 office workers coming and going
daily. It's a fascinating district to wander, but since almost nobody
actually lives there, it's dull at night and on weekends.

▲**Old Bailey**—An hour sitting in the public galleries of the City's
Central Criminal Courts, known as "Old Bailey," is always interesting (free, Mon–Fri 10:30–13:00, 14:00–16:30, quiet in August,
ask at door which trials are where, no cameras, no bags, no cloakroom, no kids under 14, at Old Bailey and Newgate Streets, tube:
St. Paul's, tel. 020/7248-3277).

▲▲▲**St. Paul's Cathedral**—Wren's most famous church is the
great St. Paul's, its elaborate interior capped by a 365-foot dome.
During World War II, when Nazi bombs failed to blow it up,
St. Paul's became Britain's symbol of resistance.

This was the wedding church of Prince Charles and the late
Princess Diana (1981). Sit under the second-largest dome in the
world and eavesdrop on guided tours. Climb the dome for some
fun in the whispering gallery (where the precisely designed barrel
of the dome lets sweet nothings circle audibly around to the
opposite side) and a great city view. The crypt (free with admission) is a world of historic tombs and memorials, including Admiral Nelson's tomb and interesting cathedral models. (£4 entry, free
on Sun but restricted viewing due to services, £3.50 extra to climb
dome—allow an hour to climb up and down the dome, daily 9:00–
16:30, last entry 16:00, £3.50 for guided 90-min cathedral and
crypt tours offered at 11:00, 11:30, 13:30, and 14:00, or £3 for a
Walkman tour anytime, Sun services are at 8:00, 10:00, 11:30,
15:15, and 18:00, evensongs Mon–Fri at 17:00, good restaurant
and cheap and cheery café in the crypt, tube: St. Paul's, tel. 020/
7236-8348.) ✪ See St. Paul's Tour on page 117.

▲**Museum of London**—Stroll through London history from
pre-Roman times to the Blitz up through today (£5, free after
16:30, Mon–Sat 10:00–18:00, Sun 12:00–18:00, tube: Barbican or
St. Paul's, tel. 020/7600-3699). This regular stop for the local
schoolkids gives the best overview of London history in town.

THE CITY

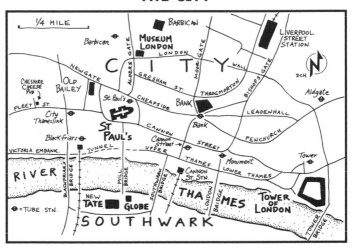

▲▲▲**Tower of London**—The Tower has served as a castle in wartime, a king's residence in peace, and, most notoriously, as the prison and execution site of rebels. This historic fortress is host to more than 3 million visitors a year. Enjoy the free, riotously entertaining 50-minute Beefeater tour (leaves regularly from inside the gate, last one is usually at 15:25). The crown jewels, dating from the Restoration, are the best on earth—and come with hour-long lines for most of the day. To avoid the crowds, arrive at 9:00 and go straight for the jewels, doing the tour and tower later; or do the jewels after 16:30 (£10.50, Mon–Sat 9:00–18:00, Sun 10:00–18:00, the long but fast-moving ticket line is worst on Sun, last entry at 17:00, tube: Tower Hill, tel. 020/7709-0765, recorded info: 020/7680-9004). ✪ See Tower of London Tour on page 122.

Ceremony of Keys: Every night at 21:30, with pageantry-filled ceremony, the Tower of London is locked up (as it has been for the last 700 years). To attend this 30-minute-long free event, you need to request an invitation at least five weeks before your visit. Write to: Ceremony of Keys, H.M. Tower of London, London EC3N 4AB. Include your name; the names, addresses, and ages of all people attending (up to seven, nontransferable); requested date and alternative dates; and an international reply coupon (buy at a U.S. post office).

Sights next to the Tower—The best remaining bit of London's **Roman Wall** is just north of the tower (at the Tower Hill tube station). Freshly painted and restored, **Tower Bridge**—

the neo-Gothic maritime gateway to London—has an 1894 to 1994 history exhibit (£6.20, daily 10:00–18:30, last entry at 17:15, good view, poor value, tel. 020/7403-3761). Just east of the Tower Bridge, the chic and newly renovated **St. Katherine Yacht Harbor** has mod shops and the classic old Dickens Inn, fun for a drink or pub lunch. Across the bridge is the South Bank, with the trendy Butlers Wharf area, museums, and promenade.

South London, on the South Bank

The South Bank is rapidly becoming a thriving arts and cultural center tied together by a riverside path. This lively, pub-crawling walk—called the Jubilee Promenade—stretches from the Tower of London Bridge to Westminster Bridge and beyond, and comes with grand views of the Houses of Parliament. (The promenade hugs the river except just east of London Bridge, where it cuts inland for a couple blocks.)

▲▲**Globe Theater**—The original Globe Theater has been rebuilt—half-timbered and thatched—exactly as it was in Shakespeare's time. It's open as a museum and hosts authentic old-time performances of Shakespeare's plays. The theater is open to tour when there are no plays (£6, May–Sept daily 9:00–12:00, Oct–Apr 10:00–17:00, includes guided 30-min tour offered on the half hour). In 2000 the Globe expands its exhibition on the history of the Globe Theater to include the beginnings of theater plus more on Shakespeare, his workplace, and his contemporaries. Expect interactive displays and possibly film presentations, a sound lab, a script factory, and a costume exhibit (included in £6 theater admission, daily 10:00–17:00, Oct–Apr 9:00–16:00, on the South Bank directly across the Thames over Southwark Bridge from St. Paul's, tube: Mansion House, tel. 020/7902-1500; for details on seeing a play, see Entertainment chapter).

▲▲**Tate Gallery of Modern Art**—Open in May of 2000, this new museum across the river from St. Paul's opens the new century with art from the old one (remember the 20th century?). This powerhouse collection of Monet, Matisse, Dalí, Picasso, Warhol, and much more is displayed in a converted powerhouse (free, special exhibitions cost extra, probably daily 10:00–18:00, Walkman tours, free guided tours, call for schedule, walk the new Millennium Bridge from St. Paul's, or tube: Southwark plus a 7-minute walk, tel. 020/7887-8000).

▲▲**Millennium Bridge**—Linking St. Paul's Cathedral and the new Tate Gallery of Modern Art, this new bridge opens in April 2000. Its sleek minimalist design—370 meters long, 4 meters wide, stainless steel with teak planks—has clever aerodynamic handrails to deflect wind over the heads of pedestrians. London's only pedestrian bridge is the city's first new bridge over the Thames in a century (free, always open).

▲▲▲Millennium Ferris Wheel (a.k.a. The British Airways London Eye)—This grand Ferris wheel towers above London opposite Big Ben on the South Bank of the Thames. It's the world's highest observational wheel, at 450 feet high, offering the highest public viewpoint in London. Built like a giant bicycle wheel, it's a pan-European undertaking: British steel and Dutch engineering, with Czech, German, French, and Italian mechanical parts. It's also very "green," running extremely efficiently, and virtually silent. Twenty-five people ride in each of its 32 capsules for the 30-minute rotation. In 2005 it will be dismantled and moved to a lower-profile location (probably £5, tel. 020/7738-8080).

▲▲Imperial War Museum—This impressive museum covers the wars of this century, from heavy weaponry to love notes and Varga Girls, from Monty's Africa campaign tank to Schwartzkopf's Desert Storm uniform. You can trace the development of the machine gun, watch footage of the first tank battles, hold your breath through the gruesome WWI trench experience, and buy WWII-era toys in the fun museum shop. The museum doesn't glorify war but chronicles the sweeping effects of humanity's most destructive century (£5.20, free for kids under 16, free for anyone after 16:30, 90 min is enough time for most visitors, daily 10:00–18:00, tube: Lambeth North, tel. 020/7416-5000).

Bramah Tea and Coffee Museum—Aficionados of tea or coffee will find this small museum fascinating. It tells the story of each drink almost passionately. The owner, Mr. Bramah, comes from a big tea family and wants the world to know how the advent of commercial television with breaks not long enough to brew a proper pot of tea required a faster hot drink. In came the horrible English instant coffee. Tea countered with finely chopped leaves in tea bags, and it's gone downhill ever since (£4, daily 10:00–18:00, in Butlers Wharf complex and behind Design Museum, just across the bridge from the Tower, tel. 020/7378-0222). Its café serves more kinds of coffees and teas than cakes (same hours as museum).

South London, on the North Bank

▲▲Tate Gallery of British Art—One of Europe's great art houses, the Tate specializes in British painting: 16th century through the 20th, including pre-Raphaelites. Commune with the mystical Blake and romantic Turner (free, daily 10:00–18:00, fine £3 CD Walkman tours, free tours weekdays: normally 11:00–British, noon–Impressionism, 14:00–Turner, 15:00–20th century, confirm schedule, tel. 020/7887-8000, tube: Pimlico). ★ See Tate Gallery of British Art Tour on page 89.

One Tate is great, but two are better. In May of 2000 the Tate's modern art collection will split off to become the new Tate Gallery of Modern Art on the South Bank (see above).

Greater London

▲**Kew Gardens**—For a fine riverside park and a palatial greenhouse jungle to swing through, take the tube or the boat to every botanist's favorite escape, Kew Gardens. While to most visitors the Royal Botanic Gardens of Kew is simply a delightful opportunity to wander among 33,000 different types of plants, it is a hardworking organization committed to understanding and preserving the botanical diversity of our planet. The Kew tube station drops you in an herbal little business community just two blocks from Victoria Gate (the main garden entry). Watch the five-minute orientation video and pick up a map brochure with a monthly listing of best blooms.

Garden lovers could spend days exploring Kew's 300 acres. For a quick visit, spend a fragrant hour wandering through three buildings: the Palm House, a humid Victorian world of iron, glass, and tropical plants; a Waterlily House—hottest in the gardens—that Monet would swim for; and the Princess of Wales Conservatory, a modern greenhouse with many different climate zones growing countless cacti, bug-munching carnivorous plants, and more (£5, Mon–Sat 9:30–18:00, Sun 9:30–19:30, until 16:30 in off-season, galleries and conservatories close a half hour earlier, entry discounted to £3.50 90 min before closing, consider the £2 narrated floral joyride on the little train that departs from Victoria gate, tube: Kew Gardens, tel. 020/8332-5000). For a sun-dappled lunch, hike 10 minutes from the Palm House to the Orangery (£6 hot meals, daily 10:00–17:30). For tea, consider the Maids of Honor (280 Kew Road, near garden entrance, tel. 020/8940-2752).

▲**Hampton Court Palace**—Fifteen miles up the Thames from downtown (£16 taxi ride from Kew Gardens) is the 500-year-old palace of Henry VIII. Actually, it was the palace of his minister, Cardinal Wolsey. When Wolsey, a clever man, realized Henry VIII was experiencing a little palace envy, he gave it to his king. The Tudor palace was also home to Elizabeth I and Charles I, and parts were updated by Christopher Wren for William and Mary. The palace stands stately overlooking the Thames with some impressive Tudor rooms including a Great Hall with its magnificent hammer-beam ceiling. The industrial-strength Tudor kitchen was capable of keeping 600 schmoozing courtesans thoroughly—if not well—fed. The sculpted garden features a rare Tudor tennis court and a popular maze. The palace, fully restored since its 1986 fire, tries hard to please, but it doesn't quite sparkle. From the information center in the main courtyard, visitors book times for

GREATER LONDON

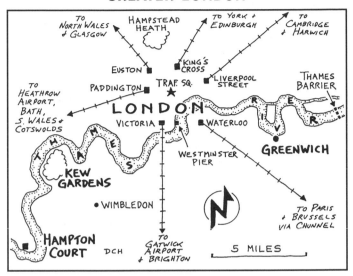

tours with tired costumed guides or grab CD-ROM wands for self-guided tours of various wings of the palace (all free). The Tudor Kitchens, Henry VIII's Apartments, and the King's Apartments are most interesting. The Georgian Rooms are pretty dull. The maze in the nearby garden is a curiosity that some find fun. The train (2/hrly, 30 min) from London's Waterloo station drops you just across the river from the palace (£10, Tue–Sun 9:30–18:00, Mon 10:15–18:00, Nov–Mar until 16:30, tel. 020/8781-9500).

▲▲▲**Greenwich and Millennium Dome**—See Day Trips chapter, page 128.

Disappointments of London

The venerable BBC broadcasts from Broadcasting House. Of all its productions, its **"BBC Experience"** tour for visitors is among the worst. On the South Bank, the **London Dungeon**, a much-visited but amateurish attraction, is just a highly advertised, overpriced haunted house—certainly not worth the £10 admission, much less your valuable London time. It comes with long and rude lines. Wait for Halloween and see one in your hometown to support a better cause. The **Design Museum** (next to Bramah Tea and Coffee Museum) and **"Winston Churchill's Britain at War Experience"** (next to London Dungeon) are also a waste of time. The **Kensington Palace State Apartments** are lifeless and not worth a visit.

WESTMINSTER WALK

4

london

From Big Ben to Trafalgar Square

London is the N.Y., L.A., and D.C. of Britain. This walk starts with London's "star" attraction, continues to its "Capitol," passes its "White House," and ends at "Times Square"... all in about an hour.

Just about every visitor to London strolls the historic White-hall boulevard from Big Ben to Trafalgar Square. This quick nine-stop guided walk gives meaning to that touristy ramble. Under London's modern traffic and big-city bustle lie 2,000 fascinating years of history. You'll get a whirlwind tour as well as a practical orientation to London.

Start halfway across Westminster Bridge (tube: Westminster), first looking upstream (Parliament) and then downstream (at the Ferris wheel).

1. Westminster Bridge: View of Big Ben and Parliament

Ding dong ding dong. Dong ding ding dong. Yes, indeed, you are in London. Big Ben is actually "Not the clock, not the tower, but the bell that tolls the hour." However, since the 13-ton bell is not visible, everyone just calls the whole works Big Ben. Ben (named for a fat bureaucrat) is scarcely older than my great-grandmother, but it has quickly become the city's symbol. The tower is 320 feet high and the clock faces are 23 feet across. The 14-foot minute hands sweep the length of your body every five minutes.

Big Ben is the north tower of a long building, the Houses of Parliament, stretching along the Thames. Britain is ruled from this building. For five centuries it was the home of kings and queens. Then, as democracy was foisted on tyrants, a parliament of nobles was allowed to meet in some of the rooms. Soon, com-moners were elected to office, the neighborhood was shot, and the royalty moved to Buckingham Palace. The current building,

— WESTMINSTER BRIDGE —

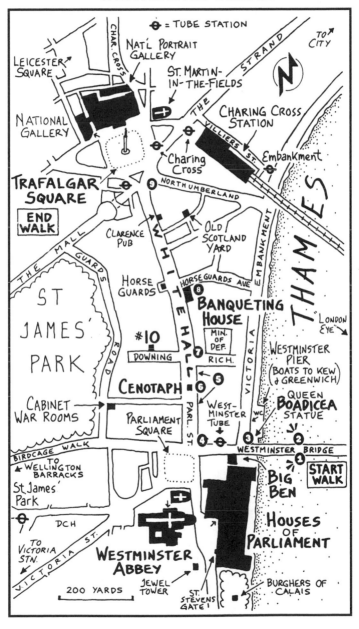

⊕ = TUBE STATION

NAT'L PORTRAIT GALLERY

CHAR. CROSS

LEICESTER SQUARE

ST. MARTIN-IN-THE-FIELDS

STRAND

TO CITY

N

CHARING CROSS STATION

NATIONAL GALLERY

THE

VILLIERS ST.

EMBANKMENT

CHARING CROSS

TRAFALGAR SQUARE

END WALK

NORTHUMBERLAND

9

THAMES

CLARENCE PUB

OLD SCOTLAND YARD

WHITEHALL

THE MALL

GUARDS

ST JAMES' PARK

HORSE GUARDS

HORSEGUARDS AVE

8

BANQUETING HOUSE

LONDON EYE

#10 DOWNING

MIN. OF DEF.

7

RICH.

WESTMINSTER PIER (BOATS TO KEW & GREENWICH)

CENOTAPH

5

6

VICTORIA

QUEEN BOADICEA STATUE

CABINET WAR ROOMS

PARLIAMENT SQUARE

WEST-MINSTER TUBE

WC

PARL. ST.

4

3

2

BIRDCAGE WALK

TO WELLINGTON BARRACKS

WESTMINSTER BRIDGE

1

START WALK

St James' Park

DCH

BIG BEN

TO VICTORIA STN.

VICTORIA ST.

WESTMINSTER ABBEY

HOUSES OF PARLIAMENT

200 YARDS

JEWEL TOWER

ST. STEVENS GATE

BURGHERS OF CALAIS

though it looks medieval, was built in the 1800s after a fire gutted old Westminster Palace.

Today, the House of Commons, which is more powerful than the queen and prime minister combined, meets in the north half of the building. The rubber-stamp House of Lords grumbles and snoozes in the south end of this 1,000-room complex and provides a tempering effect on extreme governmental changes. The two houses are very much separate: Notice the riverside tea terraces with the color-coded awnings—royal red for lords, common green for commoners.

• *Look downstream (Ferris wheel side).*

2. Westminster Bridge: City View

Aside from Big Ben, London's skyline is not overwhelming; it's a city that wows from within.

Downstream and on the other side of the river stands the huge former city hall, now a hotel complex. Shut down a decade ago, this bastion of London liberals still seems to snarl across the river at the home of the national government. The building marks the start of London's vibrant new gentrified arts and cultural zone along the South Bank of the Thames. The Jubilee Promenade, hugging the bank, makes a great one-hour walk. From Westminster Bridge (tube: Westminster), this pleasant riverside walking path runs all the way to Tower Bridge (tube: Tower Hill), leading you past several trendy new restaurants, shops, and pubs, the National Theater, the new Tate Gallery of Modern Art, the Millennium Bridge, and Shakespeare's Globe Theater. Along the way are great views across the Thames of St. Paul's dome and the City.

The 450-foot Millennium Ferris Wheel (the "London Eye"), built by British Air so people can fly BA without leaving London, will spin here for five years, giving you the highest view in town.

On the other side of the river, notice the Westminster Pier; boats depart here for the Tower of London, Greenwich, and Kew. Beyond the pier are little green copper lions' heads with rings for tying up boats. Before the construction of the Thames Barrier (the world's largest movable flood barrier, downstream near Greenwich), floods were a recurring London problem. The police measured the river by these lions. "When the lions drink, the city's at risk."

London's history is tied to the Thames, the highway that links the interior of England with the North Sea. Until 1750 only London Bridge crossed the Thames. Then a bridge was built here. Early in the morning of September 3, 1803, William Wordsworth stood where you're standing and described what he saw:

This city now doth like a garment wear
The beauty of the morning; silent, bare,
Ships, towers, domes, theaters, and temples lie
Open unto the fields, and to the sky;
All bright and glittering in the smokeless air.

• *Walk to Big Ben's side of the river. Near Westminster Pier is a big statue of a lady on a chariot (nicknamed "the first woman driver"... no reins).*

3. Boadicea, Queen of the Iceni

Riding in her two-horse chariot, daughters by her side, this Celtic Xena leads her people against Roman invaders. Julius Caesar had been the first Roman to cross the Channel, but even he was weirded out by the island's strange inhabitants who worshiped trees, sacrificed virgins, and went to war painted blue. Later Romans subdued and civilized them, building roads and making this spot on the Thames—"Londinium"—into a major urban center.

But Boadicea refused to be Romanized. In A.D. 60, after Roman soldiers raped her daughters, she rallied her people, liber-

ated London, and massacred 70,000 Romans. But the brief revolt was snuffed out, and she and her family took poison rather than surrender.

• *There's a civilized public toilet down the stairs behind Boadicea. Continue past Big Ben, one block inland to the busy intersection of Parliament Square.*

4. Parliament Square

To your left is the orange-hued Parliament. Ahead, the two white towers of Westminster Abbey rise above the trees. And broad Whitehall (here called Parliament Street) stretches to your right up to Trafalgar Square.

This is the heart of what was once a suburb of London—the medieval City of Westminster. Like Buda and Pest, London is two cities which grew into one. The City of London, centered near St. Paul's Church and the Tower of London, was the place to live. But King Edward the Confessor decided to build an abbey here, west of the city walls—hence Westminster. And to oversee its construction, he moved his court here and built the Palace of Westminster. The palace gradually evolved into a meeting place for debating public policy, which is why to this day the Houses of Parliament are still called the "Palace of Westminster."

Across from Parliament, the cute little church with the blue

sundials, snuggling under the
Abbey "like a baby lamb under a
ewe," is St. Margaret's Church.
Since 1480 this has been the place
for politicians' weddings—like
Churchill's.

Parliament Square, the small
park between Westminster Abbey
and Big Ben, is filled with statues
of famous Brits. The statue of
Winston Churchill, the man who
saved Britain from Hitler, is
shown in the military coat he wore
as he limped victoriously onto the
beaches at Normandy after D day.
According to tour guides, the
statue has a current of electricity
running through it to honor Churchill's wish that if a statue is
made of him, his head shouldn't be soiled by pigeons.

In 1868 the world's first traffic light was installed on the corner here where Whitehall now spills double-decker buses into the square. And speaking of lights, the little yellow lantern atop the concrete post on the street corner closest to Parliament says "Taxi." When a member of Parliament needs a taxi, this blinks to hail one.

• *If you have time, consider taking the Westminster Abbey Tour (page 110). Otherwise, turn right, walk away from the Houses of Parliament and the abbey, and continue up Parliament Street, which becomes Whitehall.*

5. Walking along Whitehall

Today Whitehall is choked with traffic, but imagine the effect this broad street must have had on out-of-towners a century ago. In your horse-drawn carriage, you'd clop along a tree-lined boulevard past well-dressed lords and ladies; dodging street urchins, gazing left, then right, you'd try to take it all in, your eyes dazzled by the bone-white walls of this man-made, marble canyon.

Today, Whitehall is the most important street in Britain, lined with the ministries of finance, treasury, and so on. As you walk, notice the security measures. For example, iron grates seal off the concrete ditches between the buildings and sidewalks for protection against explosives. Why so much security? London is the N.Y./L.A./D.C. of Britain, yes, but it's also the Babylon of a former colonial empire that sometimes resents its lingering control.

Notice also the ornamental arrowhead tops of the iron fences. Originally these were colorfully painted. When Prince Albert died in 1861, Queen Victoria ordered them all painted black. Probably the world's most determined mourner, when her beloved Albert died ("the only one who called her Vickie"), she wore black for the standard two-and-one-half-year period of mourning for a Victorian widow—and added an extra 38 years.

• *Continue toward the tall, square, concrete monument in the middle of the road. On your right is a colorful pub, the Red Lion. Across the street a 225-yard detour down King Charles Street leads to the Cabinet War Rooms, the underground bunker of 20 rooms that was the nerve center for Britain's campaign against Hitler (see page 29).*

6. Cenotaph

This big white stone monument honors those who died in the two events that most shaped modern Britain—World Wars I and II. The monumental devastation of these wars helped turn a colonial superpower into a cultural colony of an American superpower.

The actual "cenotaph" is the slab that sits atop the pillar— a tomb. You'll notice no religious symbols on this memorial. The dead honored here came from many creeds and all corners of Britain's empire. It looks lost in noisy traffic, but on each Remembrance Sunday (closest to November 18) Whitehall is closed off to traffic, the royal family fills the balcony overhead in the foreign ministry, and a memorial service is held around the cenotaph.

It's hard for an American to understand the impact of the Great War on Europe. It's said that if all the WWI dead from the British Empire were to march four abreast past the cenotaph, the sad parade would last for seven days.

Eternally pondering the cenotaph is an equestrian statue just up the street. Earl Haig, commander-in-chief of the British army from 1916 to 1918, was responsible for ordering so many brave and not-so-brave British boys out of the trenches and onto the killing fields of World War I.

• *Just past the cenotaph, on the other (west) side of Whitehall, is an iron security gate guarding the entrance to Downing Street.*

7. #10 Downing Street and the Ministry of Defense

Britain's version of the White House is where the prime minister and his family live, at #10—in the black-brick building a hundred yards down the blocked-off street, on the right. It looks modest, but the entryway does open up into fairly impressive digs. Britain's current prime minister is Tony Blair, a young Clinton-esque politician who prefers persuasive charm to rigid dogma. There's not much to see here unless a VIP happens to drive up. Then the bobbies snap to and check credentials, the gates open, the traffic barrier midway down the street drops into its bat cave, the car drives in, and then . . . the bobbies go back to mugging with the tourists.

The huge bleak building across Whitehall from Downing Street is the Ministry of Defense (MOD). This place looks like a Ministry of Defense should. When the building was being built, in the 1930s, they discovered and restored Henry VIII's wine cellar. English soldiers and politicians have drunk together here for 500 years . . . that's continuity.

One more security note: The drapes of the MOD are too long for good reason. They come with lead weights on the bottom. If a bomb blew out the windows, the drapes would billow in and contain the flying glass.

In front of the MOD are statues of illustrious defenders of Britain. "Monty" is Field Marshal Montgomery, the great British general of WWII fame. Monty beat the Nazis in North Africa (defeating "the Desert Fox" at El Alamein) and gave the Allies a jumping-off point to retake Europe. Along with Churchill, Monty breathed confidence back into a demoralized British army, persuading them they could ultimately beat Hitler.

Nearby, the statue of Walter Raleigh marks the spot where he was presented in glory to Queen Elizabeth. Nothing marks the spot—a few hundred yards back toward Big Ben—where he was beheaded a few years later. He's buried in St. Margaret's Church.

You may be enjoying the shade of London's plane trees. They do well in polluted London: roots which work well in clay, waxy leaves which self-clean in the rain, and bark that sheds so the pollution doesn't get into its vascular system.

• *At the equestrian statue you'll be flanked by the Welsh and Scottish government offices. At the corner (same side as the MOD) you'll find the Banqueting House.*

8. Banqueting House

The Banqueting House is just about all that remains of what was once the biggest palace in Europe—Whitehall Palace, stretching from Trafalgar Square to Big Ben. Henry VIII started it when he moved out of the Palace of Westminster (now the Parliament) and into the residence of the archbishop of York. Queen Elizabeth I and other monarchs added on as England's worldwide prestige grew. Finally, in 1698, a roaring fire destroyed everything at Whitehall except the name and the Banqueting House.

The kings held their parties and feasts in the Banqueting House's grand ballroom on the first floor. At 110 feet wide by 55 feet tall and 55 feet deep, the Banqueting House is a perfect double cube. London's first Renaissance building must have been a wild contrast to the higgledy-piggledy sprawl of the Whitehall palace complex around it.

On January 27, 1649, a man dressed in black appeared at one of the Banqueting House's first floor windows and looked out at a huge crowd that surrounded the building. He stepped out the window and onto a wooden platform. It was King Charles I. He gave a short speech to the crowd, framed by the magnificent backdrop of the Banqueting House. His final word was, "Remember." Then he knelt and laid his neck on a block as another man in black approached. It was the executioner—who cut off the King's head.

Plop—the concept of divine monarchy in Britain was decapitated. But there would still be kings after Cromwell. In fact, the royalty was soon restored and Charles' son, Charles II, got his revenge here in the Banqueting Hall... by living well. His elaborate parties under the chandeliers of the Banqueting House celebrated the Restoration of the monarchy. But from then on, every king would know that he rules by the grace of Parliament.

Charles I is remembered today with a statue at one end of Whitehall (in Trafalgar Square at the base of the tall column), while his killer, Oliver Cromwell, is given equal time with a statue at the other (at the Houses of Parliament).

• *Cross the street for a close look at the Horse Guards (11:00 changing of the guard Mon–Sat, 10:00 on Sun, dismounting ceremony daily at 16:00). Until the Ministry of Defense was created, the Horse Guards were the headquarters of the British army. It's still the home of the queen's private guard.*

Continue up Whitehall, dipping into the guarded entry court of the next big building with the too-long Ionic columns. This holds the offices of the Old Admiralty, headquarters of the British Navy. Ponder the scheming that must have gone on behind these walls as the British Navy built the greatest empire the earth has ever seen. Across the street, behind the old Clarence Pub, stood the original Scotland Yard, headquarters of London's crack police force in the days of Sherlock Holmes. Finally, Whitehall opens up into the grand, noisy, traffic-filled...

9. Trafalgar Square

London's "Times' Square" bustles around the monumental column with Admiral Horatio Nelson standing 170 feet tall in the crow's nest. Nelson saved England at a time as dark as World War II. In 1805, Napoleon (the Hitler of his day) was poised on the other side of the Channel, threatening to invade England. Meanwhile, a thousand miles away, the one-armed, one-eyed, and one-minded Lord Nelson attacked the French fleet off the coast of Spain at Trafalgar. The French were routed, Britannia ruled the waves, and the once-invincible French army would be slowly worn down and defeated at Waterloo.

Nelson—while victorious—was shot by a sniper in the battle. He died gasping, "Thank God, I have done my duty."

Surrounding the column are bronze reliefs—cast from melted-down enemy cannons—and four huggable lions, dying to have their photo taken with you. The artist had never seen a lion before so he used his dog as a model. The legs look like doggie paws.

In front of the column (nearer you) stands the statue of Charles I on horseback (the oldest such statue in town). Directly behind Charles is a pavement stone marking the center of London.

In medieval times, Westminster was the seat of government, but the financial action was downstream in London. When people from "the City" and the government needed to meet halfway, it was here. Today Trafalgar is the center of modern London.

Trafalgar Square feels cohesive because of a banister that cuts from building to building right around the square. Follow it counterclockwise from the South Africa house on the right, past the steeple of St. Martin-in-the-Fields, across the domed National Gallery, and, finally, along the Canada House on the left. Harmony.

St. Martin-in-the-Fields was built in 1722. Many Americans feel at home with this church because its style—a church spire atop a classical building—inspired many town churches in New England.

You're smack-dab in the center of London, a thriving city atop thousands of years of history. You may see me here on Trafalgar Square on December 31, 2000, gazing down Whitehall, waiting for Big Ben to ring me into the future.

BRITISH MUSEUM TOUR

In the 19th century, the British flag flew over one-fourth of the world. London was the world's capital, where women in saris walked the streets with men in top hats. And England collected art as fast as it collected colonies. In the British Museum, you'll see much of the world's greatest art from ancient Egypt, Assyria, and Greece.

The British Museum is the chronicle of Western civilization. History is a modern invention. Three hundred years ago people didn't care about crumbling statues and dusty columns. Nowadays, we value a look at past civilizations, knowing that "those who don't learn from history are condemned to repeat it."

The British Museum is the only place I know where you can follow the rise and fall of three great civilizations in a few hours with a coffee break in the middle. And, while the sun never set on the British Empire, it will on you, so on this tour we'll see just the most exciting two hours.

Orientation

Hours: Mon–Sat 10:00–17:00, Sun 12:00–18:00, closed on Good Friday, Dec 24–26, and Jan 1

Cost: Free, but £2 donation requested

Tour length: Two hours

Getting there: Tube to Russell Square, Tottenham Court Road, or Holborn, and a four-block walk. Bus 7, 8, 10, 19, 22b, 24, 25, 29, 38, 55, 68, 73, 91, 98, 134, or 188. Taxis are reasonable if you buddy up.

Information: The main-lobby information booth (English spoken) serves a free museum plan. Free 50-minute talks on particular subjects run nearly hourly; check the schedule at the entrance. Guided 90-minute £7 tours are offered daily (4/day); call museum for times. Rainy days and Sundays always get me down because

— BRITISH MUSEUM OVERVIEW —

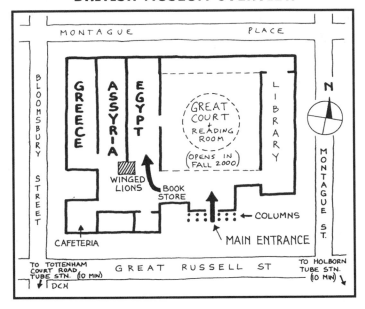

they're most crowded. Tel. 020/7636-1555, recorded information tel. 020/7388-2227, www.british-museum.ac.uk.

Cloakroom: Check your bags—anything left lying around that looks like a bomb will be treated as one. If the line is long and not moving, the cloakroom may be full.

Photography: Photos allowed, flash OK, no tripod

Cuisine art: Cheap and decent museum café and restaurant. The more comfortable and less crowded restaurant has a good salad bar and free tap water. There are lots of fast, cheap, and colorful cafés, pubs, and markets along Great Russell Street. Marx picnicked on the benches near the entrance and in Russell Square.

Starring: Rosetta Stone, Egyptian mummies, Assyrian lions, and Elgin Marbles

The Tour Begins

Our tour starts at the two huge winged Assyrian lions who stand guard over the exhibit halls covering Egypt, Assyria, and Greece. Expect construction until autumn of 2000, when the museum opens its new "Great Court" in the center of the museum.

Enter through the south entrance off Great Russell Street. Ahead is the Great Court with the round Reading Room in the

THE ANCIENT WORLD

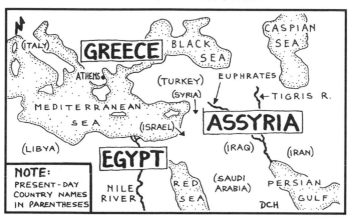

center (open in autumn of 2000), providing access to all wings. To the right is the King's Library. To the left (here on the ground floor) are Egypt, Assyria, and Greece—our tour.

From the south entrance, turn left, head through the bookshop to Room 26, and look down the long Egyptian Gallery. Introduce yourself to the Assyrian lions (with bearded human heads). We'll rendezvous here after our hikes through Egypt, Assyria, and Greece.

EGYPT (3000 B.C.–A.D. 1)

Egypt was one of the world's first "civilizations," that is, a group of people with a government, religion, art, free time, and a written language. The Egypt we think of—pyramids, mummies, pharaohs, and guys who walk funny—lasted from 3000 to 1000 B.C. with hardly any change in the government, religion, or arts. Imagine two millennia of Eisenhower.

• *Enter the Egyptian Gallery (Room 25), walking between the two black statues of pharaohs on their thrones. On your left you'll see a crowd of people surrounding a big black rock with writing on it.*

The Rosetta Stone (196 B.C.)

When this rock was unearthed in the Egyptian desert in 1799, it caused a sensation in Europe. Picture a pack of scientists (I think of the apes in that scene from *2001: A Space Odyssey*) screeching with amazement, dancing around it, and poking curiously with their fingers. This black slab caused a quantum leap in the evolution of history. Finally, Egyptian writing could be decoded.

EGYPT

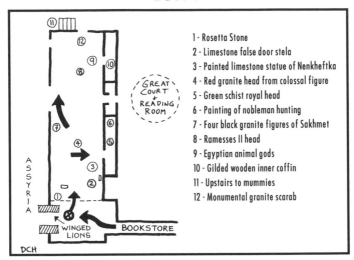

1 - Rosetta Stone
2 - Limestone false door stela
3 - Painted limestone statue of Nenkheftka
4 - Red granite head from colossal figure
5 - Green schist royal head
6 - Painting of nobleman hunting
7 - Four black granite figures of Sakhmet
8 - Ramesses II head
9 - Egyptian animal gods
10 - Gilded wooden inner coffin
11 - Upstairs to mummies
12 - Monumental granite scarab

The writing in the upper part of the stone is known as hieroglyphics. For a thousand years no one knew how to read this mysterious ancient language. Did a picture of a bird mean "bird"? Or was it a sound, forming part of a larger word, like "burden"? As it turned out, hieroglyphics are complex combination of the two.

The Rosetta Stone allowed them to break the code. It con-

tains a single inscription repeated in three languages. The bottom third is plain old Greek (find your favorite frat or sorority), while the middle is more modern Egyptian. By comparing the two known languages with the one they didn't know, they figured it out.

The breakthrough came from the large oval in the sixth line from the top. They discovered that the bird symbol represented the sound "a," part of the name Cleo-pa-tra. Simple.

• *Move on, passing between two lion statues. On your right you'll find...*

Limestone False Door (c. 2400 B.C.)
In ancient Egypt, you could take it with you. They believed that after you died, your soul lived on, enjoying its earthly possessions. This small statue represents the soul of a dead man.

It decorated his tomb, which contained all that he'd need in the next life: his mummified body, a resume of his accomplishments on earth, and his possessions—sometimes including his servants who might be buried alive with their master. The great pyramids, besides being psychic UFO power stations, were also elaborate tombs for the rich and powerful. But most tombs were small rectangular rooms of brick or stone.

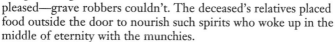

"False doors" like this were slapped on the outside of the tomb. The soul of the deceased, like the statue, could come and go through the "door" as he pleased—grave robbers couldn't. The deceased's relatives placed food outside the door to nourish such spirits who woke up in the middle of eternity with the munchies.

• *Just a few steps farther down the gallery, in a glass case on the right, you'll find the...*

Painted Limestone Statue of Nenkheftka (2400 B.C.)

After a snack the soul might wander through the nether lands

(somewhere north of Belgium) searching for paradise, meeting strange beings and weird situations. If things got too hairy, the soul could always find temporary refuge in statues like this one. It was helpful to have as many statues of yourself as possible to scatter around the earth, in case your soul needed a safe resting place.

This statue, like most Egyptian art, is not terribly lifelike—the figure is stiff, hands at the sides, left leg forward, mask-like face, stylized anatomy, and an out-of-date skirt. And talk about uptight—he's got a column down his back! But it does have all the essential features, like the simplified human figures on international traffic signs. To a soul caught in the fast lane of astral travel, this symbolic statue would be easier to spot than a detailed one.

You'll see the same rigid features in almost all the statues in the gallery.

• *Head past two tall columns that give a sense of the grandeur of the Egyptian temples. Find a huge head with a broken-bowling-pin hat.*

Red Granite Head from a Colossal Figure of a King

Art also served as propaganda for the pharaohs, kings who called themselves gods on earth. Put this head on top of an enormous body (which still stands in Egypt) and you have the intimidating image of an omnipotent ruler who demands servile obedience. Next to the head is, appropriately, the pharaoh's powerful fist— the long arm of the law.

The crown is also symbolic. It's actually two crowns in one. The pointed upper half is the royal cap of Upper Egypt. This rests on the flat fez like crown symbolizing Lower Egypt. A pharaoh wearing both crowns together is bragging that he rules a united Egypt.

• *Enter Room 25a, to the right. In a glass case you'll find . . .*

Green Schist Royal Head (c. 1490 B.C.)

This pharaoh has several symbols of authority—the familiar pointed crown of Upper Egypt, a cobra-headed "hat pin" on the forehead, and a stylized "chin strap" beard. These symbols tell us that clearly he's a powerful pharaoh, but which one?

Scholars aren't even sure if he's a he. Is it bearded King Tuthmosis III . . . or the smooth-skinned Queen Hatshepsut, one of phour phemale pharaohs who actually did wear ceremonial "beards" as symbols of royal power?

• *Ponder the mystery of this AC/DC monarch, then turn to the painting at the end of the room.*

Painting of a Nobleman Hunting in the Marshes (1425 B.C.)

This nobleman walks like Egypt-ian statues look—stiff. We see his torso from the front and every-thing else—arms, legs, face—in profile, creating the funny walk that has become an Egyptian cliché. (Like an early version of cubism, we see various perspec-tives at once.)

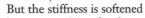

But the stiffness is softened by a humanness. It's a family scene; a snapshot of loved ones from a happy time to be remembered for all eternity. The nobleman, taking a break from his courtly duties, is hunting. He's standing in a reed boat, gliding through the marshes. His arm is raised, ready to bean a bird with a snakelike hunting stick. On the right, his wife looks on, while his daughter crouches between his legs, a symbol of fatherly protection.

Though this two-dimensional hunter looks as if he were just run over by a pyramid, the painting is actually quite realistic. The birds above and fish below are painted like encyclopedia entries. The first "paper" came from papyrus plants like the bush on the left. The only truly unrealistic element is the house cat (thigh-high, in front of the man) acting as a retriever—just possibly the only cat in history that ever did anything useful.

• *Back in the main gallery, cross over to find four black lion-headed statues.*

Four Black Granite Figures of the Goddess Sakhmet (1400 B.C.)

This goddess was a good one to have on your side. She looks pretty sedate here, but this lion-headed woman could spring into a fierce crouch when crossed. Gods were often seen as part animal, admired for being stronger, swifter, or more fierce than puny Homo sapiens.

The gods ruled the Egyptian cosmos like a big banana republic (or the American Congress). To get a favor, Egyptians bribed their gods with offerings of food, animals, or money, or by erecting statues like these to them.

Notice the ankh that Sakhmet is holding. This key-shaped cross was the hieroglyph meaning "life" and was a symbol of eternal life. Later, it was adopted as a Christian symbol because of its cross shape and religious overtones.

• *Continue to the big glass case in the middle with leftovers from an ancient Egyptian arts-and-crafts fair. Respect that bronze cat with the nose ring. Cats were the sacred cows of Egypt. You could be put to death for harming one. Walk farther on to the eight-foot granite head and torso.*

Upper Half of Colossal Statue of Rameses II of Granite (1270 B.C.)

When Moses told the king of Egypt, "Let my people go!" this was the stony-faced look he got. Rameses II (reigned c. 1290–1223 B.C.) was likely in power when Moses led the Israelites out of captivity in Egypt to their homeland in Israel. According to the Bible, Moses, a former Egyptian prince himself, appealed to the pharaoh to let them go peacefully. When the pharaoh refused, Moses cursed the land

with a series of plagues. Finally, the Israelites just bolted with the help of their God, Yahweh, who drowned the Egyptian armies in the Red Sea. Egyptian records don't exactly corroborate the tale, but this Rameses here looks enough like Yul Brynner in *The Ten Commandments* to make me a believer.

This statue, made from two different colors of granite, is a fragment from a temple in Thebes. Rameses was a great builder of temples, palaces, tombs, and statues of himself. There are probably more statues of him in the world than there are cheesy fake *Davids*. He was so concerned about achieving immortality that he even chiseled his own name on other people's statues. Very cheeky.

Imagine, for a second, what the archaeologists saw when they came upon this: a colossal head and torso separated from the enormous legs and toppled into the sand—all that remained of the works of a once-great pharaoh. Kings, megalomaniacs, and workaholics, take note.

• *Say, "Ooh, heavy," and climb the ramp behind Rameses, looking for animals.*

Various Egyptian Gods as Animals

Before technology made humans the alpha animal on earth, it was easier to appreciate our fellow creatures. The Egyptians saw the superiority of animals and worshiped them as incarnations of the gods. The lioness was stronger, so she portrayed (as we saw earlier) the fierce goddess Sakhmet.

The powerful ram is the god Amun, protecting a puny pharaoh under his powerful head. The clever baboon is Thoth, the god of wisdom, and Horus has a falcon's head. The standing hippo is Theoris, protectress of childbirth. See her stylized breasts and pregnant belly supported by ankhs, symbols of life.

• *Continuing up the ramp into Room 25b, you'll come face to face with a golden coffin.*

Gilded Wooden Inner Coffin of the Chantress of Amen-Re Henutmehit (1290 B.C.)

Look into the eyes of the deceased, a well-known singer, painted on the coffin. The Egyptians tried to cheat death by preserving their corpses. In the next life, the spirit was homeless without its body. They'd mummify the body, place it in a wooden coffin like this one, and, often, put that coffin inside a larger stone one. The result is that we now have Egyptian bodies that are as well preserved as Dick Clark.

The coffin is decorated with scenes of the deceased praising the gods, as well as magical spells to protect the body from evil and to act as crib notes for the confused soul in the netherworld.

• *You can't call Egypt a wrap until you visit the mummies upstairs. If you can handle four flights of stairs (if not, cut straight to the Assyria section from here), continue to the end of the gallery past the giant stone scarab (beetle) and up the stairs lined with Roman mosaics, then left into Rooms 59*

and 60. Snap a death-mask photo of your partner framed by an open coffin, then step into the action . . . Room 60.

Mummies

To mummify a body, disembowel it, fill the body cavities with pitch or other substances, and dry the body with natron, a natural form of sodium carbonate (and, I believe, the active ingredient in Twinkies). Then carefully bandage it head to toe with fine linen strips. Place in a coffin, wait 2,000 years, and . . . voilà! Or just dump the corpse in the desert and let the hot, dry Egyptian sand do the work—you'll get the same results.

The mummies in the glass cases here are from the time of the Roman occupation. The X-ray photos on the cases tell us more about these people. On the walls are murals showing the Egyptian burial rites as outlined in the *Book of the Dead*. In Roman times Egyptians painted a fine portrait in wax on the wrapping. And don't miss the animal mummies.

• *Linger here, but remember that eternity is about the amount of time it takes to see this entire museum. Head back down the stairs to the huge stone beetle in the center of the room at the end of the gallery.*

Monumental Granite Scarab (200 B.C.)

This species of beetle would burrow into the ground then reappear—like dying and rebirth—a symbol of resurrection.

Like the scarab, Egyptian culture was buried, first by Greece, then by Rome. Knowledge of the ancient writing died, condemning the culture to obscurity. But since the discovery of the Rosetta Stone, Egyptology is booming and Egypt has come back to life.

• *Backtrack to the Rosetta Stone. Meet you on a bench in the shadow of those bearded Assyrian human-headed lions.*

ASSYRIA (1000–600 B.C.)

Assyria was the lion, the king of beasts of early civilizations. From its base in northern Mesopotamia (northern Iraq), it conquered and dominated the Middle East—from Israel to Iran—for more than three centuries. The Assyrians were a nation of warriors—hardy, disciplined, and often cruel conquistadors—whose livelihood depended on booty and slash-and-burn expansion.

Two Winged Lions with Human Heads (c. 870 B.C.)

These lions stood guard at key points in Assyrian palaces to intimidate enemies and defeated peoples. With lion body, eagle wings, and human head, these magical beasts—and therefore the Assyrian people—had the strength of a lion, the speed of an eagle, the brain of a man, and the beard of Z. Z. Top. They protected the palace from evil spirits and they scared the heck out of foreign ambassadors and left-wing newspaper reporters. (What has five legs and flies? Take a close look. These quintrupeds appear complete from both the front and the side.)

Carved into the stone between the bearded lions' loins, you can see one of civilization's most impressive achievements—writing. This wedge-shaped ("cuneiform") script is the world's first written language, invented five thousand years ago by the Sumerians and passed down to their less-civilized descendants, the Assyrians.

• *Walk between the lions, glance at the large reconstructed wooden gates from an Assyrian palace, and turn right into the narrow red gallery lined with brown relief panels.*

Nimrud Gallery (ninth century B.C.)

This gallery is a mini-version of the main hall of Ashurnasirpal II's palace. It was decorated with these pleasant sand-colored gypsum relief panels (which were, however, originally painted).

That's Ashurnasirpal himself in the first panel on your right, with braided beard and fezlike crown, flanked by his supernatural

ASSYRIA

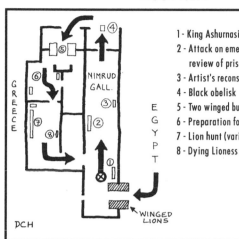

1 - King Ashurnasirpal II and protective spirits
2 - Attack on ememy town, enemy escape, review of prisoners
3 - Artist's reconstruction of palace
4 - Black obelisk
5 - Two winged bulls of Sargon II
6 - Preparation for lion hunt (various panels)
7 - Lion hunt (various panels)
8 - Dying Lioness

hawk-headed henchman. The bulging muscles tell us that Ashurnasirpal was a conqueror's conqueror who enjoyed his reputation as a savage, merciless warrior who tortured and humiliated the vanquished. The room's panels chronicle his bloody career.

The cuneiform inscription running through the center of the panel is Ashurnasirpal's résumé: "The king who has enslaved all mankind, the mighty warrior who steps on the necks of his enemies, tramples all foes and shatters the enemy; the weapon of the gods, the mighty king, the King of Assyria, the king of the world, B.A., M.B.A., Ph.D., etc...."

• *Ten yards farther down, on your left, you'll find an upper panel labeled...*

Attack on an Enemy Town

Many "nations" conquered by the Assyrians consisted of little more than a single walled city. Here, the Assyrians lay siege with a crude "tank" that shields them as they advance to the city walls to smash down the gate with a battering ram. The king stands a safe distance away behind the juggernaut and bravely shoots arrows.

• *Next, to the right, you'll find...*

Enemy Escape

Soldiers flee the slings and arrows of outrageous Assyrians by swimming across the Euphrates, using inflated animal bladders as life preservers. Their friends in the castle downstream applaud their ingenuity.

• *Below, you'll see…*

Review of Prisoners

The Assyrian economy depended on booty. Here a conquered nation is paraded before the Assyrian king, who is shaded by a parasol. Ashurnasirpal sneers and tells the captured chief: "Drop and give me 50." Above the prisoners' heads we see the rich spoils of war—elephant tusks, metal pots, and so on.

• *Notice the painted reconstruction of the palace on the opposite wall, then find the black obelisk.*

Black Obelisk of Shalmaneser III (c. 840 B.C.)

The cruel Assyrians demanded that the vanquished people pay tribute once every year (on April 15, I believe). The obelisk shows people bringing tribute to Shalmaneser from all corners of the empire. The second band from the top shows the Israelites carrying their offerings to the king, where they prostrate before him. Parts of Israel were under Assyrian domination from the ninth century B.C. on. Old Testament prophets like Elijah and Elisha constantly warned their people of the corrupting influence of the Assyrian gods.

Also check out the third band with its parade of exotic animals, especially the missing-link monkeys.

• *At the end of the Nimrud Gallery, exit and hang a U-turn left into Room 16.*

Two Winged Bulls from the Khorsabad Palace of Sargon II (c. 710 B.C.)

These 16-ton bulls guarded the palace of Sargon II. And speaking of large amounts of bull, "Sargon" wasn't his real name. It's obvious to savvy historians that Sargon must have been an insecure usurper to the throne, since the name meant "true king."

• *Sneak between these bulls and veer right into Room 17 where horses are being readied for the big hunt.*

Royal Lion Hunts

Lion hunting was Assyria's sport of kings. On the right wall we see horses being readied for the hunt. On the left wall, hunting dogs. And next to them are beautiful lions. They rest peacefully in their idyllic garden, unaware that they will shortly be rousted, stampeded, and slaughtered.

Lions lived in Mesopotamia up until modern times, and it had long been the duty of kings to keep the lion population down to protect farmers and herdsmen. This duty soon became sport as the kings of men proved their power by taking on the king of beasts. They actually bred lions to stage hunts. As we'll see, these "hunts" were as sporting as shooting fish in a barrel. The last Assyrian kings had grown soft and decadent, hardly the raging warriors of Ashurnasirpal's time.

• *Enter the larger lion-hunt room. Reading the panels like a comic strip, start on the right and gallop counterclockwise.*

The Lion-Hunt Room (c. 650 B.C.)

They release the lions from their cages. Above, soldiers on horseback herd them into an enclosed arena. The king has them cornered. Let the slaughter begin. The chariot carries decrepit King Ashurbanipal. The last of Assyria's great kings, he's ruled now for 50 years. He shoots the wrong way while spearmen hold off lions attacking from the rear.

• *At about the middle of the long wall...*

The fleeing lions, cornered by hounds, shot through with arrows and weighed down with fatigue, begin to fall, tragically. The lead lion carries on valiantly even while vomiting blood.

This, perhaps the low point of Assyrian cruelty, is the high point of their artistic achievement. It's a curious coincidence that civilizations often produce their greatest art in their declining years. Hmm.

Dying Lioness

• *On the wall opposite the vomiting lion...*

A dying lioness roars in pain and frustration. She tries to run but her body is too heavy. Her muscular hind legs, once the source of her power, are now paralyzed.

Did the sculptor sense the coming death of his own civilization? Like these brave, fierce lions, Assyria's once-great warrior nation was slain. Shortly after Ashurbanipal's death, Assyria was conquered, sacked, and

looted by an ascendant Babylon. The mood of tragedy, of dignity, of proud struggle in a hopeless cause makes this Dying Lioness simply one of the most beautiful of all human creations.
• *Return to the winged lions (where we started) by exiting the lion-hunt room at the far end. Take a break.*

To reach the Greek section, enter the doorway opposite the bookstore (Room 1), walking past early Greek Barbie and Ken dolls from the Cycladic period (2500 B.C.). Then turn right, passing through Rooms 3 and 4 to the long Room 5. Relax on a bench and read, surrounded by vases and statues.

GREECE (600 B.C.–A.D. 1)

The history of ancient Greece could be subtitled "making order out of chaos." While Assyria was dominating the Middle-Eastern world, "Greece"—a gaggle of warring tribes roaming the Greek peninsula—was floundering in darkness. But by around 700 B.C. these tribes began settling down, experimenting with democracy, forming self-governing city-states and making ties with other city-states. Scarcely two centuries later, they would be a united community and the center of the civilized world.

During its "Golden Age" (500–430 B.C.), Greece set the tone for all of Western civilization to follow. Modern democracy, theater, literature, mathematics, philosophy, science, art, and architecture, as we know them, were all virtually invented by a single generation of Greeks in a small town of maybe 80,000 citizens.
• *On the wall in Room 5, find . . .*

Map of Greek World (500–430 B.C.)

Athens was the most powerful of the city-states and the center of the Greek world. Golden Age Greece was never really a full-fledged empire, but more a common feeling of unity among Greek-speaking peoples on the peninsula.

A century after the Golden Age, Greek culture was spread still further by Alexander the Great, who conquered the Mediterranean world and beyond. By 300 B.C., the "Greek" world stretched from Italy to India to Egypt (including most of what used to be the Assyrian Empire). Two hundred years later this Greek-speaking "Hellenistic Empire" was conquered by the Romans.
• *There's a nude male to the left of the map.*

Boy (Kouros) (490 B.C.)

The Greeks saw the human body as a perfect example of the divine orderliness of the universe. For the Greeks, even the gods themselves had human forms. The ideal man was geometrically

——— EARLY GREECE ———

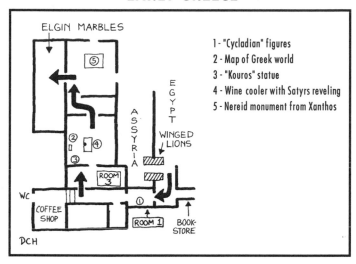

ELGIN MARBLES

⑤

E
G
Y
P
T

A
S
S
Y
R
I
A

WINGED
LIONS

②
④
③

ROOM
3

WC

COFFEE
SHOP

ROOM 1

①

BOOK-
STORE

DCH

1 - "Cycladian" figures
2 - Map of Greek world
3 - "Kouros" statue
4 - Wine cooler with Satyrs reveling
5 - Nereid monument from Xanthos

perfect, a balance of opposites, the "Golden Mean." In a statue, that meant finding the right balance between motion and stillness, between realistic human anatomy (with human flaws) and the perfection of a Greek god. This Boy is still a bit uptight, stiff as the rock from which he's carved. But—as we'll see—in just a few short decades, the Greeks would cut loose and create realistic statues that seemed to move like real humans.

• *Look in the glass case by the map, filled with decorated vases. One in the center is marked...*

Red-Figured Psykter (Wine Cooler) with Satyrs Reveling (490 B.C.)

This clay wine cooler, designed to float in a bowl of cooling water, is decorated with satyrs holding a symposium, or drinking party. These half-man/half-animal creatures (notice their tails) had a reputation for lewd behavior, reminding the balanced and moderate Greeks of their rude roots.

The reveling figures painted on this jar are more realistic, more three-dimensional, and suggest more natural movements than even the literally three-dimensional but quite stiff Kouros

statue. The Greeks are beginning to conquer the natural world in art. The art, like life, is more in balance. And speaking of "balance," if that's a Greek sobriety test, revel on.
• *Carry on into Room 7 and sit facing the Greek temple at the far end.*

Nereid Monument from Xanthos (c. 400 B.C.)

Greek temples (like this reconstruction of a temple-shaped tomb) housed a statue of a god or goddess. Unlike Christian churches, which serve as meeting places, Greek temples were the gods' homes. Worshipers gathered outside, so the most impressive part of the temple was its exterior. Temples were rectangular buildings surrounded by rows of columns and topped by slanted roofs.

The triangle-shaped roof, filled in with sculpture (reliefs or statues), is called the "pediment." The cross beams that support the roof are called "metopes" (MET-o-pees). Now look through the columns to the building itself. Above the doorway is another set of relief panels running around the building (under the "eaves") called the "frieze."

Next, we'll see pediment, frieze, and metope decorations from Greece's greatest temple.
• *Leave the British Museum. Take the Tube to Heathrow and fly to Athens. In the center of the old city, on top of the high, flat hill known as the Acropolis, you'll find . . .*

The Parthenon

The Parthenon—the temple dedicated to Athena, goddess of wisdom and the patroness of Athens—was the crowning glory of an enormous urban renewal plan during Greece's Golden Age. After Athens was ruined in a war with Persia, the city, under the bold leadership of Pericles, constructed the greatest building of its day. The Parthenon was a model of balance, simplicity, and harmonious elegance, the symbol of the Golden Age. Phidias, the greatest Greek sculptor, decorated the exterior with statues and relief panels.

While the building itself remains in Athens, many of the Parthenon's best sculptures are right here in the British

Museum—the so-called Elgin Marbles, named for the shrewd British ambassador who acquired them in the early 1800s. Though the Greek government complains

about losing its marbles, the Brits feel they rescued and preserved the sculptures.

• *Enter through the glass doors labeled "Sculptures of the Parthenon."*

THE ELGIN MARBLES (450 B.C.)

The marble panels you see lining the walls of this large hall are part of the frieze that originally ran around the exterior of the Parthenon. The statues at either end of the hall once filled the Parthenon's triangular-shaped pediments. Near the pediment sculptures, we'll also find the relief panels known as metopes. Let's start with the frieze.

The Frieze

These 56 relief panels show Athens' "Fourth of July" parade, celebrating the birth of their city. On this day, citizens marched up the Acropolis to symbolically present a new robe to the 40-foot gold and ivory statue of Athena housed in the Parthenon.

• *Start at the panels to your right (#134) and work counterclockwise.*

Men on horseback, chariots, musicians, animals for sacrifice, and young maidens with offerings are all part of the grand parade, all heading in the same direction. Prance on.

Notice the muscles and veins in the horses' legs (#128) and the intricate folds in the cloaks and dresses (#115). Some panels have holes drilled in them, where gleaming bronze reins were fitted to heighten the festive look. Of course, all these panels were originally painted in realistic colors. Despite the bustle of figures posed every which way, the frieze has one unifying element—all the heads are at the same level, creating a single ribbon around the Parthenon.

• *Cross to the opposite wall.*

A three-horse chariot (#59) cut out of only two inches of marble is more lifelike and three-dimensional than anything the Egyptians achieved in a freestanding statue.

Enter the girls (#61), the heart of the procession. Dressed in pleated robes they shuffle past the parade marshals, carrying jugs of wine and bowls to pour out an offering to the thirsty gods.

The procession culminates (#35) in the presentation of the

ELGIN MARBLES

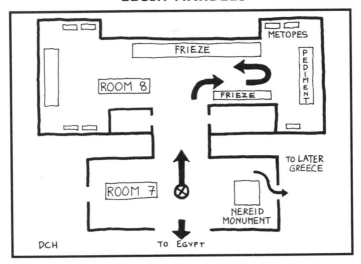

robe to Athena. A man and a child fold the robe for the goddess while the rest of the gods look on. There's Zeus and Hera (#29), the king and queen of the gods, seated, enjoying the fashion show and wondering what length hemlines will be this year.

• *Head for the set of pediment sculptures at the right end of the hall.*

The Pediment Sculptures

These statues nestled nicely in the triangular pediment above the columns at the Parthenon's east entrance. The missing statues at the peak of the triangle once showed the birth of Athena. Zeus had his head split open, allowing Athena, the goddess of wisdom, to rise from his brain fully grown and fully armed.

The other gods at this Olympian banquet slowly become aware of the amazing event. The first to notice is the one closest to them, Hebe, the cup bearer of the gods (tallest surviving fragment). Frightened, she runs to tell the others, her dress whipping behind her. A startled Demeter (just left of Hebe) turns toward Hebe.

The only one that hasn't lost his head is laid-back Dionysus (the cool guy on the far left). He just raises another glass of wine to his lips. Over on the right, Aphrodite, goddess of love, leans back into her mother's lap, too

busy admiring her own bare shoulder to even notice the hubbub. A horse screams, "These people are nuts—let me out of here!" The scene had a message. Just as wise Athena rose above the lesser gods who are scared, drunk, or vain, so would her city, Athens, rise above her lesser rivals.

This is amazing workmanship. Compare Dionysus, with his natural, relaxed, reclining pose, to all those stiff Egyptian statues standing eternally at attention. The realism of the muscles is an improvement even over the Kouros we saw, sculpted only 50 years earlier.

Appreciate the folds of the clothes on the female figures (on the right half), especially Aphrodite's clinging, rumpled robe. Some sculptors would build a model of their figure first, put real clothes on it, and study how the cloth hung down before actually sculpting in marble. Others found inspiration at the tavern on wet T-shirt night.

Even without their heads, these statues with their detailed anatomy and expressive poses speak volumes.

Wander behind. The statues originally sat 40 feet above the ground. The backs of the statues—which were never intended to be seen—are almost as detailed as the fronts. That's quality control....

• *The metopes are the panels on the walls to either side. Start with "South Metope XXXI" on the right wall, center.*

The Metopes

In #XXXI, a centaur grabs a man by the throat while the man

pulls his hair. The human Lapiths have invited some centaurs—wild half-man/half-horse creatures—to a wedding feast. All goes well until the brutish centaurs, the original party animals, get too drunk and try to carry off the Lapith women. A battle ensues.

The Greeks prided themselves on creating order out of

Centaurs slain around the world. *Dateline 500 B.C.—Greece, China, India: Man no longer considers himself an animal. Bold new ideas are exploding simultaneously around the world. Socrates, Confucius, Buddha, and others are independently discovering a non-material, unseen order in nature and in man. They say man has a rational mind or soul. He's separate from nature and different from the other animals.*

chaos. Within just a few generations, they went from nomadic barbarism to the pinnacle of early Western civilization. These metopes tell the story of this struggle between the forces of civilization (Lapiths) and barbarism (centaurs).

In #XXVIII (opposite wall, center), the centaurs start to get the upper hand as one rears triumphant over a fallen man. The leopard skin draped over the centaur's arm roars a taunt at the prone man. The humans lose face.

In #XXVII (to the left), the humans finally rally and drive off the brutish centaurs. A centaur, wounded in the back, tries to run, but the man grabs him by the neck and raises his right hand (missing) to deliver the final blow. Notice how the Lapith's cloak drapes a rough-textured background that highlights the smooth skin of this graceful, ideal man. The centaurs have been defeated. Civilization has triumphed over barbarism, order over chaos, and rational man over his half-animal alter ego.

Why are the Elgin Marbles so treasured? The British of the 19th century saw themselves as the new "civilized" race subduing "barbarians" in their far-flung empire. Maybe these rocks made them stop and wonder—will our great civilization also turn to rubble?

The Rest of the British Museum

You've toured only the foundations of Western civilization on the ground floor, west wing. Upstairs you'll find still more artifacts from these lands, plus Rome and the medieval world that sprang from it. But, of course, history doesn't begin and end in Europe. In the north wing (ground floor) are remnants of the sophisticated and exotic cultures of Asia, Africa, and Mexico—all part of the totem pole of the human family.

NATIONAL GALLERY TOUR

6

london

The National Gallery lets you tour Europe's art without ever crossing the Channel. With so many exciting artists and styles, it's a fine overture to art if you're just starting a European trip and a pleasant reprise if you're just finishing. The "National Gal" is always a welcome interlude from the bustle of London sightseeing.

Orientation

Hours: Daily 10:00–18:00, Wed until 21:00, closed on Good Friday, Dec 24–26, and Jan 1
Cost: Free
Tour length: 90 minutes
Getting there: It's central as can be, overlooking Trafalgar Square, a 15-minute walk from Big Ben, 10 minutes from Piccadilly. Tube: Charing Cross or Leicester Square. Bus: 3, 6, 9, 11, 12, 13, 15, 23, 24, 29, 53, 88, 91, 94, 109.
Information: Information desk with a free, handy floor-plan brochure in lobby. Excellent CD audioguide tours (£3) let you dial up info on any painting in the museum. The latest events schedule and a listing of free lunch lectures is in the free "National Gallery News" flier. Free one-hour general overview tours are offered most weekdays at 11:30 and 14:30. Don't miss the "Micro Gallery," a computer room even your dad could have fun in (closes 30 minutes earlier than museum). You can study any artist, style, or topic in the museum and even print out a tailor-made tour map. Tel. 020/7839-3321, recorded information 020/7747-2885.
Cloakroom: Free cloakrooms at each entrance welcome your coat and umbrella but maybe not your bag. You can take in a bag.
Photography: Strictly forbidden
Cuisine art: The Brasserie (first floor, Sainsbury Wing) is classy with reasonable prices and a petite menu. The Pret a Manger Café

(in basement, near end of this tour, just before the Impressionists) is a bustling, inexpensive, self-service cafeteria with realistic salads, Rubens sandwiches, and Gauguin juices. A block away there's a good cafeteria in the crypt of St. Martin-in-the-Fields church (facing Trafalgar Square). For pub grub, walk a block toward Big Ben and dip into the Clarence.

Starring: You name it—Leonardo, Van Eyck, Raphael, Titian, Caravaggio, Rembrandt, Rubens, Velázquez, Monet, Renoir, and van Gogh.

The Tour Begins

Of the two entrances that face Trafalgar Square, enter through the smaller building (50 yards left of the main entrance as you face it). Pick up the free map and climb the stairs. At the top, turn left and grab a seat in Room 51, facing Leonardo's *Virgin of the Rocks*.

The National Gallery offers a quick overview of European art history. We'll stay on one floor, and after a brief preview of Leonardo, we'll work chronologically through medieval holiness, Renaissance realism, Dutch detail, Baroque excess, British restraint, and the colorful French Impressionism that leads to the modern world. Cruise like an eagle with wide eyes for the big picture, seeing how each style progresses into the next.

THE ITALIAN RENAISSANCE (1400–1550)

Leonardo da Vinci—*The Virgin of the Rocks*

Mary, the mother of Jesus, plays with her son and little Johnny the Baptist (with cross, at left) while John's mother looks on. Leonardo brings this holy scene right down to earth, sitting among rocks, stalactites, water, and plants. But looking closer we see that Leonardo has deliberately posed his people into a pyramid shape, with Mary's head at the peak, creating an oasis of maternal stability and serenity amid the hard rock of the earth. Leonardo, who was illegitimate, may have sought after the young mother he never knew, in his art. Freud thought so.

The Renaissance—or "rebirth" of the culture of ancient Greece and Rome—was a cultural boom that changed people's thinking about

NATIONAL GALLERY OVERVIEW

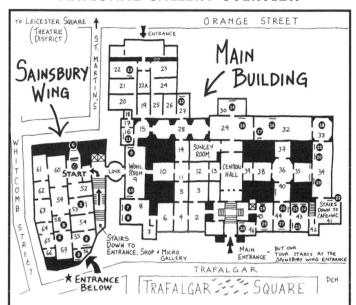

Medieval and Early Renaissance
1. Wilton Diptych
2. UCCELLO—Battle of San Romano
3. VAN EYCK—Arnolfini Marriage
4. CRIVELLI—Annunciation with St. Emidius
5. BOTTICELLI—Venus and Mars

High Renaissance
6. LEONARDO DA VINCI—Virgin and Child (painting and cartoon)
7. MICHELANGELO—Entombment
8. RAPHAEL—Pope Julius II

Venetian Renaissance
9. TINTORETTO—Origin of the Milky Way
10. TITIAN—Bacchus and Ariadne

Northern Protestant Art
11. VERMEER—Young Woman Standing at a Virginal
12. REMBRANDT—Self-Portrait
13. REMBRANDT—Belshazzar's Feast

Baroque and Rococo
14. RUBENS—The Judgment of Paris

15. VAN DYCK—Charles I on Horseback
16. VELÁZQUEZ—The Rokeby Venus
17. CARAVAGGIO—Supper at Emmaus
18. BOUCHER—Pan and Syrinx

British
19. CONSTABLE—The Hay Wain
20. TURNER—The Fighting Téméraire
21. TURNER—Rain, Steam, Speed

Impressionism and Beyond
22. DELAROUCHE—The Execution of Lady Jane Grey
23. MONET—Gare St. Lazare
24. MANET—The Waitress (La Servante de Bocks)
25. DEGAS— Miss La La at the Cirque Fernando
26. RENOIR—The Umbrellas
27. SEURAT—Bathers at Asnieres
28. VAN GOGH—Sunflowers
29. CÉZANNE—Bathers
30. MONET—Water Lilies

every aspect of life. In politics, it meant democracy. In religion, it meant a move away from Church dominance and toward the assertion of man (humanism) and a more personal faith. Science and secular learning were revived after centuries of superstition and ignorance. In architecture, it was a return to the balanced columns and domes of Greece and Rome.

In painting, the Renaissance meant realism. Artists rediscovered the beauty of Nature and the human body. With pictures of beautiful people in harmonious surroundings they expressed the optimism and confidence of this new age.

• *We'll circle back around to Leonardo in a couple hundred years. But first, turn your back on the Renaissance and cruise through the medieval world in Rooms 52, 53, and 54.*

Medieval and Early Renaissance (1260–1510)

Shiny-gold paintings of saints, angels, Madonnas, and crucifixions. One thing is very clear: Middle Ages art was religious, dominated by the Church. The illiterate faithful could meditate on an altar piece and visualize heaven.

Medieval heaven was different from medieval earth. The holy wore gold plates on their heads. Faces were serene and generic. People posed stiffly, facing directly out or to the side, never in between. Saints are recognized by the symbols they carry (a key, a sword, a book), rather than their human features. They floated in an ethereal nowhere of gold leaf. In other words, medieval artists had no need to master the techniques of portraying the "real" world of rocks, trees, and distinguished noses, because their world was... otherworldly.

• *One of the finest medieval altar pieces is in a glass case in Room 53.*

The Wilton Diptych—anonymous (c. 1395)

In this two-paneled altarpiece, a glimmer of human realism peeks through the gold leaf. The kings on the left have distinct, down-to-earth faces as they adore Mary and the baby on the right. And the back side shows not a saint, not a god, not a symbol, but a real-life deer lying down in the grass of this earth.

Still, the anonymous artist is struggling with reality. Look at the panel with the kings—John the Baptist is holding a "lamb of God" that looks more like a chihuahua. Nice try. In the right panel, the angels with their flame-like wings and cloned faces

bunch together single file across the back rather than receding real-istically into the distance. Mary's exquisite fingers hold an anatomi-cally impossible little foot. The figures are flat, scrawny, and sinless with cartoon features—far from flesh-and-blood human beings.
• *Walking straight into Room 55, you'll leave this gold-leaf peace and you'll find...*

Uccello—*Battle of San Romano* (c. 1450)

This colorful battle scene shows the victory of Florence over Siena—and the battle for literal realism on the canvas. It's an early Renais-sance attempt at a realistic, nonreligious, three-dimensional scene.

Uccello challenges his ability by posing the horses and soldiers at every conceivable angle. The background of farmyards, receding hedges, and tiny soldiers creates a 3-D illusion of distance. In the fore-ground, Uccello actually constructs a 3-D grid out of fallen lances, then places the horses and warriors within it. Still,  Uccello hasn't quite worked out the bugs—the figures in the dis-tance are far too big, and the fallen soldier on the left isn't much big-ger than the fallen shield on the right.
• *In Room 56, you'll find...*

Van Eyck—*The Arnolfini Marriage* (1434)

Called by some "The Shotgun Wedding," this painting of a sim-ple ceremony (set in Bruges, Belgium) is a masterpiece of down-to-earth details. Van Eyck has built us a medieval dollhouse, then invites us to linger over the finely crafted details. Feel the texture of the fabrics, count the terrier's hairs, trace the shadows gener-ated by the window. In fact, each object is painted at an ideal angle, with the details you'd see if you were only a foot away. So the strings of beads hanging on the back wall are as crystal-clear as the bracelets on the bride.

And to top it off, look into the round mirror on the far wall—the whole scene is reflected backward in miniature, showing the loving couple and two mysterious visitors. Is it the concerned par-ents? The minister? Van Eyck himself at his easel? Or has the artist painted you, the home viewer, into the scene?

In medieval times (this was painted only a generation after *The Wilton Diptych*) everyone could read the hidden meaning of

certain symbols—the chandelier with its one lit candle (love), the fruit on the windowsill (fertility), the dangling whisk broom (the bride's domestic responsibilities), and the terrier (Fido—fidelity).

By the way, she may not be pregnant. The fashion of the day was to wear a pillow to look pregnant in hopes you'd soon get that way. At least, that's what they told their parents.

The surface detail is extraordinary, but the painting lacks true Renaissance depth. The tiny room looks unnaturally narrow, cramped, and claustrophobic, making us wonder: Where will the mother-in-law sleep?

• *Continue into Room 57.*

Crivelli—*The Annunciation with Saint Emidius*

Mary, in green, is visited by the dove of the Holy Ghost who beams down from the distant heavens in a shaft of light.

Like Van Eyck's wedding, this is a brilliant collection of realistic details. Notice the hanging rug, the peacock, the architectural minutiae that lead you way, way back, then, bam, you've got a giant pickle in your face.

It combines meticulous detail with Italian spaciousness. The floor tiles and building bricks recede into the distance. We're sucked right in, accelerating through the alleyway, under the arch and off into space. The Holy Ghost spans the entire distance, connecting heavenly background with earthly foreground. Crivelli creates an Escher-esque labyrinth of rooms and walkways that we want to walk through, around, and into—or is that just a male thing?

Renaissance Italians were interested in—even obsessed with—portraying 3-D space. Perhaps they focused their spiritual passion away from heaven, and toward the physical world. With such restless energy, they needed lots of elbow room. Space, the final frontier.

• *In Room 58...*

Botticelli—*Venus and Mars*

Mars takes a break from war, succumbing to the delights of Love (Venus), while impish satyrs play innocently with the discarded tools of death. In the early spring of the Renaissance, there was an optimistic mood in the air, the feeling that enlightened Man could solve all problems, narrowing the gap between mortals and the Greek gods. Artists felt free to use the pagan Greek gods as symbols of human traits, virtues, and vices. Venus has sapped man's medieval stiffness and welcomed him roundly out of the darkness and into the Renaissance.

• *Now return through Room 59 to the Leonardo in Room 51, where we started.*

The High Renaissance (1500)

With the "Big Three" of the High Renaissance—Leonardo, Michelangelo, and Raphael—painters had finally conquered realism. But these three Florentine artists weren't content to just copy Nature, cranking out photographs-on-canvas. Like Renaissance architects (which they also were), they carefully composed their figures on the canvas, "building" them into geometrical patterns that reflected the balance and order they saw in Nature.

• *Enter the small dark cave behind the rocks.*

Leonardo da Vinci—*Virgin and Child with St. John the Baptist and St. Anne*

At first glance this chalk drawing, or cartoon, looks like a simple snapshot of two loving moms and two playful kids. The two children play—oblivious to the violent deaths they'll both suffer—beneath their mothers' Mona Lisa smiles.

But follow the eyes: Shadowy-eyed Anne turns toward Mary who looks tenderly down to Jesus who blesses John who gazes back dreamily. As your eyes follow theirs, you're led back to the literal and psychological center of the composition—Jesus—the alpha and omega. Without resorting to heavy-handed medieval symbolism, Leonardo drives home a theological concept in a natural, human way. Leonardo the perfectionist rarely finished paintings. This sketch gives us an inside peek at his genius.

• *Cross to the main building and enter the large Room 9. We'll return to these big, colorful canvases, but first, turn right into Room 8.*

Michelangelo—*Entombment* (unfinished)

Michelangelo, the greatest sculptor ever, proves it here in this "painted sculpture" of the crucified Jesus being carried to the tomb. The figures are almost like chiseled statues of Greek gods, especially the musclehead in red rippling beneath his clothes. Christ's naked body, shocking to the medieval Church, was completely acceptable in the Renaissance world where classical nudes were admired as an expression of the divine.

In true Renaissance style, balance and symmetry reign. Christ is the center of the composition, flanked by two equally leaning people who support his body with strips of cloth. They in turn are flanked by two more.

Where Leonardo gave us expressive faces, Michelangelo lets the bodies do the talking. The two supporters strain to hold up Christ's body, and in their tension we, too, feel the great weight and tragedy of their dead god. Michelangelo expresses the divine through the human form.

Raphael—*Pope Julius II* (1511)

The new worldliness of the Renaissance even reached the Church. Pope Julius II, who was more a swaggering conquistador than a pious pope, set out to rebuild Rome in Renaissance style (including hiring Michelangelo to paint the Vatican's Sistine Chapel).

Raphael has captured this complex man with perfect realism and psychological insight. On the one hand the pope is an imposing pyramid of power, with a velvet shawl, silk shirt, and fancy rings boasting of wealth and success. But at the same time he's a bent and broken man, his throne backed into a corner, with an expression that seems to say, "Is this all there is?"

In fact, the great era of Florence and Rome was coming to an end. With Raphael's death in 1520, the Renaissance shifted to Venice.

• *Return to the long Room 9.*

Venetian Renaissance (1510–1600)

Big change. The canvases are bigger, the colors brighter. Madonnas and saints are being replaced by goddesses and heroes. And there are nudes—not Michelangelo's lumps of noble, knotted muscle, but smooth-skinned, sexy, golden centerfolds.

Venice got wealthy by trading with the luxurious and exotic East. Its happy-go-lucky art style shows a taste for the finer things in life. But despite all the flashiness and fleshiness, Venetian art still keeps a sense of Renaissance balance.

Titian—*Bacchus and Ariadne* (1523)

In this Greek myth, Bacchus, the God of Wine, comes leaping into the picture, his red cape blowing behind him, to cheer up Ariadne (far left), who has been jilted by her lover. Bacchus'

motley entourage rattles cymbals, bangs on tambourines, and literally shakes a leg.

Man and animal mingle in this pre-Christian orgy, with leopards, a snake, a dog, and the severed head and leg of an ass ready for the barbecue. Man and animal also literally "mix" in the satyrs—part man, part goat. The fat, sleepy guy in the background has had too much.

Titian uses a pyramid composition to balance an otherwise unbalanced scene. Follow Ariadne's gaze up to the peak of Bacchus' flowing cape, then down along the snake handler's spine to the lower right corner. In addition he "balances" the picture with harmonious colors—blue on the left, green on the right, while the two main figures stand out with loud splotches of red.

Tintoretto—*The Origin of the Milky Way*

In another classical myth, the god Jupiter places his illegitimate son, baby Hercules, at his wife's breast. Juno says, "Wait a minute.

That's not my baby!" Her milk spurts upward, becoming the Milky Way, and downward, becoming lilies.

Tintoretto places us right up in the clouds, among the gods who swirl around at every angle. An "X" composition unites it all—Juno slants one way while Jupiter slants the other. The result is more dramatic and complex than the stable pyramids of Leonardo and Raphael. Also, notice how Jupiter appears to be flying almost right at us. Such shocking 3-D effects hint at the Baroque art we'll see later.

• *Exit Room 9 at the far end and turn left into Room 16 for Dutch art.*

Northern Protestant Art (1600–1700)

We switch from CinemaScope to a nine-inch TV—smaller canvases, subdued colors, everyday scenes, and not even a bare shoulder.

Money shapes art. While Italy had wealthy aristocrats and the powerful Catholic Church to purchase art, the North's patrons were middle-class, hardworking, Protestant merchants. They wanted simple, cheap, no-nonsense pictures to decorate their homes and offices. Greek gods and Virgin Marys were out, hometown folks and hometown places were in—portraits, landscapes, still lifes, and slice-of-life scenes. Painted with great attention to detail, this is art meant not to wow or preach at you, but to be enjoyed and lingered over. Sightsee.

Vermeer—*A Young Woman Standing at a Virginal*

Here we have a simple interior of a Dutch home with a prim virgin playing a "virginal." We've surprised her and she pauses to look up at us. Contrast this quiet scene with, say, Titian's bombastic, orgiastic Bacchus and Ariadne.

The Dutch took (and still take) great pride in the orderliness of their small homes. Vermeer, by framing off such a small world to look at—from the blue chair in the foreground to the wall in back—forces us to appreciate the tiniest details, the beauty of everyday things. We can meditate on the shawl, the tiles lining the floor, the subtle shades of the white wall, and, most of all, the pale diffused light that soaks in from the window. The painting of a nude cupid on the back wall only strengthens this virgin's purity.

• *Stroll down the long, blue Room 28, and turn left into Room 27.*

Rembrandt—
Belshazzar's Feast

The wicked king has been feasting with God's sacred dinnerware when the meal is interrupted. Belshazzar turns to see the finger of God, burning an ominous message into the wall that Belshazzar's number is up. As he turns, he knocks over a goblet of wine. We see the jewels and riches of his decadent life.

Rembrandt captures the scene at the most ironic moment. Belshazzar is about to be ruined. We know it, his guests know it, and, judging by the look on his face, he's coming to the same conclusion.

Rembrandt's flair for the dramatic is accentuated by the strong contrast between light and dark. Most of his canvases are a rich, dark brown, with a few crucial details highlighted by a bright light.

Rembrandt—*Self-Portrait Aged 63*

Rembrandt throws the light of truth on... himself. This craggy self-portrait was done the year he died. Contrast it with one done three decades earlier (hanging nearby). Rembrandt, the greatest Dutch painter, started out as the successful, wealthy young genius of the art world. But he refused to crank out commercial works. Rembrandt painted things that he believed in but no one would invest in—family members, down-to-earth Bible scenes, and self-portraits like these.

Here, Rembrandt surveys the wreckage of his independent life. He was bankrupt, his mistress had just died, and he had also buried several of his children. We see a disillusioned, well-worn, but proud old genius.

• *Return to the long Room 28.*

BAROQUE (1600–1700)

Rubens

This room is full of big, colorful, emotional works by Peter Paul Rubens and others from Catholic Flanders (Belgium). While Protestant and democratic Europe painted simple scenes, Catholic and aristocratic countries turned to the style called "Baroque." Baroque art took what was flashy in Venetian art and made it flashier, gaudy and made it gaudier, dramatic and made it shocking.

Rubens painted anything that would raise your pulse—battles, miracles, hunts, and, especially, fleshy women with dimples on all four cheeks. *The Judgment of Paris*, for instance, is little more than an excuse for a study of the female nude, showing front, back, and profile all on one canvas.

• *Exit Room 28 at the far end. To the left, in Room 30, you'll see the large canvas of. . .*

Van Dyck—*Charles I on Horseback*

Kings and bishops used the grandiose Baroque style to impress the masses with their power. This portrait of England's Catholic, French-educated, Divine Right king portrays him as genteel and refined, yet very much in command. Charles is placed on a huge horse to accentuate his power. The horse's small head makes sure that little Charles isn't dwarfed. Charles ruled firmly as a Catholic king in a Protestant country until England's Civil War (1648), when Charles' genteel head was separated from his refined body by Cromwell and company.

Van Dyck's portrait style set the tone for all the stuffy, boring portraits of British aristocrats who wished to be portrayed as sophisticated gentlemen—whether they were or not.

• *For the complete opposite of a stuffy portrait bust, backpedal into Room 29 for. . .*

Velázquez—*The Rokeby Venus*

Though horny Spanish kings bought Titian-esque centerfolds by the gross, this work by the king's personal court painter is the first (and, for over a century, the only) Spanish nude. Like a Venetian model, she's posed diagonally across the canvas with flaring red, white, and gray fabrics to highlight her rosy-white skin and inflame our passion. About the only concession to Spanish modesty is the false reflection in the

mirror—if it really showed what the angle should show, Velázquez would have needed two mirrors...and a new job.

• *Turning your left cheek to hers, tango into Room 32.*

Michelangelo Merisi de Caravaggio—
The Supper at Emmaus

After Jesus was crucified, he rose from the dead and appeared without warning to some of his followers. Jesus just wants a quiet meal, but the man in green, suddenly realizing who he's eating with, is about to jump out of his chair in shock. To the right, a man spreads his hands in amazement, bridging the distance between Christ and us by sticking his hand in our face.

Baroque took reality and exaggerated it. Most artists amplified the prettiness, but Caravaggio exaggerated the grittiness. He shocked the public by using real, ugly, unhaloed people in Bible scenes. Caravaggio's paintings look like a wet dog smells. Reality.

We've come a long way since the first medieval altarpieces that wrapped holy people in a golden foil. From the torn shirts to the five o'clock shadows to the uneven part in Jesus' hair, we are witnessing a very human miracle.

• *Leave the Caravaggio room under the sign reading "East Wing, painting from 1700–1900," and enter Room 33.*

FRENCH ROCOCO (1700–1800)

As Europe's political and economic center shifted from Italy to France, Louis XIV's court at Versailles became its cultural hub. Every aristocrat spoke French, dressed French, and bought French

paintings. The Rococo art of Louis' successors was as frilly, sensual, and suggestive as the decadent French court at Versailles. We see their rosy-cheeked portraits and their fantasies: lords and ladies at play in classical gardens where mortals and gods cavort together.
• *One of the finest examples is the tiny...*

Boucher—*Pan and Syrinx* (1739)
Rococo art is like a Rubens that got shrunk in the wash—smaller, lighter pastel colors, frillier and more delicate than the Baroque style. Same dimples, though.
• *Enter Room 34.*

BRITISH (1800–1850)

Constable—*The Hay Wain*
The more reserved British were more comfortable cavorting with nature than with the lofty gods. Come-as-you-are poets like Wordsworth found the same ecstasy just being outside.

Constable spent hours in the out-of-doors, capturing the simple majesty of billowing clouds, billowing trees, and everyday human activities. Even British portraits (by Thomas Gainsborough and others) placed refined lords and ladies amid idealized greenery.

This simple style—believe it or not—was considered shocking in its day. The rough, thick paint and crude country settings scandalized art lovers used to the high-falutin', prettified sheen of Baroque and Rococo.
• *Take a hike and enjoy the English-country-garden ambience of this room.*

Turner—*The Fighting Téméraire*
Constable's landscape was about to be paved over by the industrial revolution. Soon, machines began to replace humans, factories belched smoke over Constable's hay cart, and cloud gazers had to

punch the clock. Romantics tried to resist it, lauding the forces of nature and natural human emotions in the face of technological "progress." But alas, here a modern steamboat symbolically drags a famous but obsolete sailing battleship off into the sunset to be destroyed.

Turner—*Rain, Steam, and Speed*

A train emerges from the depths of fog, rushing across a bridge toward us. The red-orange glow of the engine's furnace burns like embers of a fire. (Turner was fascinated by how light penetrates haze.) Through the blur of paints, the outline of a bridge is visible, while in the center, shadowy figures (spirits?) head down to the river.

Turner's messy, colorful style gives us our first glimpse into the modern art world—he influenced the Impressionists. Turner takes an ordinary scene (like Constable), captures the play of light with messy paints (like Impressionists), and charges it with mystery (like wow).

• *London's Tate Gallery of British Art (see page 89) has an enormous collection of Turner's work. For now, enter Room 41.*

Paul Delaroche—*The Execution of Lady Jane Grey*

The teenage queen's nine-day reign has reached its curfew. This simple girl, manipulated into power politics by cunning advisors, is now sent to the execution site in the Tower of London. As her friends swoon with grief, she's blindfolded and forced to kneel at the block. Legend has it that the confused, humiliated girl was left kneeling on the scaffold. She crawled around, groping for the chopping block, crying out, "Where is it? What am I supposed to do?" The executioner in scarlet looks on with as much compassion as he can muster.

Britain's distinct contribution to art history is this Pre-Raphaelite style, showing medieval scenes in luminous realism with a mood of understated tragedy.

• *Exit Room 41, pass the door that leads downstairs to the café and WC, and enter Room 43. The Impressionist paintings are scattered throughout Rooms 43 through 46.*

IMPRESSIONISM AND BEYOND (1850–1910)

For 500 years, a great artist was someone who could paint the real world with perfect accuracy. Then along came the camera and,

click, the artist was replaced by a machine. But unemployed artists refused to go the way of the *Fighting Téméraire*.

They couldn't match the camera for painstaking detail, but they could match it—even beat it—in capturing the fleeting moment, the candid pose, the play of light and shadow, the quick impression a scene makes on you. A new breed of artists burst out of the stuffy confines of the studio. They set up their canvases in the open air or carried their notebooks into a crowded café, dashing off quick sketches in order to catch a momentary... impression.

• *Start with the misty Monet train station.*

Monet—*Gare St. Lazare* (1877) *(shown above)*

Claude Monet, the father of Impressionism, was more interested in the play of light off his subject than the subject itself. Here, the sun filters through the glass roof of the train station and is refiltered through the clouds of steam.

Manet—*The Waitress (Corner of a Café-Concert)*

Imagine how mundane (and therefore shocking) Manet's quick "impression" of this café must have been to a public that was raised on Greek gods, luscious nudes, and glowing Madonnas.

Degas—*Miss La La at the Cirque Fernando* (1879)

Degas, the master of the candid snapshot, enjoyed catching everyday scenes at odd angles.

• *In Room 44...*

Renoir—*The Umbrellas* (1880s)

View this from about 15 feet away. It's a nice scene of many-colored umbrellas. Now move in close. The "scene" breaks up into almost random patches of bright colors. The "gray" dress of the woman in the foreground is actually built from blotches of lavender, blue, green, yellow, and orange. Up close it looks like a mess, but when you back up to a proper distance, voilà! It shimmers. This kind of rough, coarse brushwork (where you can actually see the brushstrokes) is one of the telltale signs of Impressionism.

Seurat—*Bathers at Asnieres* (1883)

Seurat took the Impressionist color technique to its logical extreme. These figures—a bather, a hat, a river—are "built," dot by dot, like newspaper photos, using small points of different colors. Only at a distance do green, orange, lavender, and white blend together to make a patch of "green" grass.
• *In Room 45...*

Van Gogh—*Sunflowers* (1888)

In military terms, van Gogh was the point man of his culture. He went ahead of his cohorts, explored the unknown, and caught a bullet young. He added emotion to Impressionism, infusing his love of life even into inanimate objects. These sunflowers, painted with characteristic swirling brushstrokes, shimmer and writhe in either agony or ecstasy—depending on your own mood.

Van Gogh painted these during his stay in southern France, a time of frenzied painting when he himself hovered between agony and ecstasy, bliss and madness. Within two years of painting this, he shot himself.

In his day van Gogh was a penniless nobody, selling only one painting in his whole career. Today, a *Sunflowers* (he did a half dozen versions) sells for $40 million (a salary of about $2,500 a day for 70 years), and it's not even his highest-priced painting. Hmm.

Cézanne—*Bathers (Les Grandes Baigneuses)*

These Bathers are arranged in strict triangles *à la* Leonardo—the five nudes on the left form one triangle, the seated nude on the right forms another, and even the background trees and clouds are triangular patterns of paint.

Cézanne uses the Impressionist technique of building a figure

with dabs of paint (though his "dabs" are often larger-sized "cube" shapes) to make more solid, 3-D geometrical figures in the style of the Renaissance. In the process, his cube shapes helped inspire a radical new art style—"cube"-ism—bringing us into the 20th century.

Monet—*Water Lilies* (1916)

We've traveled from medieval spirituality to Renaissance realism to Baroque elegance and Impressionist colors. Before you spill out into the 21st-century hubbub of busy London, relax for a second in Monet's garden at Giverny near Paris. Monet planned an artificial garden, rechanneled a stream, built a bridge, and planted these water lilies—a living work of art, a small section of order and calm in a hectic world.

TATE GALLERY TOUR

The Tate is the world's best collection of British art. This is people's art, with realistic paintings rooted in the people, landscape, and stories of the British Isles. You'll see Hogarth's stage-sets, Gainsborough's ladies, Blake's angels, Constable's clouds, Turner's tempests, and the swooning realism of the Pre-Raphaelites. Even if these names are new to you, don't worry. Guaranteed you'll exit the Tate with at least one new favorite.

Orientation

Hours: Daily 10:00–18:00, closed Dec 24–26
Cost: Free
Tour length: One hour
Getting there: Subway to Pimlico (and seven-minute walk), take bus #88 or #77A, or walk 25 minutes along Thames from Big Ben.
Information: Free current map at information desk. Free tours offered (normally 11:00–British, noon–Impressionism, 14:00–Turner, 15:00–20th century). CD Walkman tours cost £3. The bookshop is great. Tel. 020/7887-8000, recorded information 0171/7887-8008, e-mail: information@tate.org.uk.
Cloakroom: Free
Photography: Without a flash is permitted.
Cuisine art: Coffee shop (affordable gourmet buffet line) and restaurant (expensive, but delightful atmosphere)
Starring: Hogarth, Gainsborough, Reynolds, Blake, Constable, Pre-Raphaelites, and Turner

The Two Tates

Beginning in May 2000, there will be two separate Tate museums: The Tate Gallery of British Art (at Millbank) and the brand-new Tate Gallery of Modern Art (at Bankside, on the South Bank of

TATE GALLERY OVERVIEW

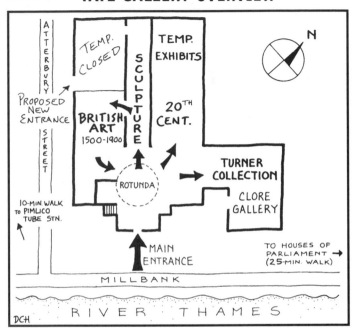

the Thames across from St. Paul's). For information on the new Tate, see page 38.

The Tour Begins

Orient yourself from the rotunda near the entrance, facing the long central sculpture gallery. The traditional British collection—the core of what we'll see—is in the left half of the museum. The 20th century is to the right. The Turner collection in the Clore Gallery is also to the right.

Warning: Expect changes. Not only is the Tate Gallery of British Art shedding its wacky modern collection (housed in the new museum on London's South Bank), it's also undergoing major construction to expand the gallery space. Until this space-odyssey ends in the summer of 2001, a painting-by-painting tour is impossible. In this chapter, we'll keep the big picture, seeing the essence of each artist and style, then let the Tate surprise us with its ever-changing wardrobe of paintings.

• *From the rotunda, walk down the central gallery, turn left into Room 1, and find Room 2.*

EARLY BRITISH ART (1500–1800)

British artists painted people, horses, countrysides, and scenes from daily life, all done realistically and without the artist passing judgment. (Substance over style.) What you won't see here is the kind of religious art so popular elsewhere. The largely Protestant English abhorred the "graven images" of Catholic saints and the Virgin Mary. Many were even destroyed during the 16th-century Reformation. They preferred landscapes of the quaint English countryside and flesh-and-blood English folk.

Portrait of Lord and Lady Whoevertheyare

These stuffy portraits of a beef-fed society try to make uncultured people look delicate and refined. English country houses often had a

long hall built specially to hang family portraits. You could stroll along and see your noble forebears looking down their noses at you. Britain's upper crust in the 1600s had little interest in art other than as a record of themselves along with their possessions— their wives, children, jewels, furs, ruffled collars, swords, and guns. You'll see plenty more portraits in the Tate, right up to modern times. Each era had its own style— some, like these, were stern and dignified; others were more relaxed and elegant.

George Stubbs—Various pictures of horses

In the 1700s, as British art came into its own, painters started doing more than just portraits. Stubbs was the Michelangelo of horse painters. He understood these creatures from the inside out, having dissected them in his studio and even using machinery to prop the corpses up into lifelike poses. He'd often paint the horses first on a blank canvas, then fill in the background landscape around them (notice the heavy outlines that make them stand out clearly from the countryside). The result is both incredibly natural—from the veins in their noses to the freshly brushed coats—and aesthetic.

William Hogarth (1697–1764)

Hogarth loved the theatre. "My picture is my stage," he said, "and my men and women my players." The curtain goes up and we see one scene that tells a whole story, often satirizing English high society. Hogarth often painted series based on popular novels or plays of the time.

William Hogarth reveled in the darker side of "merry olde England." An 18th-century Charles Dickens, Hogarth's best paintings were slices of real England. Not content to paint just pretty portraits, he chose models from real life and put them into real-life scenes.

A born Londoner, Hogarth loved every gritty aspect of the big city. You could find him in seedy pubs and brothels, at the half-price ticket booth in Leicester Square, at prizefights, cockfights, duels, and public executions—sketch pad in hand. With biting satire, he exposed the hypocrisy of the upper class...and exposed the upper classes to the hidden poverty of society's underbelly.

Thomas Gainsborough (1727–1788)

Portraits were still the bread and butter for painters, and Thomas Gainsborough was one of the best. His specialty was showcasing the elegant, educated women of his generation. The results were always natural and never stuffy. The cheeks get rosier, the poses more relaxed, the colors brighter and more pastel, showing the influence of the refined French culture of the court at Versailles. His models' clear, Ivory-soap complexions stand out from the swirling greenery of English gardens.

Sir Joshua Reynolds and the "Grand Style" (1750–1800)

Real life wasn't worthy of a painting. So said Britain's Royal Academy. People, places, and things had to be gussied up with Greek columns, symbolism, and great historic moments, ideally from classical Greece.

Sir Joshua Reynolds, the pillar of England's art establishment, stood for all that was noble, upright, tasteful, rational, brave, clean, reverent, and boring. According to Reynolds, art was meant to elevate the viewer, to appeal to his rational nature and fill him with noble sentiment.

By combining history and portraits, he could turn Lord Milquetoast into a heroic Greek patriot, or Lady Bagbody into the Venus de Milo. Combining the Grand Style with landscapes, you get Versailles-type settings of classical monuments amid landscaped greenery.

Since so much of the art we'll see from here on was painted in the looming shadow of Reynolds, and since his technique and morals are flawless, let's dedicate a minute's silence to his painting. Fifty-nine. Fifty-eight. I'll be in the next room.

Constable's Landscapes (1776–1837)

While the Royal Academy thought Nature needed makeup, Constable thought She was just fine. He painted the English landscape just as it is, realistically, and without idealizing it.

Constable's style became more "Impressionistic" near the end of his life—messier brushwork. He often painted full-scale "sketches" of works he'd perfect later (such as the Salisbury cathedral).

It's rare to find a Constable (or any British) landscape that  doesn't have the mark of man in it—a cottage, hay cart, country lane, or field hand. For him, the English countryside and its people were one.

Cloudy skies are one of Constable's trademarks. Appreciate the effort involved in sketching ever-changing cloud patterns for hours on end—the mix of dark clouds and white clouds, cumuli and strati, the colors of the sunset. His subtle genius wasn't fully recognized in his lifetime, and he was forced to paint portraits for his keep. The neglect caused him to ask a friend: "Can it therefore be wondered at that I paint continual storms?"

Other Landscapes

Compare Constable's unpretentious landscapes with the others in the Tate. Some artists mixed landscapes with intense human emotion to produce huge, colorful canvases of storms, burning sunsets, towering clouds, and crashing waves, all dwarfing puny humans. Others made supernatural, religious fantasy-scapes. Artists in the "Romantic" style saw the most intense human emotions reflected in the drama and mystery in Nature. God is found within Nature, and Nature is charged with the grandeur and power of God.

THE INDUSTRIAL REVOLUTION (1800–1900)

Think of England at midcentury. Newfangled inventions were everywhere. Railroads laced the land. You could fall asleep in Edinburgh and wake up in London, a trip that used to take days or weeks. But along with technology came factories coating towns with soot, urban poverty, regimentation, and clock punching. Machines replaced honest laborers, and once-noble Man was viewed as a naked ape.

Strangely, you'll see little of the modern world in paintings of the time—except in reaction to it. Many artists rebelled against "progress" and the modern world. They looked back to ancient Greece as a happier, more enlightened time (neoclassicism of Reynolds). Or to the Middle Ages (Pre-Raphaelites). Or they escaped the dirty cities to commune with nature (Romantics). Or they found a new spirituality in intense human emotions (dramatic scenes from history or literature). Or they left our world altogether. (Which brings us to...)

William Blake

At the age of four, Blake saw the face of God. A few years later, he ran across a flock of angels swinging in a tree. Twenty years later he was living in a run-down London flat with an illiterate wife, scratching out a thin existence as an engraver. But even in this squalor, ignored by all but a few fellow artists, he still had his heavenly visions, and he described them in poems and paintings.

One of the original space cowboys, Blake was also a unique painter who is often classed with the "Romantics" because he painted in a fit of ecstatic inspiration rather than by studied technique. He painted angels, archangels, thrones, and dominions rather than the dull material world. While Britain was conquering the world with guns and Nature with machines, and while his fellow Londoners were growing rich, fat, and self-important, Blake turned his gaze inward, painting the glorious visions of the soul.

Blake's work hangs in a darkened room to protect the watercolors. Enter his mysterious world and let your pupils dilate opium wide.

His pen and watercolor sketches glow with an unearthly aura. In visions of heaven and hell, his figures have superhero musculature. The colors are almost translucent.

Blake saw the material world as bad, trapping the divine spark inside each of our bodies and keeping us from true communion with God. Blake's prints illustrate his views on the ultimate weakness of material, scientific man. Despite their Greek-god anatomy, his men look noble, but tragically lost.

A famous poet as well as painter, Blake summed up his distrust of the material world in a poem addressed to "The God of this World," that is, Satan:

> *Though thou art worshiped by the names divine*
> *Of Jesus and Jehovah, thou art still*
> *The son of morn in weary night's decline,*
> *The lost traveler's dream under the hill.*

PRE-RAPHAELITES (1850–1880)

Millais, Rossetti, Waterhouse, Hunt, Burne-Jones, etc.

You'll see medieval damsels in dresses and knights in tights, legendary lovers from poetry, and even a very human Virgin Mary as a delicate young woman. The women wear flowing dresses, with long, wavy hair and delicate, elongated, curving bodies. Beautiful.

You won't find Pre-Raphaelites selling flowers at the airport, but this "Brotherhood" of young British artists had a cultic intensity. (You may see the initials P.R.B.—Pre-Raphaelite Brotherhood—by the artist's signature in some paintings.) After generations of the pompous Grand Style art, the Pre-Raphaelites finally said, "Enough's enough." They focused on: 1) Nature, 2) sincere human feelings, 3) medieval subjects, and 4) expressive symbolism.

They returned to a style "Pre-Raphael." The art was intended to be "medieval" in its simple style, in the melancholy mood, and often in subject matter. "Truth to Nature" was their slogan. Like the Impressionists who followed, they donned their scarves, barged out of the stuffy studio, and set up outdoors, painting trees, streams, and people as they really were. Still, they often captured nature with such a close-up clarity that it's downright unnatural.

And despite the Pre-Raphaelite claim to paint life just as it is, this is so beautiful it hurts. Be prepared to suffer, unless your heart is made of stone.

This is art from the cult of femininity, worshiping Woman's haunting beauty, compassion, and depth of soul. (Proto-feminism or

retro-chauvinism?) The artists' wives and lovers were their models and muses, and the art echoed their love lives. The people are surrounded by nature at its most beautiful, with every detail painted crystal clear. Even without the people, there is a mood of melancholy.

The Pre-Raphaelites hated gushy sentimentality and overacting. Their subjects—even in the face of great tragedy, high passions, and moral dilemmas—barely raise an eyebrow. Outwardly, they're reflective, accepting their fate. But subtle gestures and sinuous postures speak volumes. These volumes were footnoted by the small objects with symbolic importance placed around them: red flowers denoting passion, lilies for purity, pets for fidelity, and so on.

The colors—greens, blues, and reds—are bright and clear, with everything evenly lit so we see every detail. To get the luminous color, they painted a thin layer of bright paint over a pure white, still-wet undercoat, which subtly "shines" through. These canvases radiate a pure spirituality, like stained-glass windows.

Victorian (1837–1901)

Middle-class Brits loved to see Norman Rockwell–style scenes from everyday life. The style has Pre-Raphaelite realism but is too sentimental for Pre-Raphaelite tastes.

We see families and ordinary people eating, working, and relaxing. Some works tug at the heartstrings, with scenes of parting couples, the grief of death, or the joy of families reuniting. Dramatic scenes from popular literature get the heart beating. There's the occasional touching look at the plight of the honest poor, reminiscent of Dickens. And many paintings warn us to be good little boys and girls by showing the consequences of a life of sin. Then there are the puppy dogs with sad eyes.

Stand for a while and enjoy the exquisite realism and human emotions of these Victorian works... real people painted realistically. Get your fill, because beloved Queen Victoria is about to check out, the modern world is coming, and with it, new art to express modern attitudes.

• *To help ease the transition...*

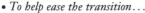

The Turner Collection

J. M. W. Turner (1775–1851)

The Tate has the world's best collection of Turners. Walking through his life's work, you can trace his progression from a painter of realistic historical scenes, through his wandering years, to "Impressionist" paintings of color-and-light patterns.

• *The Turner Collection is in the Clore Gallery, the wing that juts out to the right of the Tate. Enter through the bookstore on the other side of the rotunda.*

Start in the large square Room T1, marked "High Art, History, and the Sublime." From these early paintings, the collection runs roughly chronologically as you work your way through to Room T9.

Room T1—High Art, History, and the Sublime

Trained in the Reynolds school of grandiose epics, Turner painted the obligatory big canvases of great moments in history—*The Battle of Waterloo, Hannibal in the Alps, Destruction of Sodom, The Lost Traveler's Checks, Jason and the Argonauts,* and various shipwrecks. Not content to crank them out in the traditional staid manner, he sets them in expansive landscapes. Nature's stormy mood mirrors the human events, but is so grandiose it dwarfs them.

This is a theme we'll see throughout his works: The forces of Nature—the burning sun, swirling clouds, churning waves, gathering storms, and the weathering of Time—overwhelm men and wear down the civilizations they build.

Room T2

See his self-portrait as a young man, and read details of his life.

Room T3—Travels with Turner

Turner's true love was Nature. And he was a born hobo. Oblivious to the wealth and fame that his early paintings gave him, he set out traveling—mostly on foot—throughout England and the Continent, with a rucksack full of sketch pads and painting gear.

He found the "Sublime" not in the studio or in church, but in the overwhelming power of Nature. The landscapes throb with life and motion.

• *Walk up the hallway (T5) back toward the Tate, popping into the four rooms along the way.*

THE TURNER COLLECTION

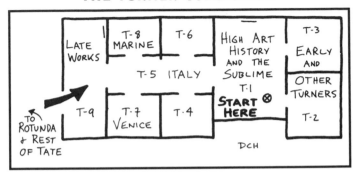

```
                                        —
  LATE    T-8      T-6    HIGH ART     T-3
  WORKS  MARINE          HISTORY      EARLY
                        AND THE        AND
          T-5  ITALY    SUBLIME
                          T·1         OTHER
                        START ⊗      TURNERS
         T-9    T·7      T·4    HERE
 ↖     ROTUNDA VENICE                  T-2
TO     & REST
OF TATE                        DCH
```

Room T5—Italy: Landscape and Antiquity

Rick Steves' guidebook in hand, Turner visited the great museums of Italy, drawing inspiration from the Renaissance masters. He painted the classical monuments and Renaissance architecture. He copied masterpieces, learned, assimilated, and fused a great variety of styles—a true pan-European vision.

Stand close to a big canvas of Roman ruins, close enough to where it fills your whole field of vision. Notice how the buildings seem to wrap around you. Turner was a master of using multiple perspectives to draw the viewer in. On the one hand, you're right in the thick of things, looking "up" at the tall buildings. Then again, you're looking "down" on the distant horizon, as though standing on a mountaintop.

Room T7—Venice

I know what color the palazzo is. But what color is it at sunset? Or after filtering through the watery haze that hangs over Venice? Can I paint the glowing haze itself? Maybe if I combine two different colors and smudge the paint on....

Venice titillated Turner's lust for reflected light. This room contains both finished works and unfinished sketches...uh, which is which?

Room T8—Marine and Coastal Subjects

Seascapes were his specialty, with waves, clouds, mist, and sky churning and mixing together, all driven by the same forces.

Turner used oils like many painters use watercolors. First he'd lay down a background (a "wash") of large patches of color, then he'd add a few dabs of paint to suggest a figure. The final product lacked photographic clarity but showed the power and constant change in the forces

of Nature. He was perhaps the most prolific painter ever, with some 2,000 finished paintings and 20,000 sketches and watercolors.

Room T9—Late Works

The older he got, the messier both he and his paintings became. He was wealthy, but died in a run-down dive where he'd set up house with a prostitute. Yet the colors here are brighter and the subjects less pessimistic than in the dark and brooding early canvases. His last works—whether landscape, religious, or classical scenes—are a blur and swirl of colors in motion, lit by the sun or a lamp burning through the mist. Even Turner's own creations are finally dissolved by the swirling forces of Nature.

These paintings are "modern" in that the subject is less important than the style. You'll have to read the title to "get" it. You could argue that an Englishman helped invent Impressionism a generation before Monet and his ilk boxed the artistic ears of Paris in the 1880s. Turner's messy use of paint to portray reflected light "chunneled" its way to France to inspire the Impressionists.

BRITISH LIBRARY TOUR

The British Empire built its greatest monuments out of paper. It's in literature that England has made her lasting contribution to history and the arts. Opened in 1998 in a fine new building, this national archives of Britain has more than 12 million books, 180 miles of shelving, and the deepest basement in London. We'll concentrate on a handful of documents—literary and historical— that changed the course of history. Start with the top 12 stops (described in this tour), then stray according to your interests.

Orientation

Open: Mon–Fri 9:30–18:00 (until 20:00 on Tue), Sat 9:30–17:00, Sun 11:00–17:00

Cost: Free

Tour length: One hour

Getting there: Tube to King's Cross/St. Pancras Station. Leaving the station, turn right and walk a block to 96 Euston Road. (Note that the British Library is no longer housed within the British Museum.)

Information: Tours are offered usually Mon, Wed, and Fri at 15:00, Sat at 10:30 and 15:00, Sun at 11:30 and 15:00, Tue at 18:30 (one hour, £4, for schedule and to reserve, tel. 020/7412-7332, library tel. 020/7412-7000, www.bl.uk).

Cloakroom: Free

No-nos: No photography, smoking, or chewing gum

Cuisine art: The library's restaurant and café, while nothing special from an eating point of view, have a 50-foot-tall wall of 65,000 old books given to the people by King George IV in 1823. This mother of all bookshelves is pretty high tech behind glass with movable lifts.

Starring: Magna Carta, Bibles, Shakespeare, English Lit 101, and the Beatles

BRITISH LIBRARY TOUR

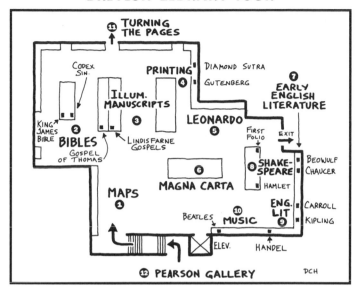

The Tour Begins

Entering the library courtyard you'll see a big statue of a naked Isaac Newton bending forward with a compass to measure the universe. The statue symbolizes the library's purpose: to gather all knowledge and promote our endless search for truth.

Stepping inside you'll see the information desk. The cloak-room, WC, and café are to the right. The Reading Rooms upstairs are not open to the public. Our tour is in the tiny but exciting area to the left, under the sign marked "Exhibitions."

The priceless literary and historical treasures of the collection are in this one carefully designed and well-lit room. The "Turning the Pages" computer room is in an adjoining room. Down a few steps you'll find the Pearson Gallery (with its recommended *History of Children's Lit* exhibit).

1. Maps

Navigate the wall of historic maps from left to right. "A Medieval Map of Britain," from 1250, puts medieval man in an unusual position—looking down on his homeland from 50 miles in the air. "The Christian World View" of 1260 has Jerusalem in the middle and God on top. The open book, from 1490, shows the best map Columbus could get—a map of everything in the world except...

what was just off the page. And then a 1506 map ("America?") shows the first depiction of America...as part of Asia. By 1562 ("America!") North America had a New Yorker's perspective—detailed East Coast, sketchy California, and "Terra Incognita" in between. By 1570 you could plan your next trip with Mercator's map of Europe.

2. Bibles

My favorite excuse for not learning a foreign language is: "If English was good enough for Jesus Christ, it's good enough for me!" I don't know what that has to do with anything, but obviously Jesus didn't speak English—nor did Moses or Isaiah or Paul or any other Bible authors or characters. As a result, our present-day English Bible is not directly from the mouth and pen of these religious figures, but the fitful product of centuries of evolution and translation.

The Bible is not a single book; it's an anthology of books by many authors from different historical periods writing in different languages (usually Hebrew or Greek). So there are three things that editors must consider in compiling the most accurate Bible: 1) deciding which books actually belong, 2) finding the oldest and most accurate version of each book, and 3) translating it accurately.

Codex Sinaiticus (c. A.D. 350)

The oldest complete "Bible" in existence (along with one in the Vatican), this is one of the first attempts to collect various books together into one authoritative anthology. It's in Greek, the language in which most of the New Testament was written. The Old Testament portions are Greek translations from the original Hebrew. This particular Bible, and the nearby *Codex Alexandrus* (A.D. 425), contain some books not included in most modern English Bibles. (Even today Catholic Bibles contain books not found in Protestant Bibles.)

Fragment of an Unknown Gospel and The Gospel of Thomas

Here are pieces—scraps of papyrus—of two such books that didn't make it into our modern Bible. The "Unknown Gospel" (an account of the life of Jesus of Nazareth) is as old a Christian manuscript as any in existence. Remember, the Gospels weren't written down for a full generation after Jesus died, and the oldest surviving manuscripts are from later than that. So why isn't this early version of Jesus' life part of our Bible right up there with Matthew, Mark, Luke, and John? Possibly because some early Bible editors didn't like the story it told about Jesus not found in the four accepted Gospels.

The "Gospel of Thomas" gives an even more radical picture of Jesus. This Jesus preaches enlightenment by mystical knowledge. He seems to be warning people against looking to gurus for the answers, a Christian version of "If you meet the Buddha on the road, kill him." This fragment dates from A.D. 150, more than a century after Jesus' death, but that's probably not the only reason why it's not in our Bible (after all, the Gospel of John is generally dated at A.D. 100). Rather, the message, which threatened established church leaders, may have been too scary to include in the Bible—whether Jesus said it or not.

The King James Bible (1611)

This Bible is in the same language you speak, but try reading it. The strange letters and archaic words clearly show how quickly languages evolve.

Jesus spoke Aramaic, a form of Hebrew. His words were written down in Greek. Greek manuscripts were translated into Latin, the language of medieval monks and scholars. By 1400 there was still no English version of the Bible, though only a small percentage of the population understood Latin. A few brave reformers risked death to make translations into English and print them with Gutenberg's new invention. Within two centuries English translations were both legal and popular.

The King James version (done during his reign) has been the most popular English translation. Fifty scholars worked for four years, borrowing heavily from previous translations, to produce the work. Its impact on the English language was enormous, making Elizabethan English something of the standard, even after all those "thees" and "thous" fell out of fashion in everyday speech.

In our century, many new translations are both more accurate (based on better scholarship and original manuscripts) and more readable, using modern speech patterns.

3. Lindisfarne Gospels (A.D. 698) and Illuminated Manuscripts

Throughout the Middle Ages, Bibles had to be reproduced by hand. This was a painstaking process usually done by monks for a rich patron. This beautifully illustrated ("illuminated") collection of the four Gospels is the most magnificent of medieval British monk-u-scripts. The text is in Latin, the language of scholars ever since the Roman Empire, but the elaborate decoration mixes Irish, classical, and even Byzantine forms.

These Gospels are a reminder that Christianity almost didn't make it in Europe. After the fall of Rome (which had established Christianity as the official religion), much of Europe reverted to

its pagan ways. This was the time of Beowulf, when people worshiped woodland spirits, smurfs, and terrible Teutonic gods. It took dedicated Irish missionaries 500 years to reestablish the faith on the Continent. Lindisfarne, an obscure monastery of Irish monks on an island off the east coast of England, was one of the few beacons of light after the fall of Rome, tending the embers of civilization through the long night of the Dark Ages. (You can virtually flip through the Lindisfarne Gospels in the adjacent "Turning the Pages" computer room.)

Browse through more illuminated manuscripts (in the cases behind the Lindisfarne Gospels). This is some of the finest art from what we call the "Dark Ages." The little intimate details offer a rare and fascinating peek into medieval life.

4. Printing

The *Diamond Sutra*, from 868, is the earliest dated printed document. Printing was common in Asia from the mid-eighth century—700 years before Gutenberg "invented" the printing press in Europe. Texts such as this "Buddhist Bible" were printed using wooden blocks carved with Chinese characters that were dipped into paint or ink. Notice also the fine wood-block illustration. This was discovered in China in 1907.

The Gutenberg Bible— The First Book Printed in Europe (c. 1455)

It looks like just another monk-made Latin manuscript, but it's the first book printed in Europe. Printing is one of the most revolutionary inventions in history. Johann Gutenberg (c. 1397–1468), a German goldsmith, devised a convenient way to reproduce written materials quickly, neatly, and cheaply—by printing with movable type. You scratch each letter onto a separate metal block, then arrange them into words, ink them up, and press them onto paper. When one job was done you could reuse the same letters for a new one.

This simple idea had immediate and revolutionary consequences. Knowledge became cheap and accessible to a wide audience, not just the rich. Books became the "mass media" of Europe, linking people by a common set of ideas. And, like a drug, this increased knowledge only created demand for still more.

Suddenly the Bible was available for anyone to read. Church authorities, more interested in "protecting" than spreading the word of God, passed laws prohibiting the printing of Bibles. As the Church feared, when people read the Bible they formed their own opinions of God's message, which was often different from the version spoon-fed to them by priests. In the resulting Reformation, Protestants broke away from the Catholic Church, confident they could read the Bible without a priest's help.

5. Leonardo da Vinci's Notebook

Books also spread secular knowledge. Renaissance men turned their attention away from heaven, to the nuts and bolts of the material world around them. These pages from Leonardo's notebook show his powerful curiosity, his genius for invention, and his famous backward and inside-out handwriting.

One person's research inspired another's, and books allowed knowledge to accumulate. While Galileo championed the counter-commonsense notion that the earth spun around the sun, Isaac Newton perfected the mathematics of those moving bodies.

6. Magna Carta

How did Britain, a tiny island with a few million people, come to rule a quarter of the world? Not by force but by law. The Magna Carta was the basis for England's constitutional system of government.

In the year 1215, England's barons rose in revolt against the slimy King John. After losing London, John was forced to negotiate. The barons presented him with a list of demands ("The Articles of the Barons"). John, whose rule was worthless without the support of the barons, had no choice but to fix his seal to it.

This was a turning point in the history of government. Kings had ruled by God-given authority. They were above the laws of men, acting however they pleased. Now for the first time there were limits—in writing—on how a king could treat his subjects. More generally, it established the idea of "due process"—that is, the government can't infringe on people's freedom without a legitimate legal reason. This small step became the basis for all constitutional governments, including yours.

A few days after John agreed to this original document, it was rewritten in legal form, and some 35 copies of this final version of the "Great Charter" were distributed around the kingdom ("Magna Carta" and "Burnt Magna Carta").

So what did this radical piece of paper actually say? Not much by today's standards. The specific demands had to do with things like inheritance taxes, the king's duties to widows and orphans, and so on. It wasn't the specific articles that were important, but the simple fact that the king had to abide by them as law.

Around the corner there are many more historical documents in the library—letters by Queen Elizabeth I, Isaac Newton, Wellington, Gandhi, and so on. But for now, let's trace the evolution of...

7. Early English Literature

Four out of every five English words have been borrowed from other languages. The English language, like English culture (and London today), is a mix derived from foreign invaders. Some of the historic ingredients that make this cultural stew are:

1. The original Celtic tribesmen
2. Romans (A.D. 1–500)
3. Germanic tribes called Angles and Saxons (making English a Germanic language and naming the island "Angle-land"— England)
4. Vikings from Denmark (A.D. 800)
5. French-speaking Normans under William the Conqueror (1066–1250).

Beowulf (c. 1000)

This Anglo-Saxon epic poem written in Old English, the early version of our language, almost makes the hieroglyphics on the Rosetta Stone look easy. The manuscript here is from A.D. 1000, although the poem itself dates to about 750. This is the only existing medieval manuscript of this first English literary masterpiece.

In the story, the young hero Beowulf defeats two half-human monsters threatening the kingdom. Beowulf symbolizes England's emergence from Dark Age chaos and barbarism.

The Canterbury Tales (c. 1410)

Six hundred years later, England was Christian but it was hardly the pious, predictable, Sunday-school world we might imagine. Geoffrey Chaucer's bawdy collection of stories, told by pilgrims on their way to Canterbury, gives us the full range of life's experiences—happy, sad, silly, sexy, and pious. (Late in life, Chaucer wrote an apology for those works of his "that tend toward sin.")

While most serious literature of the time was written in scholarly Latin, *The Canterbury Tales* was written in Middle

English, the language that developed when the French invasion (1066) added a Norman twist to Old English.

8. Shakespeare

William Shakespeare (1564–1616) is the greatest author in any language. Period. He expanded and helped define modern English. In one fell swoop he made the language of everyday people as important as Latin. In the process, he gave us phrases like "one fell swoop" that we quote without knowing it's Shakespeare.

Perhaps as important was his insight into humanity. With his stock of great characters—Hamlet, Othello, Macbeth, Falstaff, Lear, Romeo and Juliet—he probed the psychology of human beings 300 years before Freud. Even today, his characters strike a familiar chord.

Shakespeare as a Collaborator

Shakespeare cowrote a play titled *The Booke of Sir Thomas More*. Some scholars have wondered if maybe Shakespeare had help on other plays as well. After all, they reasoned, how could a journey-man actor, with little education, have written so many master-pieces? Modern scholars, though, unanimously agree that Shakespeare did indeed write the plays ascribed to him.

The Good and Bad Quarto of *Hamlet*

Shakespeare wrote his plays to be performed, not read. He published a few, but as his reputation grew, unauthorized "bootleg" versions also began to circulate. Some of these were written out by actors, trying (with faulty memories) to recreate a play they'd been in years before. Here are two different versions of *Hamlet*: "good" and "bad."

The Shakespeare First Folio (1623)

It wasn't until seven years after his death that this complete-works collection of his plays came out. The editors were friends and fellow actors.

The engraving of Shakespeare on the title page is one of only two likenesses done during his lifetime. Is this what he really looked like? No one knows. The best answer probably comes from his friend and fellow poet Ben Jonson in the introduction on the facing page. He concludes: "Reader, look not on his picture, but his book."

9. Other Greats in English Literature

The rest of the "Beowulf/Chaucer wall" is a greatest-hits sampling of British literature featuring the writing of Wordsworth, Blake, Dickens, and James Joyce. Especially interesting may be:

Coleridge—Xanadu, an Earthly Paradise
from *Kubla Khan*

One day Samuel Taylor Coleridge took opium. He fell asleep while reading about the fantastic palace of the Mongol emperor, Kubla Khan. During his three-hour drug-induced sleep, he composed in his head a poem of "from two to three hundred lines." When he woke up, he grabbed a pen and paper and "instantly and eagerly wrote down the lines that are here preserved." But just then, a visitor on business knocked at the door and kept Coleridge busy for an hour. When Coleridge finally kicked him out, he discovered that he'd forgotten the rest! The poem *Kubla Khan* is only a fragment, but it's still one of literature's masterpieces.

Coleridge (aided by his Muse in the medicine cabinet) was one of the Romantic poets. Check out his fellow Romantics—Keats, Shelley, and Wordsworth—nearby.

Dickens

In 1400, few people could read. By 1850 almost everyone in England could and did. Charles Dickens gave them their first taste of "literature." Periodicals serialized his books, and the increasingly educated masses read them avidly. Stories recount mobs of American fans waiting at the docks with "Who shot J. R.?" enthusiasm for the latest news of their favorite character.

Dickens also helped raise social concern for the underprivileged—of whom England had more than her share. When Dickens was 12 years old, his father was thrown into debtor's prison, and young Charles was put to work to support the family. The ordeal of poverty scarred him for life and gave him experiences he'd draw on later for books such as *Oliver Twist* and *David Copperfield*.

Lewis Carroll—The Original
Alice in Wonderland

I don't know if Lewis Carroll ever dipped into Coleridge's medicine jar or not, but his series of children's books makes *Kubla Khan* read like the phone book. Carroll was a stammerer, which made him uncomfortable around everyone but children. For them he created a fantasy world where grown-up rules and logic were turned upside down.

10. Music

The Beatles
Future generations will have to judge whether this musical quartet ranks with artists like Dickens and Keats, but no one can deny its historical significance. The Beatles burst onto the scene in the early 1960s to unheard-of popularity. With their long hair and loud music, they brought counterculture and revolutionary ideas to the middle class, affecting the values of a whole generation.

Look for the photos of John Lennon, Paul McCartney, George Harrison, and Ringo Starr before and after their fame.

Most interesting are the manuscripts of song lyrics written by Lennon and McCartney, the two guiding lights of the group. "I Wanna Hold Your Hand" was the song that launched them to superstardom. John's song, "Help," was the quickly written title song for one of the Beatles' movies. Some call "A Ticket to Ride" the first heavy-metal song. "Yesterday," by Paul, was recorded with guitar and voice backed by a string quartet—a touch of sophistication by the producer George Martin. Also glance at the rambling, depressed, cynical, but humorous letter by John on the left. Is that a self-portrait at the bottom?

Music Manuscripts
Kind of an anticlimax after the Fab Four, I know, but here are manuscripts by Handel, Mozart, Beethoven, Schubert, and others.

11. Turning the Pages—Virtual Reality Room
For a chance to virtually flip though the pages of a few of the most precious books in the collection, drop by the "Turning the Pages" room. Grab a computer and let your fingers do the walking.

12. Pearson Gallery and Printing Workshop
As you leave, browse through the Pearson Gallery for a chance to trace the story of writing, the evolution of printing and bookmaking, and the history of children's books. "W is for the woman, who not overly nice, made very short work of the three blind mice."

WESTMINSTER ABBEY TOUR

Westminster Abbey is the greatest church in the English-speaking world. England's kings and queens have been crowned and buried here since 1066. The history of Westminster Abbey and of England are almost the same. A thousand years of English history—3,000 tombs, the remains of 29 kings and queens, and hundreds of memorials—lie within its walls and under its stone slabs.

Orientation
Hours: Mon–Fri 9:00–16:45, also Wed 18:00–19:45, Sat 9:00–14:45, closed Sun to sightseers but open for services, last admission 60 minutes before closing. Mornings are most crowded. On weekdays, 15:00 is less crowded; come then and stay for the 17:00 evensong (not held on Wed).
Cost: £5, half-price Wed evening. Praying is free, thank God; use separate marked entrance.
Tour length: 90 minutes
Getting there: Near Big Ben and houses of Parliament (tube: Westminster)
Information: Informative audioguide tours cost £2 (offered until 15:00 weekdays or until 13:00 Sat). Vergers, the church equivalent of docents, give more entertaining guided tours for £3 (up to 6/day, 90 min, tel. 020/7222-7110 to get times). Tour themes are the historic church, the personalities buried here, and the great coronations. Evensong is on Mon, Tue, Thu, and Fri at 17:00, Sat and Sun at 15:00; an organ recital is held Sun at 17:45 (confirm times, tel. 020/7222-5152).
Photography: Prohibited, except on Wed evening
Starring: Edwards, Elizabeths, Henrys, Annes, Richards, Marys, and the Poets' Corner

WESTMINSTER ABBEY TOUR

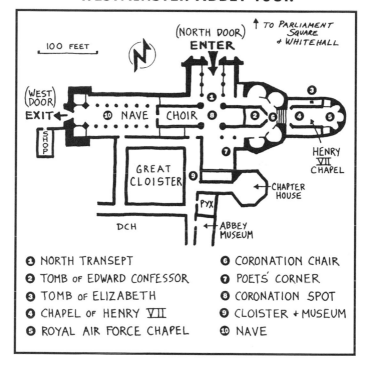

❶ NORTH TRANSEPT
❷ TOMB of EDWARD CONFESSOR
❸ TOMB of ELIZABETH
❹ CHAPEL of HENRY VII
❺ ROYAL AIR FORCE CHAPEL

❻ CORONATION CHAIR
❼ POETS' CORNER
❽ CORONATION SPOT
❾ CLOISTER + MUSEUM
❿ NAVE

The Tour Begins
You'll have no choice but to follow the steady flow of tourists in through the north transept, wandering among tombstones, circling behind the altar, into Poets' Corner in the south transept, detouring through the cloisters and finally back out through the west end of the nave. It's all one way and the crowds can be a real crush. Here are the Abbey's top-10 stops:
• *Walk straight in, pick up the map flier that locates the most illustrious tombs, and belly up to the barricade in the center.*

1. North Transept
Look down the long and narrow center aisle of the church. Lined with the praying hands of the Gothic arches, glowing with light from the stained glass, it's clear that this is more than a museum. With saints in stained glass, heroes in carved stone, and the bodies of England's greatest under the floor stones, Westminster Abbey is the religious heart of England.

You're standing at the center of a cross-shaped church.
The main altar (with cross and candlesticks) sits on the platform
up the five stairs in front of you. To the right stretches the long,
high-ceilinged nave. Nestled in the nave is the elaborately carved
wooden seating of the choir (or "quire").

The Abbey was built in 1065. Its name, Westminster, means
Church in the West (west of St. Paul's). For the next 250 years the
abbey was redone and remodeled to become essentially the church
you see today, notwithstanding an extensive resurfacing in the
19th century. Thankfully, later architects—ignoring building
trends of their generation—honored the vision of the original
planner and the building was completed in one relatively harmonious style. The 10-story nave is the tallest in England. The chandeliers, 10 feet tall, look small in comparison. (Sixteen were given
to the Abbey by the Guinness family.)

The north transept (through which you entered) is nicknamed
"Statesmen's Corner" and specializes in famous prime ministers.
Find Gladstone and the novelist/politician Disraeli, who presided
over England's peak of power under Queen Victoria.

Musicians may want to hum "Pomp and Circumstance"
and detour to the right where Edward Elgar, Vaughn-Williams,
and others are honored. (Is there a slab awaiting Lloyd-
Webber yet?)

• *Now turn left and follow the crowd. Walk under Robert Peel, the
prime minister whose policemen were nicknamed "bobbies," and stroll a
few yards into the land of dead kings and queens. Stop at the blocked
wooden staircase on your right.*

2. Tomb of Edward the Confessor

The most holy part of the church is the raised area behind the
altar (where the wooden staircase leads). Step back and peek over
the dark coffin of Edward I to see the green and gold wedding-
cake tomb of King Edward the Confessor—the man who built
Westminster Abbey.

God had told pious Edward to visit St. Peter's Basilica in
Rome. But, with Normans thinking conquest, it was too dangerous
for him to leave England. Instead, he built this grand church
and dedicated it to St. Peter. It was finished just in time to bury
Edward (1065) and to crown his foreign rival, William the
Conqueror (1066). After Edward's death, people prayed on his
tomb and, after getting fine results, canonized him (he was the
only English king ever to be sainted). This elevated, central tomb
is surrounded by the tombs of eight kings and queens.

• *Continue on. At the top of the large staircase, detour left into the
private burial chapel of Queen Elizabeth I.*

3. Tomb of Queen Elizabeth I and Mary I

Although there's only one effigy on the tomb (Elizabeth's), there are two queens buried beneath it, both daughters of Henry VIII (by different mothers). Bloody Mary—meek, pious, sickly, and Catholic—enforced Catholicism during her reign by burning "heretics" at the stake and executing young Lady Jane Grey.

Elizabeth—strong, clever, "virginal," and Protestant—steered England on an Anglican course. Her long reign was one of the greatest in English history, a time when England ruled the seas and Shakespeare explored human emotions. The effigy, taken from Elizabeth's death mask, is considered a very accurate take on this virgin queen.

The two half-sisters disliked each other in life—Mary even had Elizabeth locked up in the Tower of London. Now they lie side by side for eternity—with a prayer for Christians of all persuasions to live peacefully together.

• *Continue into the ornate room behind the main altar.*

4. Chapel of King Henry VII (a.k.a. the Lady Chapel)

The light from the stained-glass windows and the colorful banners overhead give the room the festive air of a medieval tournament. The prestigious Knights of Bath meet here, under the magnificent ceiling studded with gold pendants. Unless you're going to Cambridge's King's College Chapel, this ceiling is the finest English Perpendicular Gothic and fan vaulting you'll see. The brilliant stone ceiling was built in 1509, capping the Gothic period and signaling the vitality of the coming Renaissance.

The knights sit in the wooden stalls with churches on their heads, capped by their own insignia. When the queen worships here, she sits in the corner chair under the carved wooden throne.

Behind the small altar is an iron cage housing tombs of the old warrior Henry VII of Lancaster and his wife, Elizabeth of York. Their love and marriage finally settled the "War of the Roses" between the two clans. The combined red-and-white rose symbol decorates the ironwork. Henry VII was the first Tudor king, the father of Henry VIII, and grandfather of Elizabeth I. This exuberant chapel heralds a new optimistic postwar era in English history.

• *Walk past Henry and Elizabeth to the far end of the chapel. Stand at the banister in front of the modern set of stained-glass windows.*

5. Royal Air Force Chapel

Saints in robes and halos mingle with pilots in bomber jackets and parachutes in this tribute to World War II flyers who earned their angel wings in the Battle of Britain. Hitler's air force ruled the skies in the early days of the war, bombing at will, threatening to snuff Britain out without a fight. These were the fighters about whom Churchill said, "Never has so much been owed by so many to so few."

The abbey survived the blitz virtually unscathed. As a memorial, a bit of bomb damage—the little glassed-over hole in the wall—is left below the windows in the lower left-hand corner. The book of remembrances lists each casualty of the Battle of Britain.

Hey. Look down at the floor. You're standing on the grave of Oliver Cromwell, leader of the rebel forces in England's Civil War. Or rather, Cromwell was buried here from 1658 to 1661. Then his corpse was exhumed, hanged, drawn, quartered, and decapitated, with the head displayed on a stake as a warning to future king-killers.

• *Exit the Chapel of Henry VII and step out of the flow of traffic. To your left is a door to a side chapel with the tomb of Mary Queen of Scots (beheaded by Elizabeth). Ahead of you, at the foot of the stairs, is the Coronation Chair. Behind the chair, again, is the tomb of the church's founder, Edward the Confessor.*

6. Coronation Chair

The gold-painted wooden chair waits here—with its back to the high altar—for the next coronation. For every English coronation since 1296, it's been moved to its spot before the high altar to receive the royal buttocks. The chair's legs rest on lions, England's symbol. The space below the chair originally held a big rock from Scotland called the Stone of Scone (pronounced "skoon"), symbolizing Scotland's unity with England's king. Recently, however, Britain gave Scotland more sovereignty, its own Parliament, and the stone.

• *Continue on. Turn left into the south transept. You're in Poets' Corner.*

7. Poets' Corner

England's greatest contribution to art is the written word. Here lie buried the masters of arguably the world's most complex and expressive language. (Many writers are honored with plaques and monuments; relatively few are actually buried here.)

• *Start with Chaucer, buried in the wall under the blue windows. The plaques on the floor before Chaucer are memorials to other literary greats.*

Geoffrey Chaucer is often considered the father of English literature. Chaucer's *Canterbury Tales* told of earthy people speaking everyday English. He was buried here first. Later, Poets' Corner was built around his tomb.

Lord Byron, the great lover of women and adventure: "Though the night was made for loving, and the day returns too soon/Yet we'll go no more a-roving by the light of the moon."

Dylan Thomas, alcoholic master of modernism with a

Romantic's heart: "Oh as I was young and easy in the mercy of his means/Time held me green and dying/Though I sang in my chains like the sea."

W. H. Auden: "May I, composed like them of Eros and of dust/Beleaguered by the same negation and despair/Show an affirming flame."

Lewis Carroll, creator of *Alice in Wonderland*: "'Twas brillig, and the slithy toves did gyre and gimble in the wabe...."

T. S. Eliot, the dry voice of modern society: "This is the way the world ends/Not with a bang but a whimper."

Alfred, Lord Tennyson, conscience of the Victorian Age: "'Tis better to have loved and lost/Than never to have loved at all."

Robert Browning: "Oh, to be in England/Now that April's there."

• *Farther out in the south transept, you'll find...*

William Shakespeare: Although he's not buried here, a fine statue of this greatest of English writers stands near the end of the transept, overlooking the others: "All the world's a stage/And all the men and women merely players./They have their exits and their entrances/And one man in his time plays many parts."

George Handel: High on the wall opposite Shakespeare is the man famous for composing "The Messiah": "Hallelujah, hallelujah, hallelujah." His actual tomb is on the floor next to...

Charles Dickens, whose serialized novels brought "literature" to the masses: "It was the best of times, it was the worst of times."

You'll also find tombs of Samuel Johnson (who wrote the first English dictionary) and the great English actor Lawrence Olivier. (Olivier disdained the "Method" style of experiencing intense emotions in order to portray them. When his costar stayed up all night in order to appear haggard for a scene, Olivier said, "My dear boy, why don't you simply try acting?")

• *Walk to the center of the abbey in front of the high altar. Stand directly under the central spire.*

8. The Coronation Spot

Here is where every English coronation since 1066 has taken place. The nobles in robes and powdered wigs look on from the carved wooden stalls of the choir. The archbishop stands at the high altar (table with candlesticks, up five steps). The coronation chair is placed in the center of the church, directly below the design-work cross on the ceiling high in the middle of the central tower. Surrounding the whole area are temporary bleachers for VIPs, creating a "theatre." At Queen Elizabeth's 1953 coronation, 7,000 sat on bleachers going halfway up the rose windows of each transept.

Imagine the day when Prince William becomes king. Long

silver trumpets hung with banners will be raised and sound a fanfare, as the monarch-to-be enters the church. The congregation
will sing, "I will go into the house of the Lord," as he parades
slowly down the center of the nave and up the steps to the altar.
After a church service, he'll be seated in the chair, facing the nobles
in the choir. A royal scepter and orb will be placed in his hands,
and—dut, dutta dah—the archbishop will lower the Crown of St.
Edward the Confessor onto his royal head. Finally, King William
will stand up, descend the steps, and be presented to the people for
their approval. The people will cry, "God save the king!"
• *Royalty are also given funerals here. Princess Diana's coffin lay here
before her funeral service. She was then buried on her family estate.
Exit the church (temporarily) at the south door, leading to...*

9. Cloisters and Museum
The church is known as the "Abbey" because it was the headquarters
of Benedictine monks—until Henry VIII kicked them out in 1540.
The buildings that adjoin the church housed the monks. Cloistered
courtyards gave them a place to meditate on God's creation.

Look back at the church through the cloisters. Notice the
flying buttresses—the stone bridges that push in on the church
walls—that allowed Gothic architects to build so high.

Historians should pay £1 extra for three more rooms. The
Chapter House, where the monks had daily meetings, features fine
architecture with faded but well described medieval art. The tiny
Pyx Chamber has an exhibit about the King's Treasury. The Abbey
Museum, formerly the monks' lounge with a cozy fireplace and
snacks, now has fascinating exhibits on royal coronations, funerals,
abbey history, and a close-up look at medieval stained glass.
• *Go back into the church for the last stop.*

10. Nave
On the floor near the west entrance of the abbey is the flower-
lined Tomb of the Unknown Warrior, one ordinary WWI soldier
buried in soil from France with lettering made from melted-down
weapons from that war. Think about that million-man army from
the Empire and Commonwealth that gave their lives. Hanging on
a column next to the tomb is the U.S. Congressional Medal of
Honor presented to England's WWI dead by General Pershing in
1921. Closer to the door is a memorial to Winston Churchill.

Look back down the nave of the abbey, filled with the
remains of the people who made Britain great—saints, royalty,
poets, musicians, soldiers, politicians. Now step back outside into a
city filled with the same kind of people.

ST. PAUL'S
TOUR

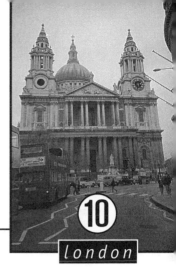

10

london

No sooner was Christopher Wren selected to refurbish Old St. Paul's church than the Great Fire of 1666 incinerated it. Within six days, Wren had a plan for a whole new building... and for the city around it, complete with some 50 new churches. For the next four decades he worked to achieve his vision—a spacious church, topped by a dome, surrounded by a flock of Wrens.

St. Paul's is England's national church. There's been a church on this spot since 604. It was the symbol of London's rise from the Great Fire of 1666 and of London's survival of the blitz of 1940.

Orientation

Hours: Daily 9:30–16:30, last entry at 16:00
Cost: £4, free on Sun but restricted viewing due to services, £3.50 extra to climb dome—allow an hour for the climb up and down
Tour length: One hour (two if you climb dome)
Getting there: Located in "The City" in east London, tube: St. Paul's
Information: Guided £3.50 90-minute cathedral and crypt tours are offered at 11:00, 11:30, 13:30, and 14:00. Audioguide tours cost £3. Sunday services are at 8:00, 10:00, 11:30, 15:15, and 18:00; weekday communion is at 8:00 and 12:30; evensong is at 17:00 on weekdays. Tel. 020/7236-4128.
Photography: Allowed without a flash
Starring: Christopher Wren, Wellington, and World War II

The Tour Begins

Even now, as skyscrapers encroach, the 365-foot dome of St. Paul's rises majestically above the rooftops of the neighborhood. The tall dome is set on classical columns, capped with a lantern, topped by a six-foot ball, and iced with a cross. As the first

ST. PAUL'S TOUR

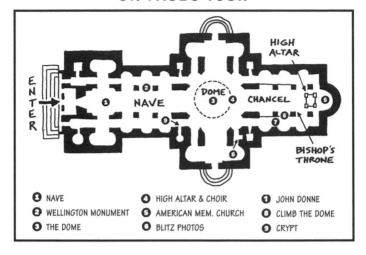

❶ NAVE   ❹ HIGH ALTAR & CHOIR   ❼ JOHN DONNE
❷ WELLINGTON MONUMENT   ❺ AMERICAN MEM. CHURCH   ❽ CLIMB THE DOME
❸ THE DOME   ❻ BLITZ PHOTOS   ❾ CRYPT

Anglican cathedral built in London after the Reformation, it is
Baroque: St. Peter's filtered through clear-eyed English reason.
• *Enter, buy your ticket, and stand at the back of the nave.*

1. Nave

Look down the nave through the choir stalls to the stained glass at
the far end. This big church feels big. Its spaciousness is accentuated by the lack of decoration. The simple cream-colored ceiling
and the clear glass in the windows light everything evenly. Wren
wanted this: a simple, open church with nothing to hide. Unfortunately, only this entrance area keeps his original vision—the rest
was crusted with Baroque decoration after his death.
• *Glance up and behind. The organ trumpets say "come to the 17:00
evensong." Ahead and on the left is the towering...*

2. Wellington Monument

It's so tall that even Wellington's horse has to duck to avoid
bumping his head. Wren would have been appalled, but his
church has become so central to England's soul that many national
heroes are buried here (in the basement crypt). General Wellington, Napoleon's conqueror at Waterloo and the embodiment of
British stiff-upper-lippedness, was honored here in a funeral
packed with 13,000 fans.
• *Stroll up the same nave Prince Charles and Lady Diana walked on
their 1981 wedding day. Grab a chair underneath the dome.*

3. The Dome

The dome you see, painted with scenes from the life of St. Paul, is only the innermost of three domes. From the painted interior dome #1, look up through the tunnel burrowing inside the structural core of dome #2, which is capped by the light-filled lantern. Finally, the whole thing is covered on the outside by dome #3, the shell of lead-covered wood, which is what you saw from the street. Wren's ingenious three-in-one design was psychological as well as functional—he wanted a low inner dome so the worshiper wouldn't feel dwarfed.

You'll see tourists walking around the base of the dome in the "Whispering Gallery." The dome is constructed with such precision that whispers from one side of the dome are heard on the other side, 170 feet away.

Christopher Wren (1632–1723) was the right man at the right time. While the 31-year-old math professor had never built a major building in his life when he got the commission for St. Paul's, his reputation for brilliance and a unique ability to work with others carried him through. The church has the clean lines and geometric simplicity of the age of Newton, when reason was holy and God set the planets spinning in perfect geometrical motion.

For over 40 years Wren worked on this site, overseeing every detail. At age 75 he got to look up and see his son place the cross on top of the dome, completing the masterpiece.

On the floor directly beneath the dome is a brass grate—part of a 19th-century attempt to heat the church. Encircling it is Christopher Wren's name and epitaph, written in Latin: *Lector, si monumentum requiris circumspice* (Reader, if you seek his monument, look around you).

Now review the ceiling: Behind is Wren simplicity and ahead is Baroque ornate.

• *The choir area blocks your way to the altar at the far end, but belly up to the entrance between two sets of organ pipes and look at the far end under a golden canopy.*

4. High Altar and Choir

The altar (the marble slab with crucifix and candlesticks—you'll get a close-up look later) was destroyed in World War II. Today it lies under a huge canopy with corkscrew columns. It looks ancient, but was actually built in 1958 according to sketches by Wren.

English churches, unlike most in Europe, often have an area like this in their center known as the choir (or quire or chancel), where church officials and the singers sit. St. Paul's—a cathedral since 604—is home to the local bishop, who presides in the chair closest to the altar on the south or right side (the carved bishop's hat hangs over the chair).

The ceiling above the choir is a riot of glass mosaic representing God and his creation.

• *Walk to the altar, pausing at the modern statue on the left:* Mother and Child, *by Britain's greatest modern sculptor, Henry Moore. After donating this to St. Paul's, he was rewarded with a burial spot in the crypt. Continue to the far end of the church where you'll find three bright and modern stained-glass windows.*

5. American Memorial Church

Each of the three windows has a central core of religious scenes, but the brightly colored panes that arch around them have some unusual iconography: American. Spot the American eagle (center window, to the left of Christ) and look for George Washington (right window, upper right corner) and symbols of all 50 states (find your state seal). In the carved wood beneath the windows you'll see birds and foliage native to the States. And at the very far right, check out the tiny tree "trunk" beneath the bird behind the carved leaves—it's a U.S. rocket circa 1958, shooting up to the stars.

Britain is very grateful to its WWII saviors, the Yanks, and remembers them religiously here immediately behind the altar with the Roll of Honor. This book under glass lists the names of 28,000 U.S. servicemen based in Britain who gave their lives.

• *Take a close look at the high altar and the view back to the entrance from here, then continue on around the altar where you'll find a glass case of photographs.*

6. St. Paul's in Wartime

Nazi planes firebombed a helpless London in 1940. While "the City" around it burned to the ground, St. Paul's survived, giving hope to the citizens. Some swear that bombs bounced miraculously off Wren's dome, while others credit the heroic work of local firefighters. (There's a memorial chapel to the firefighters who kept watch over St. Paul's with hoses cocked.) Still, these photos make it clear St. Paul's was not fully blitz-proof.

• *Across the aisle, standing white in a black niche, is a statue of...*

7. John Donne

This statue survived the Great Fire of 1666. Donne, shown here wrapped in a burial shroud, was a passionate preacher in Old St. Paul's as well as a great poet.

Imagine hearing Donne deliver a funeral sermon here, with the huge church bell tolling in the background: "No man is an island...Any man's death diminishes me, because I am involved in

Mankind. Therefore, never send to know for whom the bell tolls—it tolls for thee."

• *And also for dozens of people who lie buried beneath your feet, in the crypt where you'll end your tour. But first...*

8. Climb the Dome

There are no elevators, and you must pay extra, but the 530-step climb is worthwhile. First you get to the Whispering Gallery (with views of the church interior). Have fun in the gallery and whisper sweet nothings into the wall; your partner (and anyone else) on the far side can hear you. Then, after another climb you're at the Stone Gallery (views of London, high enough if you're exhausted). Finally a long, tight, metal 150-step staircase takes you to the very top of the cupola for stunning unobstructed views of the city. A tiny window allows you to peek directly down on the church floor.

9. Crypt

Grand tombs of General Wellington and Admiral Nelson dominate the center of the crypt. Nelson, who defeated the French fleet in 1805 and ensured that Britannia ruled the waves, lies buried directly beneath the dome (and heating grate). Christopher Wren's tomb is in the far right corner (right of chapel altar). Also find painters Turner, Reynolds, and others (near Wren); Florence Nightingale (near Wellington); and memorials to many others (including George Washington, who lies buried back in old Virginny). There are interesting exhibits about the building of the cathedral, a fine gift shop, a WC, and the tasty if grim-sounding Crypt Café.

TOWER OF LONDON TOUR

William I, still getting used to his new title of "the Conqueror," built the stone "White Tower" (1077–1097) to keep the Londoners in line. The tower served as an effective lookout for invaders coming up the Thames. His successors enlarged it to its present 18-acre size. Because of the security it provided, it has served over the centuries as the Royal Mint, the Royal Jewel House, and, most famously, as the prison and execution site of those who dared oppose the crown. The Tower's hard stone and glittering jewels represent the ultimate power of the king. So does the executioners' block. You'll find more bloody history per square inch in this original tower of power than anywhere in Britain.

Orientation

Hours: Mon–Sat 9:00–18:00, Sun 10:00–18:00, last entry at 17:00. In winter (Nov 1–Feb 28) Tue–Sat 9:00–17:00, Sun–Mon 10:00–17:00, last entry at 16:00; closed Dec 24–26 and Jan 1. To avoid the crowds, arrive at opening time and go straight for the jewels, doing the tour and White Tower later (or do the jewels after 16:30). The crowd hits after the 9:30 cheap tube passes start. The long but fast-moving line is worst on Sunday. Also on Sunday, visitors are welcome on the grounds to worship in the Royal Chapel (free, 11:00 service with fine choral music). For information on participating in the evening Ceremony of Keys, see page 37.
Cost: £10.50
Tour length: Two hours
Getting there: Located in East London (tube: Tower Hill). For speed, take the tube there; for romance, take the boat back. Boats run between the Tower of London and Westminster Pier near

—— TOWER OF LONDON TOUR ——

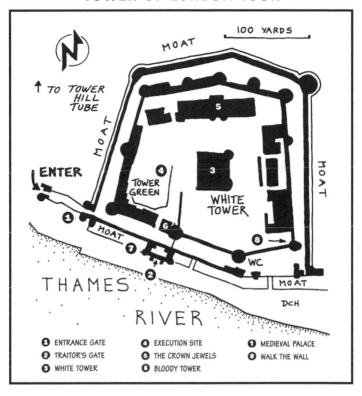

100 YARDS

MOAT

↑ N

↑ TO TOWER
HILL
TUBE

MOAT

ENTER

TOWER
GREEN

5

3

WHITE
TOWER

MOAT

❶

MOAT

❻

❼

❽ →

WC

❷

MOAT

THAMES

DCH

RIVER

❶ ENTRANCE GATE	❹ EXECUTION SITE	❼ MEDIEVAL PALACE
❷ TRAITOR'S GATE	❺ THE CROWN JEWELS	❽ WALK THE WALL
❸ WHITE TOWER	❻ BLOODY TOWER	

Big Ben (£4.60, round-trip £5.80, 3/hrly from 10:20–21:00 in peak
season, until 18:00 in winter, 30-min cruise).

Information: The free, worthwhile 50-minute Beefeater tour
leaves regularly from inside the gate (last one usually at 15:30).
Tel. 020/7709-0765.

Photography: Yes, but not of the jewels

Starring: Crown jewels, Beefeaters, William the Conqueror, and
Henry VIII

1. Entrance Gate

Even an army the size of the ticket line couldn't storm this castle.
After they pulled the drawbridge up and slammed the iron
portcullis down, you'd have to swim the 40-yard moat (now grass)
then toss a grappling hook onto the wall and climb while the
enemy poured boiling oil on you. Yes, it was difficult to get into

the Tower... but almost impossible to get out.

• *The entertaining 50-minute tours by the Yeoman Warders (nicknamed "Beefeaters" for the rations of beef they earned) begin just inside the entrance gate. The information booth is nearby, and toilets are 100 yards straight ahead. Otherwise, go 50 yards straight ahead to the...*

2. Traitor's Gate

This entrance into the Tower was a waterway passage from the Thames. Princess Elizabeth I, who was a prisoner here before she became Queen, was poled through this gate on a barge, as were many other leaders who fell from grace. Nixon wasn't the only politician with Water-gate problems. (That's a Beefeater joke, if you're still considering a tour.)

• *Pass underneath the "Bloody Tower" into the inner courtyard. The big white tower in the middle is the...*

3. White Tower

This is the "Tower" that gives this castle complex of 20 towers its name. William the Conqueror built it 900 years ago to put 15 feet of stone between himself and his conquered. Over the centuries the other walls and towers were built around it.

The Tower represents the king's absolute power over his subjects. If you made the wrong move here, you could be feasting on roast boar in the banqueting hall one night, and chained to the walls of the prisons the next. Torture ranged from stretching on the rack, to hanging by the neck until blue, to drawing and quartering with your giblets displayed on the walls as a warning. (Or in the case of Guy Fawkes, who tried to blow up Parliament, all of the above.) Any cries for help were muffled by the thick stone walls—15 feet at the base, a mere 11 feet at the Tower top.

Inside the Tower today, you can see models of the Tower and exhibits recreating medieval life, as well as suits of armor (including that of Henry VIII and other kings), guns, swords, and Charles Brandon's exceptionally large lance. The rare and lovely Norman chapel (St. John's Chapel, 1080), where Lady Jane Grey offered up a last unanswered prayer, is simple, plain, and moving.

• *Left of the Tower is the Tower Green, where you'll find a granite-paved square marked "Site of Scaffold."*

4. Execution Site

Here is where enemies of the crown would kneel before the king for the final time and, with their hands tied behind their backs, say a final prayer, lay their heads on a block, and—shlit!—the blade would slice through their necks as their heads tumbled to the ground.

The headless corpses were buried in unmarked graves in the Tower Green or under the floor of the stone church ahead of you. The heads were stuck on a stick and displayed at London Bridge. Passersby did not see heads but spheres of parasites.

Henry VIII axed his exes here—Anne Boleyn, whom he called a witch and an adulteress, and the forgettable Catherine Howard. Next.

Henry even beheaded his friend, Thomas More (a Catholic), because he refused to recognize (Protestant) Henry as head of the Church of England. (Thomas died at the less-prestigious Tower Hill site just outside the walls—near the Tube stop—where most Tower executions took place.)

The most tragic victim was 17-year-old Lady Jane Grey, a simple girl who was manipulated into claiming the crown during the scramble for power after Henry's death. When "Bloody" Mary took control, she forced Jane to kneel at the block. Jane's young husband, locked in the nearby Beauchamp Tower, could vent his grief only by scratching "Jane" into the tower's stone (in the upstairs room find graffiti #85—"IANE").

A Beefeater, tired of what he called "Hollywood coverage" of the Tower, grabbed my manuscript, read it, and told me that in over 900 years as a fortress, palace, and prison, the place held 8,500 prisoners. But only 120 were executed and of those only six were executed inside the Tower. And, stressing the hospitality of the Tower, he added, "Torture was actually quite rare here."

• *Look past the White Tower on the left to the line leading to the crown jewels. Like a Disney ride, the line is still very long once you get inside. But great videos help pass the time pleasantly. First you'll pass through a room of wooden chairs and coats of arms—one for every monarch who wore jewels like these, from William the Conqueror (1066) to Elizabeth I, with her lion-and-dragon crest, to Queen Elizabeth II. Next, you'll see a film of Elizabeth's 1953 coronation—a chance to see the jewels in*

action. You'll also see video close-ups of the jewels. Finally, you pass
into a huge vault and reach…

5. The Crown Jewels
In the first display case notice the 12th-century coronation spoon
for anointing (used in 1953). Most of the original crown jewels

were lost during the 1648 Revolution, so
this is the most ancient object here. After
scepters, robes, trumpets, and wristlets, a
moving sidewalk takes you past the most
precious of the crown jewels.

• *The crowns are all facing you as you*
approach them (ride the nearest walkway).
You're welcome to circle back and glide by the
back side and hang out on the elevated viewing
area with the Beefeater guard. Chat with the
guard. Ask him what happens if you shoot a
photo.

These are the most important pieces:
• **St. Edward's Crown**, in the first glass case, is placed by the
archbishop upon the head of each new monarch in Westminster
Abbey on coronation day. It's worn for 20 minutes, then locked
away until the next coronation. Although remodeled, this five-
pound crown is older than the Tower itself, dating back to 1061,
the time of King Edward the Confessor, "the last English king"
before William the Conqueror invaded (1066).
• **The Sovereign's Scepter**, in the second case, is encrusted with
the world's largest cut diamond—the 530-carat Star of Africa, as
beefy as a quarter-pounder.
• **The Crown of the Queen Mother** (Elizabeth's aged mom),
the highest crown in the fourth case, has the 106-carat Koh-i-
Noor diamond glittering on the front.
• **The Imperial Crown**, in the fifth and last case, is for when the
monarch slips into something a little less formal—for coronation
festivities, official state functions, and the annual opening of
Parliament. Among its 3,733 jewels are Queen Elizabeth I's
former earrings (the hanging pearls) and Edward the Confessor's
ring (the sapphire on top).
• *Leave the jewels. Back near the Traitor's Gate you'll find sights #6*
and #7…

6. Bloody Tower
Not all prisoners died at the block. During the War of the Roses,
13-year-old future king Edward and his kid brother were kid-
napped by their uncle Richard III ("Now is the winter of our

discontent. . . .") and locked in the Bloody Tower, never to be seen again (until two centuries later when two children's bodies were discovered).

Sir Walter Raleigh—poet, explorer, and political radical— was imprisoned here for 13 years. In 1603 the English writer and adventurer was accused of plotting against King James and sentenced to death. The king commuted the sentence to life imprisonment in the Tower. While in prison, Raleigh wrote the first volume of his *History of the World*. See his rather cushy bedroom, study, and walkway (courtesy of the powerful tobacco lobby?). Raleigh promised the king a wealth of gold if he would release him to search for El Dorado. The expedition was a failure. Upon Raleigh's return, the displeased king had him beheaded in 1618.

More recent prisoners in the complex include Rudolf Hess, Hitler's henchman who parachuted into Scotland in 1941 (kept in bell tower). Hess claimed to have dropped in to negotiate a separate peace between Germany and Britain. Hitler denied any such plan.

7. Medieval Palace
The Tower was a royal residence as well as a fortress. These rooms are furnished as they might have been during the reign of Edward I in the 13th century.
• *Enter near where you leave the Medieval Palace to...*

8. Walk the Wall
The Tower was defended by state-of-the-art walls and fortifications in the 13th century. This walk offers a good look. From the walls, you also get a good look at...

Tower Bridge
The famous bridge straddling the Thames with the twin towers and blue spans is not London Bridge (which is the nondescript bridge just upstream), but Tower Bridge. It looks medieval, but this drawbridge was built in 1894 of steel and concrete. Sophisticated steam engines raise and lower the bridge, allowing tall-masted ships to squeeze through.

Gaze out at the bridge, the river, and life-filled London, then turn back and look at the stern stone walls of the tower. Be glad you can leave.

DAY TRIPS
IN ENGLAND

⑫

london

Greenwich • Cambridge • Bath

Near London are some great day-trip possibilities: Greenwich, Cambridge, and Bath (listed from nearest to farthest). Greenwich, England's maritime capital, sports a Millennium Dome; Cambridge is England's best university town; and Bath is an elegant spa town dating from Roman times.

You could fill a book with the many easy and exciting day trips from London (Earl Steinbicker did: *Daytrips London: Fifty-One Day Adventures by Rail or Car, in and around London and Southern England*).

Getting Around
By Bus Tour: Several tour companies take London-based travelers out and back every day. Stonehenge and Bath tours are popular: Evan Evans' tours come fully guided for £46 or with just the bus transportation for £25 (leave from behind Victoria Station daily at 9:00, tel. 020/7950-1777). Travelline also offers a Stonehenge/Bath tour (office in Fountain Square directly south of Victoria Station, tel. 020/8668-7261). If you want to stay in Bath, consider using a bus tour as a "free" way to get to there (saving you the £32.50 London-to-Bath train ticket); just stow your luggage under the bus, and when the tour drops you in Bath, stay there, rather than return to London.

By Train: The British rail system uses London as a hub and normally offers round-trip fares (after 9:30) that cost virtually the same as one-way fares. You can save even more if you purchase Super Advance tickets before 14:00 on the day before your trip.

By Train Tour: Original London Walks offers a variety of day trips using the train for about £10 plus transportation costs (see their black-and-white walking-tour brochure at TIs, pubs, and hotels; for recorded schedule, tel. 020/7624-3978, www.walks.com).

GREENWICH

The palace at Greenwich was favored by the Tudor kings. Henry VIII was born here. Later kings commissioned Inigo Jones and Chris Wren to beautify the town and palace. In spite of Greenwich's architectural and royal treats, this is England's maritime capital, and visitors go for things salty. Greenwich hosts historic ships, nautical shops, and hordes of tourists. Now, in 2000, the home of the zero meridian will host more visitors than ever.

Planning Your Time

If you plan to tour the Millennium Dome and Greenwich, do the dome first (to get your money's worth out of the hefty ticket price—£25). Take the tube from London straight to the dome (on the Jubilee Line, tube: North Greenwich). If you decide to roam the dome all day, it's easy to return to Greenwich another day to see the sights.

When you tour the town of Greenwich, visit the two great ships upon arrival. Then walk the shoreline promenade with a possible lunch or drink in the venerable Trafalgar Tavern before heading up to the National Maritime Museum and Old Royal Observatory. Or, if you're rushed or tired, consider taking the handy shuttle bus that runs from Greenwich Pier (near the *Cutty Sark*) to the Old Royal Observatory, saving a 15-minute gradual uphill walk; then walk down, sightseeing as you go (£1.50, Apr–Sept 10:45–17:00, 4/hrly, Meridian Line Shuttle).

Tourist Information

The TI is on 46 Greenwich Church Street (daily 10:00–17:00, tel. 020/8858-6376). Most of Greenwich's sights are covered by combo tickets—there's a pricier one that covers nearly everything, and sometimes there's a cheaper one that covers just a couple of sights. Each year the combination of sights is shuffled slightly and the prices go up. Greenwich throbs with day-trippers on weekends, particularly on Sunday when the arts-and-crafts market takes place. To avoid crowds, visit on a weekday.

Sights—Greenwich

▲▲*Cutty Sark*—The Scottish-built *Cutty Sark* was the last of the great China tea clippers. Handsomely restored, she was the queen of the seas when first launched in 1869. With 32,000 square feet of sail, she could blow with the wind 300 miles in a day. Below deck you'll see the best collection of merchant ships' figureheads in Britain and exhibits giving a vivid peek into the lives of Victorian sailors back when Britain ruled the waves. Stand at the big wheel and look up at the still-rigged main mast towering 150 feet

GREENWICH

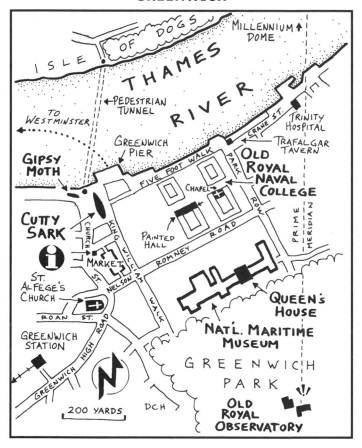

above. During summer afternoons costumed storytellers tell tales of the high seas (£3.50, £12 combo ticket covers most Greenwich town sights, Mon–Sat 10:00–18:00, Sun 12:00–18:00; Oct–Apr Mon–Sat 10:00–17:00, Sun 12:00–17:00, tel. 020/8858-3445, www.cuttysark.org.uk).

▲*Gipsy Moth IV*—Tiny next to the *Cutty Sark*, the 53-foot *Gipsy Moth IV* is the boat Sir Francis Chichester used for the first solo circumnavigation of the world in 1966 and 1967. Upon Chichester's return, Queen Elizabeth II knighted him in Greenwich using the same sword Elizabeth I had used to knight Francis Drake in 1582 (free, viewable anytime, but interior not open to public).

Stroll the Thames to Trafalgar Tavern—From the *Cutty Sark* and *Gipsy Moth*, pass the pier and wander east along the Thames on Five Foot Walk (the width of the path) for grand views in front of the Old Royal Naval College (listed below). Founded by William III as a naval hospital and designed by Wren, the college was split in two because Queen Mary didn't want the view from Queen's House to be blocked. The riverside view's good, too, with the twin-domed towers of the college (one giving the time; the other, the direction of the wind) framing Queen's House and the Old Royal Observatory crowning the hill beyond.

Continuing downstream, just past the college, you'll see the Trafalgar Tavern. Dickens knew the pub well, and even used it as the setting for the wedding breakfast in *Our Mutual Friend*. Built in 1837 in the Regency style to attract Londoners downriver, the tavern is still popular with Londoners for its fine lunches. And the upstairs Nelson Room is still used for weddings. Its formal moldings and elegant windows with balconies over the Thames are a step back in time (Mon–Sat 11:30–23:00, Sun 12:00–23:00, lunch 12:00–15:00, dinner 17:00–21:00, CC:VM, Park Row, tel. 020/8858-2437).

From the Trafalgar Tavern you can walk the two long blocks up Park Row and turn right into the park leading up to the Old Royal Observatory.

Old Royal Naval College—Now that the Royal Navy has moved out, the public is invited in to see the elaborate Painted Hall and Chapel, grandly designed by Wren and completed by other architects in the 1700s (fee not yet set, Mon–Sat 10:00–17:00, Sun 12:00–17:00, in the two College buildings farthest from river, choral service Sun at 11:00 in chapel—all are welcome).

▲**Queen's House**—In 2000 this royal house—the architectural centerpiece of Greenwich—will host an exhibit entitled *The Story of Time*. The building, the first Palladian-style villa in Britain, was designed in 1616 by Inigo Jones for James I's wife, Anne of Denmark. Exploring its Great Hall and Royal Apartments offers a sumptuous look at royal life in the 17th century—or lots of stairs if you're suffering from manor house fatigue (£12 combo ticket covers most Greenwich town sights, daily 10:00–17:00).

▲▲▲**National Maritime Museum**—At the largest and most important maritime museum in the world, visitors can taste both the romance and harshness of life at sea. Experience 20th-century naval warfare on a WWII frigate or get to know Britain's greatest naval hero, Nelson, whose display covers both his public career and scandalous private life (don't miss the uniform coat in which he was fatally shot). The museum's newly opened Neptune Court greatly increases the number of galleries and better profiles the sweep of Empire and the role of the sea in British history (£12 combo ticket

covers most Greenwich town sights, daily 10:00–17:00, look for
events board at entrance, tel. 020/8312-6565, www.nmm.ac.uk).

▲▲**Old Royal Observatory**—Whether you think the millennium
starts in 2000 or 2001, it happened/happens here first. All time is
measured from zero longitude degrees, the prime meridian line—
the point from which the millennium began/begins. However, the
observatory's early work had nothing to do with coordinating the
world's clocks to GMT, Greenwich mean time. The observatory
was founded in 1675 by Charles II to find a way to determine
longitude at sea. Today the Greenwich time signal is linked with
the BBC (which broadcasts the "pips" worldwide at the top of the
hour). In the courtyard, set your wristwatch to the digital clock
showing GMT to a 10th of a second, and straddle the prime meridian (called the Times meridian at the Observatory, in deference to
the *London Times*, which paid for the courtyard sculpture and inset
meridian line that runs banner headlines of today's *Times*—I wish
I were kidding). It's less commercial—and cheaper—to straddle the
meridian marked on the path outside the museum's courtyard.
Nearby (also outside the courtyard), see how your foot measures up
to the foot where the public standards of length are cast in bronze.
Look up to see the orange Time Ball, also visible from the Thames,
which drops daily at 13:00. Inside, check out the historic astronom-
ical instruments and camera obscura. Finally, enjoy the view: the
symmetrical royal buildings, the Thames, the square-mile "City"
of London with its skyscrapers and the dome of St. Paul's, the
Docklands with its busy cranes, and the Millennium Dome itself
(£12 combo ticket covers most Greenwich town sights, daily
10:00–17:00). Planetarium shows twinkle on weekdays at 14:30,
sometimes on weekends—ask (£2, buy tickets at observatory, a
two-minute walk from planetarium).

Greenwich Town—Save time to browse the town. Sunday is
best for markets: The arts-and-crafts market is an entertaining
mini–Covent Garden between College Approach and Nelson
Road (Fri–Sun, best on Sun), and the antique market sells old
ends and odds at high prices on Greenwich High Road near the
post office. Wander beyond the touristy Church Street and
Greenwich High Road to where flower stands spill into the side
streets and antique shops sell brass nautical knickknacks. King
William Walk, College Approach, Nelson Road, and Turnpin
Lane are all worth a look. Covered markets and outdoor stalls
make weekends colorful and lively.

Sights—Near Greenwich

▲▲▲**Millennium Dome**—Housed under a vast dome a mile
from Greenwich, the show's theme is "who we are, how we live,

what we do." The dome—at 20 acres the largest ever built— is separated into 14 zones, each with a focus: body, mind, spirit, work, rest, and so on. In the body zone, listen to the magnified sounds of human organs as you walk through the 90-foot-tall sculptures of a reclined man and woman (exit through leg). Each day the town zone features a different British town telling its story. At center stage, an acrobatic drama performs five times daily. Your admission includes a filmed 30-minute joke history of Britain written by Mr. Bean (Rowan Atkinson) and shown at the Skyscape "Baby Dome" 5,000-seat theatre, which boasts the two biggest screens in Britain (in the Millennium Plaza in front of the dome).

The organizers plan (or pray) for 12 million visitors this year; a maximum of 35,000 tickets will be sold daily. Even from the outside the dome is a spectacle, especially on the nights it becomes an out-door light show with bright lights flickering over its white surface.

Skeptical media, an upset church, and problems organizing transportation connections have tempered this Y2K blowout. Still, it's an awesome building and the show promises to be a happening worth the steep admission price of £25 (Jan 1–Dec 31 daily 10:00–18:00, until 23:00 during peak times). Tickets are sold at the door or in advance at National Lottery Ticket outlets in Britain or over the phone at tel. 0870-606-2000, www.dome2000.co.uk and www.greenwich2000.com). At the end of 2000 the contents of the dome will be dismantled and the dome will be sold.

Thames Barrier—The world's largest movable flood barrier is east of Greenwich. Visitors are treated to a good video and exhibition on what is supposedly the cleanest urban waterway in the world, its floods, and how it was tamed (£3.40, Mon–Fri 10:00–17:00, Sat–Sun 10:30–17:30; catch a 70-minute boat from Westminster Pier or take a 30-minute boat from Greenwich Pier— the first boats from either location leave at around 11:00; or catch a 20-minute train ride from London's Charing Cross station to Charlton, then a 15-minute walk; tel. 020/8305-4188).

Transportation Connections—Greenwich

To Greenwich: Getting to Greenwich is a joy by boat or a snap by tube. You have good choices: Cruise down the Thames from central London's piers at Westminster, Charing Cross, or Tower of London; tube to Cutty Sark in Zone 2 (free with tube pass); or catch the train from Charing Cross (2/hrly, £2). I'd take the tube to Greenwich, see the sights, and take a leisurely cruise back.

To the Millennium Dome: From London, it's quickest to reach the dome by tube. The new Jubilee Line Extension, with the largest tube station in Europe, zips up to 22,000 people an hour from central London directly to the Millennium Dome in

12 minutes (tube: North Greenwich). Boats offer a more scenic trip and shuttle people in about 45 minutes (6/hrly from Westminster Pier). To get to the dome from the town of Greenwich, take any of the frequent boats or buses or walk the mile-long path.

CAMBRIDGE

Cambridge, 60 miles north of London, is world famous for its prestigious university. Wordsworth, Isaac Newton, Tennyson, Darwin, and Prince Charles are a few of its illustrious alumni. This historic town of 100,000 people is more pleasant than its rival, Oxford. Cambridge is the epitome of a university town with busy bikers, stately residence halls, plenty of bookshops, and proud locals who can point out where electrons and DNA were discovered and where the first atom was split.

In medieval Europe, higher education was the domain of the Church and was limited to ecclesiastical schools. Scholars lived in "halls" on campus. This scholarly community of residential halls, chapels, and lecture halls connected by peaceful garden courtyards survives today in the colleges that make the universities at Cambridge and Oxford. By 1350 Cambridge had eight colleges (Oxford is roughly 100 years older), each with a monastic-type courtyard and lodgings. Today Cambridge has 31 colleges. While a student's life revolves around his or her independent college, the university organizes lectures, presents degrees, and promotes research.

The university dominates—and owns—most of Cambridge. The approximate term schedule is late January to late March (called Lent term), mid-April to mid-June (called Easter term), and early October to early December (called Michaelmas term). The colleges are closed to visitors during exams, from mid-April until late June, but King's College Chapel and the Trinity Library stay open. The town is never sleepy.

Planning Your Time

Cambridge is worth most of a day, but not an overnight. Catch a train from London's King's Cross station (2/hrly, one-hour trip) and arrive in Cambridge in time for the 11:30 walking tour, an essential part of any visit. Spend the afternoon touring King's College and the Fitzwilliam Museum (closed Mon), and simply enjoying the ambience of this stately old college town.

Orientation (tel. code: 01223)

Cambridge is small but congested. There are two main streets separated from the river by the most interesting colleges. The town center, brimming with tearooms, has a TI and a colorful open-air market (daily 9:00–16:00 on Market Hill Square; on Sunday arts

CAMBRIDGE

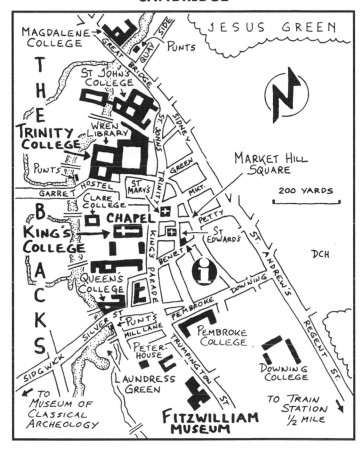

and crafts, otherwise clothes and produce). Also on the main square is a Marks & Spencer grocery (Mon–Sat 8:30–19:00, Sun 11:00–17:00). A J. Sainsbury supermarket, with longer hours and a better deli, is three blocks away on Sidney Street, just north of Green Street. A good picnic spot is Laundress Green, a grassy park on the river at the end of Mill Lane near the Silver Street punts. Everything is within a pleasant walk.

Tourist Information: At the station, a Guide Friday TI dispenses free Guide Friday maps of Cambridge and sells more detailed ones. The official TI, well signed and just off Market Hill Square, is more harried than helpful (40p maps, Mon–Fri

10:00–18:00, Sat 10:00–17:00, Sun 11:00–16:00; Nov–Easter
Mon–Sat 10:00–17:00, closed Sun, tel. 01223/322-640).

Arrival in Cambridge: To get to downtown Cambridge from
the train station, take a 20-minute walk (the Guide Friday map is
fine for this), a £3 taxi ride, or bus #3 (90p, every 10 minutes).

Tours of Cambridge

▲▲Walking Tour of the Colleges—A walking tour is the best
way to understand Cambridge's mix of "town and gown." Walks
give a good rundown on the historic and scenic highlights of the
university, as well as some fun local gossip. Walks are run by and
leave from the tourist office. From mid-June through August, tours
start at 10:30, 11:30, 13:30, and 14:30; September 10:30, 11:30,
13:30; the rest of the year often at 11:30 and always at 13:30. Tours
cost £6.50 and include admission to King's College Chapel. Drop by
the TI 30 minutes early to snare a spot; off-season you can call
ahead and book with your credit card (TI tel. 01223/322-640 or
01223/463-290). Try calling to at least confirm that a tour is scheduled and not full. Private guides are also available.

Bus Tours—Guide Friday hop-on, hop-off bus tours are informative and cover the outskirts (£8, departing every 15 minutes, can
use CC if you buy tickets in office in train station), but walking
tours go where the buses can't—right into the center.

Sights—Cambridge

▲▲King's College Chapel—Built from 1446 to 1515 by Henrys VI
through VIII, England's best example of Perpendicular Gothic is the
single most impressive building in town. Stand inside, look up, and
marvel, as Christopher Wren did, at what was the largest single span
of vaulted roof anywhere—2,000 tons of incredible fan vaulting.
Wander through the Old Testament via the 25 16th-century stained-
glass windows (the most Renaissance stained glass anywhere in one
spot; it was taken out for safety during World War II, then painstak-
ingly replaced). Walk to the altar and admire Rubens' masterful
Adoration of the Magi (£3.50, erratic hours depending on school and
events, but usually daily 9:30–15:30 in term, till 16:30 otherwise).
During term you're welcome to enjoy an evensong service (Mon–
Sat at 17:30, Sun at 15:30).

▲▲Trinity College—Half of Cambridge's 63 Nobel Prize
winners came from this richest and biggest of the town's colleges,
founded in 1546 by Henry VIII. Don't miss the Wren-designed
library with its wonderful carving and fascinating original manuscripts (free, 10p leaflet, Mon–Fri noon–14:00; also Sat 10:30–
12:30 during term). Just outside the library entrance, Sir Isaac
Newton, who spent 30 years at Trinity, clapped his hands and

timed the echo to measure the speed of sound as it raced down the side of the cloister and back. In the library's display cases you'll see handwritten work by Newton, Milton, Byron, Tennyson, and Housman, as well as A. A. Milne's original *Winnie the Pooh* (the real Christopher Robin attended Trinity College).

▲▲**Fitzwilliam Museum**—Britain's best museum of antiquities and art outside of London is the Fitzwilliam. Enjoy its wonderful paintings (Old Masters and a fine English section featuring Gainsborough, Reynolds, Hogarth, and others, plus works by all the famous Impressionists), old manuscripts, and Greek, Egyptian, and Mesopotamian collections (free, £2 guided tour at 14:30 on Sun only, Tue–Sat 10:00–17:00, Sun 14:15–17:00, closed Mon, tel. 01223/332-900).

Museum of Classical Archeology—While this museum contains no originals, it offers a unique chance to see accurate copies (19th-century casts of the originals) of virtually every famous ancient Greek and Roman statue. More than 450 statues are on display (free, Mon–Fri 10:00–17:00; sometimes also Sat 10:00–13:00 during term; Sidgwick Avenue, tel. 01223/335-153). The museum is a five-minute walk west of Silver Street Bridge; after crossing the bridge, continue straight till you reach "Sidgwick Site" (museum is on your right).

▲**Punting on the Cam**—For a little levity and probably more exercise than you really want, try hiring one of the traditional (and inexpensive) flat-bottom punts at the river and pole yourself up and down (around and around, more likely) the lazy Cam. Once you get the hang of it, it's a fine way to enjoy the scenic side of Cambridge. After 17:00 it's less crowded and less embarrassing. Three places, one at each bridge, rent punts (£25–50 deposit required, CC OK) and offer chauffeured rides (minimum £25 for 40-minute ride). Trinity Punt, at Garrett Hostel Bridge near Trinity College, has the best prices (£6/hour rental, ask for short free lesson). Scudamore runs the other two locations: the central Silver Street (£10/hr rentals) and the less-convenient Quayside at Great Bridge, at the north end of town (£8/hr). Depending on the weather, punting season runs daily Easter through October, with Silver Street open weekends year-round.

Transportation Connections—Cambridge

By train to: London's King's Cross or Liverpool Station (departures at :15 and :45 past each hour, 1 hr, one-way £13.40, cheap day-return for £13.50), **York** (hrly, 2.5 hrs, transfer in Petersborough), **Birmingham** (6/day, 3 hrs), **Liverpool** (5/day, 5 hrs), **Heathrow** (hrly buses, 3.5 hrs). Train info tel. 0345-484-950.

BATH

The best city to visit within easy striking distance of London is Bath—just a 75-minute train ride away. Two hundred years ago this city of 80,000 was the trend-setting Hollywood of Britain. If ever a city enjoyed looking in the mirror, Bath's the one. It has more "government-listed" or protected historic buildings per capita than any other town in England. The entire city, built of the creamy warm-tone limestone called "Bath stone," beams in its cover-girl complexion. An architectural chorus line, it's a triumph of the Georgian style. Proud locals remind visitors that the town is routinely banned from the "Britain in Bloom" contest to give other towns a chance to win. Bath's narcissism is justified. Even with its mobs of tourists, it's a joy to visit.

Long before the Romans arrived in the first century, Bath was known for its hot springs. What became the Roman spa town of Aquae Sulis has always been fueled by the healing allure of its 116-degree mineral hot springs. The town's importance carried through Saxon times when it had a huge church on the site of the present-day abbey and was considered the religious capital of Britain. Its influence peaked in 973 when England's first king, Edgar, was crowned in the abbey. Bath prospered as a wool town.

Bath then declined until the mid-1600s, when it was just a huddle of huts around the abbey and a hot springs with 3,000 residents oblivious to the Roman ruins 18 feet below their dirt floors. Then, in 1687, Queen Mary, fighting infertility, bathed here. Within 10 months she gave birth to a son…and a new age of popularity for Bath.

The town boomed as a spa resort. Ninety percent of the buildings you'll see today are from the 18th century. Local architect John Wood was inspired by the Italian architect Palladio to build a "new Rome." The town bloomed in the neoclassical style and streets were lined not with scrawny sidewalks but with wide "parades," upon which the women in their stylishly wide dresses could spread their fashionable tails.

Beau Nash (1673–1762) was Bath's "master of ceremonies." He organized both the daily regimens of the aristocratic visitors and the city—lighting and improving security on the streets, banning swords, and opening the Pump Room. Under his fashionable baton, Bath became a city of balls, gaming, concerts, and the place to see and be seen in England. This most civilized place became even more so with the great neoclassical building spree that followed.

Planning Your Time

Bath needs at least two nights. There's plenty to do and it's a joy to do it. On a one-week trip to London, consider spending two nights

BATH

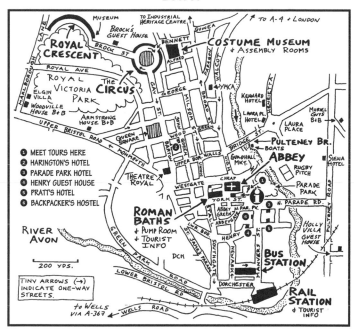

MUSEUM TO INDUSTRIAL GUINEA TO A-4 & LONDON
HERITAGE CENTRE

BROCK'S GUEST HOUSE BENNETT

ROYAL CRESCENT BROCK ST COSTUME MUSEUM
& ASSEMBLY ROOMS

ALFRED

ROYAL AVE

ROYAL THE CIRCUS GEORGE

ELGIN VILLA VICTORIA PARK YMCA KENWARD HOTEL

WOODVILLE HOUSE B+B LAURA PL HOTEL MURIEL GUYS B+B

ARMSTRONG HOUSE B+B LAURA PLACE

UPPER BRISTOL ROAD

QUEEN SQUARE PULTENEY BR.

BOATS

❶ MEET TOURS HERE ABBEY SIENA HOTEL
❷ HARINGTON'S HOTEL WALLS GUILDHALL MKT.
❸ PARADE PARK HOTEL RUGBY PITCH
❹ HENRY GUEST HOUSE THEATRE ROYAL PARADE PARK
❺ PRATT'S HOTEL WESTGATE CHEAP
❻ BACKPACKER'S HOSTEL YORK ST.
ABBEY N. PAR. PK. N. PARADE RD.

ROMAN BATHS ABBEY GREEN HOLLY VILLA GUEST HOUSE
+ PUMP ROOM
+ TOURIST INFO HENRY

RIVER AVON DCM BUS STATION

200 YDS.

LOWER BRISTOL RD DORCHESTER RAIL STATION

TINY ARROWS (→) INDICATE ONE-WAY STREETS. & TOURIST INFO

to WELLS VIA A-367 WELLS ROAD

in Bath with one entire day for the city. Ideally, use Bath as your jet-lag recovery pillow and do London at the end of your trip.

Consider starting a London vacation this way:

Day 1: Land at Heathrow. Catch the National Express bus to Bath (10/day, 2.5-hr trip).

Day 2: 9:00–Tour the Roman Baths, 10:30–Catch the free city walking tour, 12:30–Picnic on the open deck of a Guide Friday bus, 14:30–Free time in the shopping center of old Bath, 16:00–Tour the Costume Museum.

Day 3: Early train into London.

Orientation (tel. code: 01225)

Bath's town square, three blocks in front of the bus and train station, is a bouquet of tourist landmarks including the abbey, Roman and medieval baths, and royal Pump Room.

Tourist Information: The TI is in the abbey churchyard (Mon–Sat 9:30–18:00, Sun 10:00–16:00; Oct–Apr closes at 17:00 Mon–Sat, tel. 01225/477-101). Pick up the 25p Bath map/guide; the free *Museums in Bath* brochure; and the free, info-packed

This Month in Bath. Browse through scads of flyers, books, and maps (including Cotswolds) in their bookshop. Skip their room-finding service (£3 fee for walk-ins, £5 for callers) and go direct. An American Express office is tucked into the TI (decent rates, no commission on any checks, open same hours as TI).

Arrival in Bath: The Bath train station is a pleasure (small-town charm, an international tickets desk, and a Guide Friday office masquerading as a tourist information service). The bus station is immediately in front of the train station. To get to the TI, walk two blocks up Manvers Street from the bus or train station and turn left, following TI signs. My recommended B&Bs are all within a 10- or 15-minute walk or a £3.50 taxi ride from the station.

Tours of Bath

▲▲**City Bus Tours**—The Guide Friday green-and-cream open-top tour bus makes a 70-minute figure-eight circuit of Bath's main sights with an exhaustingly informative running commentary. For one £8.50 ticket (buy from driver), tourists can stop and go at will for a whole day. The buses cover the city center and the surrounding hills (17 signed pick-up points, 5/hrly in summer, hrly in winter, about 9:30–18:00, until 16:00 in winter, tel. 01225/464-446). This is great in sunny weather and a feast for photographers. You can munch a sandwich, work on a tan, and sightsee at the same time. Several competing hop-on/hop-off tour bus companies offer basically the same tour but in 45 minutes and without the swing through the countryside for a couple pounds less. (Ask a local what he or she thinks about all of these city-tour buses.) Generally, the Guide Friday guides are better. Save your ticket to get a £1 discount on a Guide Friday tour in another town.

▲▲▲**Walking Tours**—These two-hour tours, offered free by trained local volunteers who want to share their love of Bath with its many visitors, are a chatty, historical gossip–filled joy, essential for your understanding of this town's amazing Georgian social scene. How else will you learn that the old "chair ho" call for your sedan chair evolved into today's "cheerio" greeting? Tours leave from in front of the Pump Room (year-round daily at 10:30, plus May–Oct 14:00 weekdays, 14:30 Sun, and several evenings a week at 19:00; confirm at TI). For Ghost Walks and Bizarre Bath Comedy Walks, see "Nightlife," below. For a private walking tour from a local gentleman who's an excellent guide, contact Patrick Driscoll (two hours for £41, tel. 01225/462-010).

Sights—Bath

▲▲▲**Roman and Medieval Baths**—Back in ancient Roman times, high society enjoyed the mineral springs at Bath. From Londinium,

Romans traveled so often to Aquae Sulis, as the city was called, to "take a bath" that finally it became known simply as Bath. Today a fine Roman museum surrounds the ancient bath. The museum, with its well-documented displays, is a one-way system leading you past Roman artifacts, mosaics, a temple pediment, and the actual mouth of the spring piled high with Roman pennies. Enjoy some quality time looking into the eyes of Minerva, goddess of the hot springs. The included self-guided tour audio-wand makes the visit easy and plenty informative. In-depth 40-minute tours leave from the end of the museum at the edge of the actual bath for those with a big appetite for Roman history (included, on the hour, a poolside clock is set for the next departure time). You can revisit the museum after the tour. (£6.70, £8.70 combo ticket includes Costume Museum at a good savings, a family combo costs £22.60, combo tickets good for one week; daily 9:00–18:00, in Aug also 20:00–22:00, Oct–Apr closes at 17:00, tel. 01225/477-000.)

▲**Pump Room**—After a centuries-long cold spell, Bath was reheated when the previously barren Queen Mary bathed here and in due course bore a male heir to the throne (1687). Once Bath was back on the aristocratic map, high society soon turned the place into one big pleasure palace. The Pump Room, an elegant Georgian hall just above the Roman baths, offers the visitor's best chance to raise a pinky in this Chippendale elegance. Drop by to sip coffee or tea to the rhythm of a string trio or pianist (live music all year 10:00–noon, summers until 17:00, tea/coffee and pastry available for £4 anytime except during lunch, traditional high tea served after 14:30). Above the newspaper table and sedan chairs a statue of Beau Nash himself sniffles down at you. Now's your chance to have a famous (but forgettable) "Bath bun" and split (and spit) a 45p drink of the awfully curative water. Public WCs are in the entry hallway that connects the Pump Room with the Baths.

A quarter of a million gallons of mineral water still bubble through the spa daily. You can't soak in it until 2001, when a new spa facility will open.

▲**Abbey**—Bath town wasn't much in the Middle Ages. But an important church has stood on this spot since Anglo-Saxon times. In 973 Edgar, the first king of England, was crowned here. Dominating the town center, the present church—the last great medieval church of England—is 500 years old and a fine example of late Perpendicular Gothic, with breezy fan vaulting and enough stained glass to earn it the nickname "Lantern of the West" (Mon–Sat 9:00–18:00, Sun 13:00–17:30 with 15:15 evensong service; closes at 16:30 in winter; concert and evensong schedule posted on door, worth the £2 donation, handy flier narrates an 18-stop tour). The abbey's Heritage Vaults, a small but interesting exhibit, tells the story of Christianity in Bath since Roman times (£2, Mon–Sat 10:00–16:00, closed Sun). Take a moment to really appreciate the abbey's architecture from the Abbey Green square.

▲**Pulteney Bridge and Cruises**—Bath is inclined to compare its shop-lined Pulteney Bridge to Florence's Ponte Vecchio. That's pushing it. But to best enjoy a sunny Bath kind of day, pay £1 to go into the Parade Gardens below the bridge (daily 10:00–20:00, free after 20:00).

Across the bridge at Pulteney Weir, tour boats run cruises from under the bridge (£4, up to 7/day if the weather's good, 50 minutes to Bathampton and back, WCs on board). Just take whatever boat is running. Avon Cruisers stop in Bathampton if you'd like to walk back; Pulteney Cruisers come with a sundeck ideal for picnics.

▲▲**Royal Crescent and the Circus**—If Bath is an architectural cancan, these are the kickers. These first elegant Georgian "condos" by John Wood (the Elder and the Younger) are explained in the city walking tours and one is open as a museum (see "Georgian House," below). "Georgian" is British for "neoclassical," or dating from the 1770s. Stroll the Crescent after dark. Pretend you're rich. Pretend you're poor. Notice the "ha ha fence," a drop in the front yard offering a barrier, invisible from the windows, to sheep and peasants.

▲▲**Georgian House**—This museum in the Royal Crescent offers your best look into a period house. It's worth the £4 admission to get behind one of those classy exteriors. The volunteers in each room are determined to fill you in on all the fascinating details of Georgian life . . . like how high-class women shaved their eyebrows and pasted on carefully trimmed strips of furry mouse skin in their place (Tue–Sun 10:30–17:00, closed Mon, closes at 16:00 in Nov, closed Dec–Jan, "no stiletto heels, please," 1 Royal Crescent, on the corner of Brock Street and the Royal Crescent, tel. 01225/428-126).

▲▲▲**Costume Museum**—One of Europe's great museums, displaying 400 years of fashion—one frilly decade at a time—is housed within Bath's elegant Assembly Rooms. Follow the included and excellent CD-wand self-guided tour. Learn why Yankee Doodle "stuck a feather in his cap and called it macaroni" and much more (£4, £8.70 combo ticket includes Roman Baths, family combo costs £22.60, daily 10:00–17:00, tel. 01225/477-789).

▲▲**Industrial Heritage Centre**—This is the grand title for Mr. Bowler's Business, a turn-of-the-century engineer's shop, brass foundry, and fizzy-drink factory with a Dickensian office. It's just a pile of meaningless old gadgets until a volunteer guide lovingly resurrects Mr. Bowler's creative genius. Fascinating hour-long tours go regularly; just join the one in session. (£3.50, plus a few pence for a glass of genuine Victorian lemonade, daily 10:00–

17:00, weekends only in winter, two blocks up Russell Street from
the Assembly Rooms, call to be sure a volunteer is available to
give a tour, tel. 01225/318-348.) There's a Bath stone exhibit
downstairs and a café and shop upstairs.

Nightlife in Bath

This Month in Bath (available at the TI and many B&Bs) lists
events and evening entertainment.

Plays—The Theatre Royal, newly restored and one of England's
loveliest, offers a busy schedule of London West End–type plays,
including many "pre-London" dress-rehearsal runs (£10–25, cheap
standby tickets, tel. 01225/448-844). You can sometimes get late
cancellation seats for sold-out performances (drop by around 18:00).

Bizarre Bath Walks—For a walking comedy act—street theater
at its best "with absolutely no history or culture"—follow J. J. or
Noel Britten on their creative and entertaining Bizarre Bath walk.
This 90-minute "tour," which plays off local passersby as well as
tour members, is a kick (£3.50, 20:00 nightly Apr–Sept; heavy on
magic, careful to insult all kinds of minorities and sensitivities,
just racy enough but still good family fun; leave from Huntsman
pub near the abbey, confirm time and starting place at TI or call
01225/335-124). Ghost Walks are another way to pass the after-
dark hours (£4, 20:00, 2 hrs, unreliably Mon–Sat Apr–Oct; in
winter Fri only; leave from Garrick's Head pub near Theatre
Royal, tel. 01225/463-618). And for the scholarly types, there are
free historical intro-to-Bath walking tours offered several times a
week (19:00, 2 hrs, May–Oct, ask at TI).

Sleeping in Bath
(£1 = about $1.70, tel. code: 01225)

Sleep Code: S = Single, **D** = Double/Twin, **T** = Triple, **Q** = Quad,
b = bathroom, **t** = toilet only, **s** = shower only, **CC** = Credit Card
(**V**isa, **M**asterCard, **A**mex).

Bath is one of England's busiest tourist towns. To get a good
B&B, make a telephone reservation in advance. Competition is
stiff, and it's worth asking any of these places for a nonweekend,
three-nights-in-a-row, or off-season deal. Friday and Saturday
nights are tightest—especially if you're staying only one night,
since B&Bs favor those staying longer. If staying only Saturday
night, you're very bad news. In Bath, expect lots of stairs and no
lifts. A laundrette is around the corner from Brock's Guest House
on the cute pedestrian lane called Margaret's Buildings (Sun–Fri
8:00–21:00, Sat 8:00–20:00), and another scruffier laundrette,
closer to the Marlborough Lane listings, is on Upper Bristol
Road (daily 9:00–20:00, tel. 01225/429-378).

Sleeping in B&Bs near the Royal Crescent

These listings are all a 10- to 15-minute uphill walk or an easy £3.50 taxi ride from the train station.

Brock's Guest House will put bubbles in your Bath experience. Marion Dodd and her husband Geoffrey have redone their Georgian townhouse (built by John Wood in 1765) in a way that would make the famous architect proud. This charming house is perfectly located between the prestigious Royal Crescent and the elegant Circus (Db-£60–67, one deluxe Db-£72, Tb-£83–85, Qb-£95–99, reserve with a credit-card number far in advance, CC:VM, strictly nonsmoking, little library on top floor, 32 Brock Street, BA1 2LN, tel. 01225/338-374, fax 01225/334-245, e-mail: marion@brocks.force9.net). To reach Brock's from the station, consider taking the Guide Friday bus tour, get off at the Costume Museum, walk three minutes to the Guest House, check in, then continue the Guide Friday circuit. If you're in a transportation jam, Marion may be able to arrange a reasonable private car hire.

Woodville House is run by Anne and Tom Toalster. This grandmotherly little house has three charming rooms, one shared shower/WC, an extra WC, and a TV lounge. Breakfast is served at a big, family-style table (D-£40, minimum two nights, strictly nonsmoking, below the Royal Crescent at 4 Marlborough Lane, BA1 2NQ, tel. & fax 01225/319-335, e-mail: toalster @compuserve.com).

Elgin Villa is also a fine value with five comfy and well-maintained rooms (Ds-£45, Db-£50, discounts for three-night stays, kids £15 extra, parking, nonsmoking, 6 Marlborough Lane, BA1 2NQ Bath, tel. & fax 01225/424-557, www.elginvilla.co.uk, Alwyn and Carol Landman). They serve a big continental breakfast in your bedroom.

Athelney Guest House, which also serves a continental breakfast in your room, has three spacious rooms with two shared bathrooms (D-£38, T-£57, nonsmoking, parking, 5 Marlborough Lane, BA1 2NQ, tel. & fax 01225/312-031, Sue and Colin Davies).

Parkside Guest House is more upscale, renting four classy Edwardian rooms (Db-£60, nonsmoking, access to pleasant backyard, 11 Marlborough Lane, BA1 2NQ, tel. & fax 01225/429-444, e-mail: parkside@lynall.freeserve.co.uk, Erica and Inge Lynall).

Marlborough House is both Victorian and vegetarian, with five comfortable rooms and optional £12 veggie dinners (Sb-£45–55, Db-£70–85, CC:VM, room service, 1 Marlborough Lane, BA1 2NQ, tel. 01225/318-175, fax 01225/466-127, www.s-h-systems.co.uk/hotels/marlbor1.html, run by Americans Laura and Charles).

Sleeping in B&Bs East of the River
These listings are about a 10-minute walk from the city center.

Near North Parade Road: Holly Villa Guest House, with a cheery garden and a cozy TV lounge, is enthusiastically and thoughtfully run by Jill and Keith McGarrigle (Ds-£42, Db-£48, deluxe Db-£50, Tb-£65, six rooms, strictly nonsmoking, easy parking, eight-minute walk from station and city center, 14 Pulteney Gardens, BA2 4HG, tel. 01225/310-331, fax 01225/339-334, e-mail: hollyvilla.bb@ukgateway.net). From the city center, walk over North Parade Bridge, take the first right, then the second left.

Near Pulteney Road: Muriel Guy's B&B is another good value, mixing Georgian elegance with homey warmth and fine city views (Db-£48, four rooms, nonsmoking, 10-minute walk from city center, go over bridge on North Parade Road, left on Pulteney Road, cross to church, Raby Place is first row of houses on hill, 14 Raby Place, BA2 4EH, tel. 01225/465-120, fax 01225/465-283).

Siena Hotel, next door to a lawn-bowling green, has comfy, attractive rooms that hint of a more genteel time. Though this well-maintained hotel fronts a busy street, its double-paned windows make it feel tranquil inside. Rooms in the back have pleasant views of sports greens and Bath beyond (Db-£70–90, four-poster Db-£100, CC:VMA, access to garden in back, easy parking, 10-minute walk from center, 24/25 Pulteney Road, BA2 4EZ, tel. 01225/425-495, fax 01225/469-029).

Sleeping in Hotels near Pulteney Bridge
These listings are just a few minutes' walk from the center.

Kennard Hotel has 14 charming Georgian rooms. Richard Ambler runs this comfortable place with careful attention to detail (S-£48, Db-£88–98, CC:VMA, nonsmoking, just over Pulteney Bridge, turn left at Henrietta, 11 Henrietta Street, BA2 6LL, tel. 01225/310-472, fax 01225/460-054, www.kennard.co.uk).

Laura Place Hotel is another elegant Georgian place (eight rooms, two on the ground floor, Db-£80–90 from small and high up to huge and palatial, two-night minimum stay, 10 percent discount with cash and this book, CC:VMA, family suite, nonsmoking, easy parking, 3 Laura Place, Great Pulteney Street, BA2 4BH, just over Pulteney Bridge, tel. 01225/463-815, fax 01225/310-222, Patricia Bull).

Sleeping in Hotels in the Town Center
Harington's of Bath Hotel, with 13 newly renovated rooms on a quiet street in the town center, is run by Susan Pow (Db-£78–95, Tb-£95–120, prices decrease midweek and increase on weekends, CC:VMA, nonsmoking, lots of stairs, attached restaurant/bar serves

simple meals throughout day, extremely central at 10 Queen
Street, BA1 1HE, tel. 01225/461-728, fax 01225/444-804, www
.haringtonshotel.co.uk).

Parade Park Hotel, in a Georgian building, has comfortable
rooms, helpful owners, and a central location (35 rooms, Db-
£60–65, special four-poster Db-£75, Tb-£90, Qb-£105, CC:VM,
nonsmoking, *beaucoup* stairs, attached restaurant/bar, 10 North
Parade, BA2 4AL, tel. 01225/463-384, fax 01225/442-322,
www.paradepark.co.uk, Nita and David Derrick).

Henry Guest House is a plain, vertical little eight-room,
family-run place two blocks in front of the train station on a quiet
side street (S-£20, D-£40, T-£57, TVs in rooms, lots of narrow
stairs, one shower and one bath for all, 6 Henry Street, BA1 1JT,
tel. 01225/424-052). This kind of decency at this budget price is
found nowhere else in Bath.

Pratt's Hotel is as proper and old English as you'll find in
Bath. Its creaks and frays are aristocratic. Its public places make you
want to sip a brandy, and its 46 rooms are bright, spacious, and
come with all the comforts (Sb-£75, Db-£105, prices promised with
this book in 2000, dogs £2.95 but children free, CC:VMA, attached
restaurant/bar, elevator, two blocks immediately in front of the station on South Parade, BA2 4AB, tel. 01225/460-441, fax 01225/
448-807, e-mail: admin@prattshotel.demon.co.uk).

Sleeping in Dorms
The **YMCA**, institutional but friendly and wonderfully central on
a leafy square down a tiny alley off Broad Street, has industrial-
strength rooms and scuff-proof halls (S-£15, D-£28, T-£42, Q-
£55, beds in big dorms-£11, cheaper for two-night stays, includes
breakfast, day nursery for kids under five, cheap dinners, CC:VM,
Broad Street Place, BA1 5LH, tel. 01225/460-471, fax 01225/462-
065, e-mail: info@ymcabath.u-net.com).

Bath Backpackers Hostel bills itself as a totally fun-packed
place to stay. This Aussie-run dive/hostel rents bunk beds in 6- to
10-bed coed rooms (£12 per bed, nonsmoking, no lockers, Inter-
net access for nonguests as well, a couple blocks toward the city
center from the station, 13 Pierrepont Street, tel. 01225/446-787,
fax 01225/446-305, www.backpackers-uk.demon.co.uk).

Eating in Bath
While not a great pub grub town, Bath is bursting with quaint
eateries. There's something for every appetite and budget—just
stroll around the center of town. A picnic dinner of take-out fish
and chips in the Royal Crescent Park is ideal for aristocratic
hoboes.

Eating between the Abbey and the Station

Three fine and popular places share North Parade Passage, a block south of the Abbey: **Tilley's Bistro** serves healthy French, English, and vegetarian meals with ambience (£15 three-course lunches, £20 dinners, daily noon–14:30, 18:30–23:00, CC:VM, nonsmoking, North Parade Passage, tel. 01225/484-200). **Sally Lunn's House** is a cutesy, quasi-historic place for expensive doily meals, tea, pink pillows, and lots of lace (£12 meals, nightly, CC:VM, 4 North Parade Passage, tel. 01225/461-634). It's fine for tea and buns, and customers get a free peek at the basement museum (otherwise 30p). Next door, **Demuth's Vegetarian Restaurant** serves good three-course meals for £15 (daily 10:00–22:00, CC:VM, vegan options available, tel. 01225/446-059).

Crystal Palace Pub, with hearty meals under rustic timbers or in the sunny courtyard, is a handy standby (£6 meals, Mon–Fri 11:00–20:30, Sat 11:00–15:30, Sun noon–14:30, children welcome on patio, not indoors, 11 Abbey Green, tel. 01225/423-944).

Seafoods offers the best eat-in or take-out fish-and-chips deal in town (daily from noon until near midnight, 27 Kingsmeads Street, just off Kingsmead Square). For more cheap meals, try **Spike's Fish and Chips** (open very late) and the neighboring café just behind the bus station.

Eating between the Abbey and the Circus

George Street is lined with cheery eateries: Thai, Italian, wine bars, and so on. **Caffé Martini** is purely Italian with class (£9 entrees, £7 pizzas, daily noon–14:30, 18:00–22:00, CC:VM, 9 George Street, tel. 01225/460-818), while the **Mediterraneo**, also Italian, is homier (12 George Street, tel. 01225/429-008).

Eastern Eye has tasty Indian food under the sumptuous domes of a Georgian auction hall (£15 meals, £9 minimum, daily noon–14:30, 18:00–23:00, CC:VMA, 8a Quiet Street, tel. 01225/422-323).

The **Old Green Tree Pub** on Green Street is a rare pub with good grub, microbrews, and a nonsmoking room (lunch only, served noon–14:15, no children).

Browns, a popular chain, offers affordable English food throughout the day without the customary afternoon closure (£5 lunch special, Mon–Sat 11:00–23:30, Sun noon–23:30, CC:VMA, live music sometimes, half block east of the abbey, Orange Grove, tel. 01225/461-199).

Locals prize **The Moon and Sixpence** for its high quality (£7 lunch, three-course dinners £18–22, daily noon–14:30, 17:30–22:30, CC:VM, indoor/outdoor seating, 6a Broad Street, tel. 01225/460-962).

Pasta Galore serves decent Italian food and homemade pasta outside on a patio or inside. The ground floor is brighter than the basement (daily noon–14:30, 18:00–22:30, CC:VM, 1 Barton Street, tel. 01225/463-861).

Devon Savouries serves greasy but delicious take-out pasties, sausage rolls, and vegetable pies (Mon–Sat 9:00–17:30, hours vary on Sun; on Burton Street, the main walkway between New Bond Street and Upper Borough Walls).

The **Waitrose** supermarket, at the Podium shopping center, is great for groceries (Mon–Fri 8:30–20:00, Sat 8:30–19:00, Sun 11:00–17:00, just west of Pulteney Bridge and across from post office on High Street).

Guildhall Market, across from Pulteney Bridge, is fun for browsing and picnic shopping and includes an inexpensive Market Café if you'd like to sip tea surrounded by stacks of used books, bananas on the push list, and honest-to-goodness old-time locals (Mon–Sat 7:30–17:00, closed Sun).

Transportation Connections—Bath

To: London's Paddington station by train (hrly, 75 min, £32.50 one way, tel. 0345/484-950) or National Express bus (nearly hrly, 3 hrs, £11.25 one way, £19.50 round-trip, ask about £11.50 day returns, tel. 0990-808-080). To get from London to Bath, consider using an all-day Stonehenge and Bath bus tour from London. For about the same cost as the train ticket, you can see Stonehenge and Bath and leave the tour before it returns to London (they'll let you stow your bag underneath). Consider Evan Evans (£25 for transportation only, £46 includes admissions and tour, tel. 020/8332-2222) or Travelline (tel. 020/8668-7261).

To London's airports: By National Express bus to Heathrow Airport and continuing on to London (10/day, leaving Bath at 5:00, 6:30, 7:30, 8:45, 10:00, 12:00, 13:30, 15:00, 16:30, and 18:30, 2.5 hrs, £11.50, tel. 0990-808-080), and to Gatwick (2/hrly, 4.5 hrs, £19.50, change at Heathrow). Trains are faster but more expensive (hrly, 2.5 hrs, £28.20). Coming from Heathrow you can also take the tube or train (£10, 4/hrly, 15 min) from the airport to London's Paddington station, then catch the Exeter train to Bath.

DAY TRIP
TO PARIS

The most exciting single day trip from London is Paris, just a three-hour trip by Eurostar train. Paris offers sweeping boulevards, sleepy parks, world-class art galleries, chatty crêpe stands, sleek shopping malls, the Eiffel Tower, and people watching from outdoor cafés. Climb the Notre-Dame and the Eiffel Tower, master the Louvre museum, and cruise the grand Champs-Élysées boulevard. Many fall in love with Paris, one of the world's most romantic cities. (This chapter is excerpted from *Rick Steves' France, Belgium & the Netherlands 2000*, by Rick Steves and Steve Smith.)

Getting to Paris
You can order tickets for the Eurostar train from London to Paris by phone with a credit card in the United States (tel. 800/ EUROSTAR, www.eurostar.com) or in Britain at any train station or by phone (tel. 0990-186-186; pick up tickets at London's Waterloo station an hour before the Eurostar departure). For more information, see Transportation Connections chapter.

Planning Your Time
Ideally, spend the night in Paris, but if all you have is a day, here's the plan:
7:10–Depart London.
11:30–Arrive in Paris. Take a taxi or the Métro to Notre-Dame.
12:00–Explore Notre-Dame and Sainte-Chapelle.
14:00–Taxi or Métro to the Arc de Triomphe.
14:30–Walk down Champs-Élysées and through the Tuileries Gardens.
16:00–Tour the Louvre (open until 18:00, until 21:45 Mon and Wed, closed Tue, after 15:00 it's half price and not crowded).
18:00–Taxi or Métro to Trocadero, walk to Eiffel Tower (if you

— PARIS OVERVIEW —

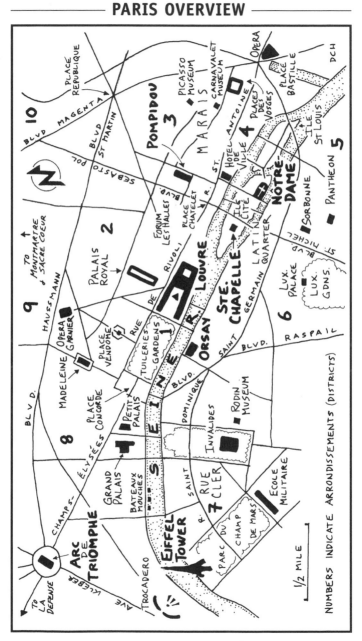

ascend, allow plenty of time for delays). One hour before departure, catch a taxi or the Métro back to Paris' Gare du Nord train station.
20:07 or 21:13–Depart Paris.
22:13 or 23:16–Arrive in London.
Note: For a trip of more than one day, it's worth getting *Rick Steves' Paris*, which includes extensive museum tours and interesting walks, along with great places to eat and sleep.

Arrival in Paris
(6F = about $1)
The Eurostar train from London zips you to Paris' Gare du Nord train station. Paris has six major train stations, each serving different regions. The Gare du Nord serves London. You'll find a handy train information booth and a Paris tourist office near track 18. There are also information booths for Eurostar trains in the center of the arrival area. Change offices, the Métro, and taxis are easy to find.

Passengers departing for London via the Eurostar must check in on the top level, opposite track 4. A peaceful waiting area overlooks the tracks.

Orientation
Paris is split in half by the Seine River. You'll find Paris easier to negotiate if you know which side of the river you're on, and which subway stop (abbreviated "Mo") you're closest to. If you're north of the river (above on any city map), you're on the Right Bank (*rive droite*). If you're south of it, you're on the Left Bank (*rive gauche*).

Tourist Information
Avoid the Paris TIs—long lines, short information, and a 5F charge for maps. This chapter and a map (cheap at newsstands or free from any hotel) are all you need for a short visit. If you're staying longer than a day, pick up a copy of *Pariscope* (or one of its clones, 3F at any newsstand), which lists museum hours, concerts, plays, movies, nightclubs, and art exhibits.

Getting around Paris
By Taxi: Two people with only one day should taxi everywhere. You'll save lots of time and spend only a few bucks per ride. Parisian cabs are comfortable, have hassle-free meters, and are easy to flag down (or ask for a nearby taxi stand).

By Métro: In Paris you're never more than a 10-minute walk from a Métro station. One ticket takes you anywhere in the system with unlimited transfers for about $1. These are your essential Métro words: *direction*, *correspondance* (transfer), *sortie* (exit), *carnet* (cheap set of 10 tickets), and *Donnez-moi mon porte-monnaie!* (Give me back my wallet!) Thieves thrive in the Métro.

Helpful Hints

On Monday, the Orsay Museum, Rodin Museum, and Versailles are closed. The Louvre is more crowded because of this. On Tuesday, when the Louvre is closed, Versailles and the Orsay Museum can be jammed.

Paris Museum Pass: Serious sightseers save time (less time in lines) and money by getting this pass. Sold at museums, major Métro stations, and tourist information offices, it pays for itself in two admissions and gets you into nearly all the sights (major exceptions: Eiffel Tower and Disneyland Paris). The pass allows you to skip to the front of lines at sights—saving hours of waiting in the summer (one day-80F, three consecutive days-160F, five consecutive days-240F).

Sights—Paris

Start your visit where the city did—on the Île de la Cité (the island of the city), facing the Notre-Dame.

▲▲**Notre-Dame Cathedral**—The 700-year-old cathedral is packed with history and tourists. Study its sculpture (Notre-Dame's forte) and windows, eavesdrop on guides, and walk all around the outside of the church dedicated to "Our Lady" (Notre-Dame). The facade is the worth a close look. Mary, cradling Jesus and surrounded by the halo of the rose window, is center stage. Adam is on the left, and Eve is on the right. Below Mary and above the arches is a row of 28 statues known as the Kings of Judah. During the French Revolution these Biblical kings were mistaken for the hated French kings. The citizens stormed the church, crying, "Off with their heads." All were decapitated but have since been recapitated. (Free, daily 8:00–18:45; treasury-15F, daily 9:30–17:30; free English tours usually offered Wed and Thu at noon and Sat at 14:30. Métro: Cité.) Climb to the top for a great gargoyle's-eye view of the city; you get 400 steps for only 35F (entrance on outside, north tower open 9:30–17:30, closed at lunch and earlier off-season). Clean 2.70F toilets are in front of the church near Charlemagne's statue.

If you're hungry near Notre-Dame, the only grocery store on the Île de la Cité is tucked away at 16 rue Chanoinesse, one block north of the church (Mon–Sat 9:00–13:30, 16:00–20:30, closed Sun). Nearby Île St. Louis has inexpensive *crêperies* and grocery stores on its main drag. Plan a picnic for the quiet bench-filled park immediately behind the church (public WC). Two blocks west of Notre-Dame is the...

▲▲▲**Sainte-Chapelle**—The triumph of Gothic church

CORE OF PARIS

architecture is a cathedral of glass like no other. It was speedily built from 1242 to 1248 for St. Louis IX (France's only canonized king) to house the supposed Crown of Thorns. Its architectural harmony is due to the fact that it was completed under the direction of one architect in only six years—unheard of in Gothic times. (Notre-Dame took more than 200 years to build.) Climb the spiral staircase to the *Chapelle Haute* and "let there be light." There are 15 huge stained-glass windows (two-thirds of them 13th-century originals) with more than 1,100 different scenes, mostly from the Bible (32F, daily 9:30–18:30, off-season 10:00–16:30, concerts nearly nightly in summer, call 01 48 01 91 35 for concert information, Métro: Cité).

▲▲▲**Arc de Triomphe**—Napoleon had the magnificent Arc de Triomphe commissioned to commemorate his victory at the Battle of Austerlitz. There's no triumphal arch bigger (50 meters high, 40 meters wide). And, with 12 converging boulevards, there's no traffic circle more thrilling to experience—either behind the wheel or on foot (take the underpass). An elevator or a spiral staircase leads to a cute museum about the arch and a grand view from the top, even after dark (40F, daily 9:30–23:00, Oct–Mar daily 9:30–22:00, tel. 01 43 80 31 31, Métro: Étoile).

▲▲**Champs-Élysées and the Place de la Concorde**—This famous boulevard, carrying the city's greatest concentration of traffic, leads to the place de la Concorde, the city's largest square. This was the place where the guillotine took the lives of thousands—including King Louis XVI. Back then it was called the place de la Revolution.

Catherine de Medici wanted a place to drive her carriage, so she started draining the swamp that would become the Champs-Élysées. Napoleon put on the final touches, and it's been the place to be seen ever since. The Tour de France bicycle race ends here, as do all parades (French or foe) of any significance. While the boulevard has become a bit hamburgerized, a walk here is a must. Take the Métro to the Arc de Triomphe (Métro: Étoile) and saunter down the Champs-Élysées. (Métro stops are located every three blocks along the boulevard.)

▲▲▲**Louvre**—This is Europe's oldest, biggest, greatest, and possibly most crowded museum. It's packed with masterpieces from ancient Greece and Rome, medieval jewels, Michelangelo statues, and paintings by the greatest artists from the Renaissance to the Romantic movement of the mid-1800s. A security check with metal detectors creates a line in front of the pyramid; if you enter directly from the Métro stop you'll get in quicker, though there is no grander entry than through the pyramid.

Pick up the free *Louvre Handbook in English* at the information desk under the pyramid as you enter. Don't try to cover the museum thoroughly. The 90-minute English-language tours, which leave six times daily except Sunday, boil this overwhelming museum down to size (33F, tour tel. 01 40 20 52 09, www.louvre.fr). Clever new 30F digital audio tours (after ticket booths, at top of stairs) give you a receiver and a directory of about 130 masterpieces, allowing you to dial a (rather dull) commentary on included works as you stumble upon them. Rick Steves' and Gene Openshaw's museum guidebook, *Rick Steves' Mona Winks* (buy in the United States), includes a self-guided tour of the Louvre.

If you can't get a guide, start in the Denon wing and visit these highlights, in this order: Michelangelo's *Slaves*, Ancient Greek and Roman (Parthenon frieze, *Vénus de Milo*, Pompeii mosaics, Etruscan sarcophagi, Roman portrait busts, Nike of Samothrace); Apollo Gallery (jewels); French and Italian paintings in the Grande Galerie (a quarter mile long and worth the hike); the *Mona Lisa* and her Italian Renaissance roommates; the nearby neoclassical collection (*Coronation of Napoleon*); and the Romantic collection, with works by Delacroix (*Liberty at the Barricades*) and Géricault (*Raft of the Medusa*).

Cost: 45F until 15:00, 26F after 15:00 and all day Sun, free on the first Sun of the month and if you're under 18.

Hours: Wed–Mon 9:00–18:00; Richelieu wing open Mon until 21:45; all wings open Wed until 21:45 and closed Tue. Tel. 01 40 20 51 51 or 01 40 20 53 17 for recorded information.

Getting to the Louvre: Using the Métro, get off at the Palais-Royal/Musée du Louvre Métro stop (not the Louvre Rivoli stop, which is farther away). Exiting the Métro, follow *Musée du Louvre* signs and head for the inverted pyramid, where you'll uncover a handy TI, glittering boutiques, a dizzying assortment of good-value eateries (up the escalator), and the underground entry to the Louvre.

▲▲▲**Eiffel Tower**—It may be crowded and expensive, but it's worth the trouble. The Eiffel Tower is 1,000 feet tall (six inches taller in hot weather), covers two and one-half acres, and requires 50 tons of paint. Its 7,000 tons of metal are spread out so well at the base that it's no heavier per square inch than a linebacker on tiptoes.

Built a hundred years after the French Revolution (and in the midst of an industrial one), the tower served no function but to impress. To a generation hooked on technology, the tower was the marvel of the age, a symbol of progress and of human ingenuity.

There are three observation platforms, at 200, 400, and 900 feet; the higher you go the more you pay. Each requires a separate elevator (and a line), so plan on at least 90 minutes if you want to go to the top and back. The view from the 400-foot-high second level is plenty. It costs 21F to go to the first level, 43F to the second, and 60F to go all the way for the 1,000-foot view (summers daily 9:00–24:00, off-season 9:30–23:00, tel. 01 44 11 23 23, Métro: Trocadero). Go early (arrive by 9:15) or late in the day (after 18:00) to avoid most crowds; weekends are worst. Pilier Nord (the north pillar) has the biggest elevator and, therefore, the fastest-moving line.

More Sights—Paris

▲▲▲**Orsay Museum**—Paris' 19th-century art museum (actually, art from 1848–1914) includes Europe's greatest collection of Impressionist works. The museum is housed in a former train station (Gare d'Orsay) across the river and 10 minutes downstream from the Louvre (the Métro stop "Solferino" is three blocks south of the Orsay).

Start on the ground floor. The "pretty" conservative establishment art is on the right. Then cross left into the brutally truthful and, at that time, very shocking art of the realist rebels and Manet. Then ride the escalators at the far end (detouring at the top for a grand museum view) to the series of Impressionist rooms (Monet, Renoir, Dégas, et al). Don't miss the Grand Ballroom (room 52, *Arts et Decors de la IIIème République*) and Art Nouveau on the mezzanine level.

Cost: 40F, 27F for the young and old, under 18 free, tickets good all day. The booth near the entrance gives free floor plans in English. English-language tours usually run daily except Sun at 11:30, cost 38F, take 90 minutes, and are also available on audio-tape. City museum passes are sold in the basement; if there's a long line you can skip it by buying a pass there, but you can't skip the metal-detector line into the museum. Tel. 01 40 49 48 48.

Hours: Tue–Sat 10:00–18:00, Thu until 21:45, Sun 9:00–18:00, closed Mon. Opens at 9:00 Jun 20–Sept 20. Last entrance 45 minutes before closing. Galleries start closing 30 minutes early. The Orsay is crowded on Tuesday, when the Louvre is closed.

▲▲**Napoleon's Tomb and the Army Museum**—The emperor lies majestically dead inside several coffins under a grand dome—a goose-bumping pilgrimage for historians. Napoleon is surround-ed by the tombs of other French war heroes and Europe's greatest military museum in the Hôtel des Invalides. Follow signs to the crypt, where you'll find Roman Empire–style reliefs listing the accomplishments of Napoleon's administration. The restored dome glitters with 26 pounds of gold (38F, daily 10:00–18:00, closes off-season at 17:00, tel. 01 44 42 37 67, Métro: La Tour Maubourg or Varennes).

▲▲**Rodin Museum**—This user-friendly museum is filled with works by the greatest sculptor since Michelangelo. See *The Kiss*, *The Thinker*, *The Gates of Hell*, and many more. Don't miss the room full of work by Rodin's student and mistress, Camille Claudel. (28F, 18F on Sun, 5F for gardens only—perhaps Paris' best deal as many works are well displayed in the beautiful gardens; Tue–Sun 9:30–17:45, closed Mon, closes off-season at 17:00, 77 rue de Varennes, tel. 01 44 18 61 10, Metro: Varennes, near Napoleon's Tomb.) Good cafeteria and idyllic picnic spots in family-friendly back garden.

▲**Latin Quarter**—The Left Bank neighborhood just opposite the Notre-Dame is the Latin Quarter. This was a center of Roman Paris, but its touristic fame relates to the Latin Quarter's intriguing artsy, bohemian character. This was Europe's leading university district in the Middle Ages—home, since the 13th century, to the prestigious Sorbonne University. Back then, Latin was the language of higher education. And, since students here came from all over Europe, Latin served as their linguistic com-mon denominator. Locals referred to the quarter by its language: Latin. In modern times this was the center of Paris' café culture.

The neighborhood's main boulevards (St. Michel and St. Germain) are lined with cafés—once the haunts of great poets and philosophers but now just places where tired tourists can hang out. While still youthful and artsy, the area has become a tourist ghetto filled with cheap North African eateries.

▲▲**Sacré-Coeur and Montmartre**—This Byzantine-looking church, while only 130 years old, is impressive. It was built as a "praise the Lord anyway" gesture, after the French were humiliated by the Germans in a brief war in 1871. The church is open daily until 23:00. One block from the church, the square called the place du Tertre was the haunt of Toulouse-Lautrec and the original bohemians. Today it's mobbed by tourists and unoriginal bohemians, but still fun. Either use the Anvers Métro stop (plus one Métro ticket for the funicular to avoid stairs) or the closer but less scenic Abbesses stop. A taxi to the top of the hill saves time and sweat.

Sights—Near Paris

▲▲▲**Palace of Versailles**—Every king's dream, Versailles was the residence of the French king and the cultural heartbeat of Europe for about 100 years—until the Revolution of 1789 ended the notion that God deputized some people to rule for Him on Earth. Louis XIV spent half a year's income of Europe's richest country turning his dad's hunting lodge into a palace fit for a divine monarch. Louis XV and Louis XVI spent much of the 18th century gilding Louis XIV's lily. In 1837, about 50 years after the royal family was evicted, King Louis Philippe opened the palace as a museum. Europe's next-best palaces are Versailles wannabes.

Information: You'll find TIs across from the Versailles' R.G. train station (tel. 01 39 50 36 22), on the approach to the palace, and at the palace (entrance C). Their free "Versailles Orientation Guide" explains your sightseeing options.

Ticket Options: The main palace self-guided, one-way palace romp, including the Hall of Mirrors, costs 45F (35F after 15:30, on Sun, or for those over 60 or ages 18–25, under 18 free). To supplement this with a private tour through the other sections, you'll need to pay the 45F base price then add 30F for a one-hour guided tour, 37F for a 90-minute guided tour, or 25F for a self-guided audiotape tour.

Hours: Tue–Sun 9:00–18:30, Oct–Apr 9:00–17:30, last entry 30 min before closing, closed Mon. In summer, Versailles is especially crowded around 10:00 and 13:00, Tue, and Sun. To minimize crowds and get a reduced entry ticket, arrive after 15:30. Tour the gardens after the palace closes. The palace is great late. Information tel. 01 30 84 76 18 or 01 30 84 74 00.

VERSAILLES

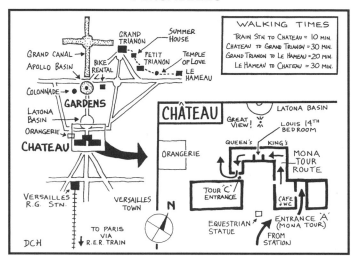

Getting to Versailles: Versailles, 12 miles from downtown Paris, is a quick and easy ride on the RER train (not covered by a standard Paris Métro ticket). Take the Métro to an RER-C station (such as Gare d'Austerlitz, St. Michel, Orsay, Invalides, Pont de l'Alma, or Champs de Mars/Tour Eiffel), follow the RER signs, and buy a round-trip ticket to Versailles (28F). Look at the schedule for trains, usually named VICK, going to Versailles R.G., the Rive Gauche station (4/hrly, 30 min; confirm that your train stops at Versailles R.G. rather than Versailles C.H., which is farther from the palace). When leaving the Versailles station, first turn right, then turn left on the major boulevard (10-minute walk to the palace).

▲▲**Disneyland Paris**—Europe's Disneyland is basically a modern remake of California's, with most of the same rides and smiles. The main difference is that Mickey Mouse speaks French (and you can buy wine with your lunch). My kids went ducky. Locals love it. It's worth a day if Paris is handier than Florida or California. Crowds are a problem. If possible, avoid Saturday, Sunday, Wednesday, school holidays, and July and August. The park can get very crowded. When 60,000 have entered, they close the gates (tel. 01 64 74 30 00 for the latest). The crowds leave after dinner, and you can walk right onto rides that had a 45-minute wait three hours earlier. Food is fun but expensive. To eat reasonably, smuggle in a picnic. Disney brochures are in every Paris hotel.

Cost: 220F for adults, 170F for kids 3–11, 25F less in spring and fall.

Hours: Daily 9:00–23:00 late Jun–early Sept and weekends year-round, shoulder-season Mon–Fri 9:00–19:00, off-season 10:00–18:00.

Getting to Disneyland Paris: The RER train drops you right in the park (43F each way, from downtown Paris to Marne-la-Vallee in 30 min). The last train back to Paris leaves shortly after midnight. Disneyland Paris is actually a stop on the London Eurostar route.

Sleeping in Paris
(6F = about $1)
Sleep Code: S = Single, **D** = Double/Twin, **T** = Triple, **Q** = Quad, **b** = bathroom, **t** = toilet only, **s** = shower only, **CC** = Credit Card (**V**isa, **M**asterCard, **A**mex), * = French hotel rating system (0–4 stars).

If you're calling Paris from the United States, dial 011-33 (from Britain dial 00-33), then dial the local number without the initial zero.

Sleeping in the Rue Cler Neighborhood
(Seventh district, Métro: École Militaire, zip code: 75007)
Rue Cler, a villagelike pedestrian street, is safe, tidy, and makes me feel like I must have been a poodle in a previous life. How such coziness lodged itself between the high-powered government/business district and the expensive Eiffel Tower and Invalides areas, I'll never know. Living here ranks with the top museums as one of the city's great experiences.

The street called rue Cler is the glue that holds this pleasant neighborhood together. On rue Cler you can eat and browse your way through a street full of tart shops, cheeseries, and colorful outdoor produce stalls.

Hôtel Leveque** has been entirely renovated. With a helpful staff and a singing maid, it's still cozy. It's a fine value with the best location on the block, comfortable rooms, cable TV, hair dryers, safes, an ice machine, and tasteful decor throughout (Sb-300F, Db-400–470F, Tb-580F, breakfast-30F, 1st free for readers of this book, CC:VMA, 29 rue Cler, tel. 01 47 05 49 15, fax 01 45 50 49 36, www.hotel-leveque.com, e-mail: leveque @gofornet.com). Laurence speaks English.

Hôtel du Champs de Mars**, with charming pastel rooms, is an even cozier rue Cler option. The hotel has a Provence-style small-town feel from top to bottom. Rooms are comfortable and a very good value. Single rooms can work as tiny doubles (Sb-390F,

Db-430–460F, Tb-550F, CC:VMA, cable TV, hair dryers, etc., 30 yards off rue Cler at 7 rue du Champs de Mars, tel. 01 45 51 52 30, fax 01 45 51 64 36, www: adx.fr/hotel-du-champ-de-mars, e-mail: stg@club-internet.fr).

Hôtel Relais Bosquet*** is bright, spacious, and a bit up-scale with sharp and comfortable rooms (Sb-600–800F, Db-650–1,000F, most at 850F, CC:VMA, 19 rue du Champs de Mars, tel. 01 47 05 25 45, fax 01 45 55 08 24, www.relaisbosquet.com). The similar **Hotel Beaugency***** offers basic three-star comfort for less (Sb-680F, Db-730F, includes buffet breakfast, 21 rue Duvivier, tel. 01 47 05 01 63, fax 01 45 51 04 96).

Hôtel de l'Alma*** is a good value with 32 small but pleasant look-alike rooms with TVs and minibars (Sb-450F, Db-500F, breakfast included, no triples but a kid's bed can be moved in for free, CC:VMA, 32 rue de l'Exposition, tel. 01 47 05 45 70, fax 01 45 51 84 47).

Hôtel La Tour Maubourg*** lies alone five minutes east of rue Cler, just off the Esplanade des Invalides, and feels like a slightly faded, elegant manor house with spacious Old World rooms. It overlooks a cheery green within sight of Napoleon's tomb (Sb-700F, Db-800–900F, suites for up to 4-1,100–1,800F, prices include breakfast with fresh-squeezed juice, prices reduced mid-Jul–mid-Aug, CC:VM, immediately at the La Tour Maubourg Métro stop, 150 rue de Grenelle, tel. 01 47 05 16 16, fax 01 47 05 16 14, e-mail: victor@worldnet.fr).

Transportation Connections—Paris

To London: The sleek Eurostar train makes the 190-mile trip in three hours, with 12 departures daily in each direction. For details and prices, see the end of the Transportation Connections chapter.

To Other Destinations: Paris is Europe's transportation hub. The city has six central rail stations, each serving different regions. You'll find trains (day and night) to almost any French or European destination. For schedule information, call 08 36 35 35 35 (3F/minute).

SLEEPING
IN LONDON

(14) *london*

London is expensive. For £50 ($80) you'll get a sleep-worthy double with breakfast in a safe, cramped, and dreary place with minimal service. For £60 ($95) you'll get a basic, clean, reasonably cheery double in a usually cramped, cracked-plaster building or a soulless but comfortable room without breakfast in a huge Motel 6–type place. My London splurges, at £100 to £140 ($170 to $240), are spacious, thoughtfully appointed places you'd be happy to entertain or make love in. Hearty English or generous buffet breakfasts are included unless otherwise noted, and TVs are nearly standard in rooms.

Reserve your London room with a phone call or e-mail as soon as you can commit to a date. A few places will hold a room with no deposit if you promise to arrive by midday. Most take your credit-card number as security. Most have expensive cancellation policies. Some fancy £120 rooms rent for half-price if you arrive late on a slow day and ask for a deal.

Sleep Code
S = Single, **D** = Double/Twin, **T** = Triple,
Q = Quad, **b** = bathroom, **t** = toilet only, **s** = shower only,
CC = Credit Card (**V**isa, **M**asterCard, **A**mex). Unless otherwise noted, prices include a generous breakfast and all taxes.
Exchange rate: £1=about $1.70. **Tel. code:** 020.

Sleeping in Victoria Station Neighborhood, Belgravia

The streets behind Victoria Station teem with budget B&Bs. It's a safe, surprisingly tidy, and decent area without a hint of the trashy, touristy glitz of the streets in front of the station. Here in

VICTORIA STATION

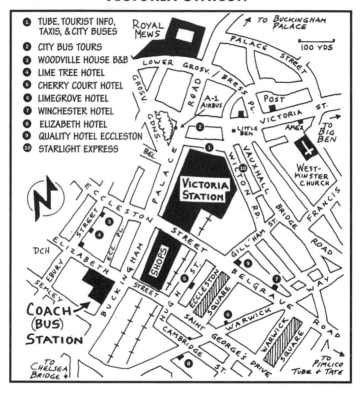

① TUBE, TOURIST INFO, TAXIS, & CITY BUSES
② CITY BUS TOURS
③ WOODVILLE HOUSE B&B
④ LIME TREE HOTEL
⑤ CHERRY COURT HOTEL
⑥ LIMEGROVE HOTEL
⑦ WINCHESTER HOTEL
⑧ ELIZABETH HOTEL
⑨ QUALITY HOTEL ECCLESTON
⑩ STARLIGHT EXPRESS

Belgravia, your neighbors include Andrew Lloyd Webber and Margaret Thatcher (her policeman stands outside 73 Chester Square). Decent eateries abound (see Eating chapter). The cheaper listings are dumpy. Don't expect £90 cheeriness in a £50 room. Off-season you can save money by arriving late without a reservation and checking around. Fierce competition softens prices, especially for multinight stays. Particularly for Warwick Way hotels (and on hot summer nights), request a quiet back room. All are within a five-minute walk of the Victoria tube, bus, and train stations. There's an £8-per-day garage and a nearby launderette (daily 8:00–20:30, self-serve or full-serve, past Warwick Square at 3 Westmoreland Terrace, tel. 020/7821-8692).

Winchester Hotel is family run and perhaps the best value with 18 fine rooms and a wise and caring management (Db-£75, Tb-£100, Qb-£115, no groups or small children, 17 Belgrave

Road, London SW1V 1RB, tel. 020/7828-2972, fax 020/7828-5191, Jimmy #1 cooks, Jimmy #2 greets).

In **Woodville House** the quarters are dollhouse tight, showers are down the hall, and several rooms are noisy on the street (doubles on quiet backside, twins and singles on street), but this well-run, well-worn place is a good value with lots of travel tips and friendly chat—especially about the local rich and famous—from Rachel Joplin (S-£42, D-£62, bunky family deals—£80–110 for up to five, CC:VM, 107 Ebury Street, SW1W 9QU, tel. 020/7730-1048, fax 020/7730-2574, e-mail: woodville.house@cwcom.net).

Lime Tree Hotel, enthusiastically run by David and Marilyn Davies, comes with spacious and thoughtfully decorated rooms and a fun-loving breakfast room. While priced a bit steep, the place has character (Sb-£75, Db-£95–105, Tb-£130, family room-£145, David deals in slow times and is good at helping travelers in a bind, CC:VMA, 135 Ebury Street, SW1W 9RA, tel. 020/7730-8191, fax 020/7730-7865).

Elizabeth House feels institutional and a bit bland—as you might expect from a former YMCA—but the rooms are clean and bright and the price is right (S-£30, D-£50, Db-£60, T-£75, Q-£85, CC:VM, 118 Warwick Way, SW1 4JB, tel. 020/7630-0741, fax 020/7630-0740).

Quality Hotel Eccleston is big, modern, well located, and a fine value for no-nonsense comfort (Db-£96, on slow days drop-ins can ask for "saver prices"—33 percent off on first night, breakfast extra, CC:VMA, nonsmoking floor, elevator, 82 Eccleston Square, SW1V 1PS, tel. 020/7834-8042, fax 020/7630-8942, e-mail: admin@gb614.u-net.com).

These three places come with cramped rooms and claustrophobic halls. While they generate a lot of reader complaints, I list them because they offer beds at youth-hostel prices and are beautifully located just a few minutes from Victoria Station: **Cherry Court Hotel** is run by the friendly and industrious Patel family (S-£30, Sb-£40, Db-£45, T-£50, Tb-£65, price promised with this book, CC:VMA, fruit-basket breakfast in room, no twins—only double beds, 23 Hugh Street, SW1V 1QJ, tel. 020/7828-2840, fax 020/7828-0393, e-mail: info@cherrycourthotel.co.uk). **Cedar Guest House**, run by a Polish organization to help Poles afford London, welcomes all (D-£38, Db-£45, T-£54, 30 Hugh Street, SW1V 1RP, tel. 020/7828-2625). The musty and run-down **Limegrove Hotel**, run by harried Joyce, serves a humble in-room breakfast (S-£28, D-£38, Db-£50, T-£48, Tb-£60, cheaper off-season, lots of stairs, 101 Warwick Way, SW1V 1QL, tel. 020/7828-0458). Back rooms are quieter.

Big, Cheap, Modern Hotels

These places—popular with budget tour groups—are well run with elevators and all the modern comforts in no-frills practical packages. Their £60 doubles are a great value for London.

London County Hall Travel Inn, literally down the hall from a $400-a-night Marriot Hotel, fills one end of London's massive former city hall. This place is wonderfully located across the Thames from Big Ben. Its 300 slick and no-frills rooms come with all the necessary comforts (Db-£60 for two adults and up to two kids under age 17, couples can request a bigger family room—same price, breakfast extra, book in advance, no-show rooms are released at 16:00, elevator, some smoke-free and easy-access rooms, CC:VMA, 500 yards from Westminster tube stop and Waterloo station where the Chunnel train leaves for Paris, Belvedere Road, SE1 7PB, tel. 020/7902-1600, fax 020/7902-1619, www.travelinn.co.uk).

Other London Travel Inns charging £60 per room include **London Euston** (141 Euston Road, NW1 2AU, tube: Euston), **Tower Bridge** (tube: London Bridge), and **London Putney Bridge** (farther out, tube: Putney Bridge). For any of these, call 01582/414-341.

Hotel Ibis London Euston, which feels classier than a Travel Inn, is located on a quiet street a block behind Euston Station (Sb-£60, Db-£63, breakfast extra, CC:VMA, nonsmoking floor, 3 Cardington Street, NW1 2LW, tel. 020/7388-7777, fax 020/7388-0001, e-mail: ho921@accor-hotels.com).

Jurys Inn rents 200 mod, compact, and comfy rooms near King's Cross station (Db/Tb-£75, two adults and two kids in one room is OK, breakfast extra, CC:VMA, nonsmoking floors, 60 Pentonville Road, Islington, N1 9LA, tube: Angel, tel. 020/7282-5500, fax 020/7282-5511).

"South Kensington," She Said, Loosening His Cummerbund

To live on a quiet street so classy it doesn't allow hotel signs, surrounded by trendy shops and colorful restaurants, call "South Ken" your London home. Shoppers like being a short walk from Harrods and the designer shops of King's Road and Chelsea. When I splurge, I splurge here. Sumner Place is just off Old Brompton Road, 200 yards from the handy South Kensington tube station (on Circle Line, two stops from Victoria Station, direct Heathrow connection). There's a taxi rank in the meridian at the end of Harrington Road. The handy "Wash & Dry" Laundromat is on the corner of Queensberry Place and Harrington Road (daily 8:00–21:00, bring 20p and £1 coins).

Aster House Hotel—run by friendly and accommodating Simon and Leona Tan—has a sumptuous lobby, a lounge, and a breakfast room. Its well-worn rooms are comfy and quiet with TV, phone, and fridge but ramshackle bathrooms. Enjoy breakfast or just lounging in the whisper-elegant Orangery, a Victorian greenhouse (Sb-£65–85, Db-£125, deluxe four-poster Db-£145, CC:VM, entirely nonsmoking, 3 Sumner Place, SW7 3EE, tel. 020/7581-5888, fax 020/7584-4925, www.welcome2london.com).

Five Sumner Place Hotel was recently voted "the best small hotel in London." In this 150-year-old building, rooms are tastefully decorated and the breakfast room is a Victorian-style conservatory/greenhouse (13 rooms, Sb-£88, Db-£141, third bed-£24; Oct–Mar 10 percent discount with this book, making it the best Sumner Place value off-season; CC:VMA, TV, phone, and fridge in rooms, nonsmoking rooms, elevator, 5 Sumner Place, South Kensington, SW7 3EE, tel. 020/7584-7586, fax 020/7823-9962, www.sumnerplace.com, e-mail: reservations@sumnerplace.com, run by Tom).

Sixteen Sumner Place—a lesser value for classier travelers—has over-the-top formality and class packed into its 37 unnumbered but pretentiously named rooms, plush lounges, and quiet garden (Db-£160 with showers, £185 with baths, CC:VMA, breakfast in your room, elevator, 16 Sumner Place, SW7 3EG, tel. 020/7589-5232, fax 020/7584-8615, U.S. tel. 800/592-5387, e-mail: reservations@numbersixteenhotel.co.uk).

Kensington Jurys Hotel is big and stately (Sb/Db/Tb-£100–170 depending upon "availability," ask for a deal, breakfast extra, CC:VMA, piano lounge, nonsmoking floor, elevator, Queen's Gate, South Kensington, SW7 5LR, tel. 020/7589-6300, fax 020/7581-1492).

The Claverley, two blocks from Harrods, is on a quiet street similar to Sumner Place. The warmly furnished rooms come with all the comforts (S-£70, Sb-£75–115, Db-£110–145, sofa bed Tb-£160–215, flexible during slow times, CC:VMA, plush lounge, nonsmoking rooms, elevator, 13–14 Beaufort Gardens, SW3 1PS, tube: Knightsbridge, tel. 020/7589-8541, fax 020/7584-3410, U.S. tel. 800/747-0398).

Sleeping in Notting Hill Gate Neighborhood

Residential Notting Hill Gate has quick bus and tube access to downtown, is on the A2 Airbus line from Heathrow, and, for London, is very "homely." It has a self-serve launderette, an artsy theater, the weekend street fair at Portobello Road, a late-hours supermarket, and lots of fun budget eateries (see Eating chapter).

Westland Hotel is comfortable, convenient, and hotelesque

──── NOTTING HILL GATE ────

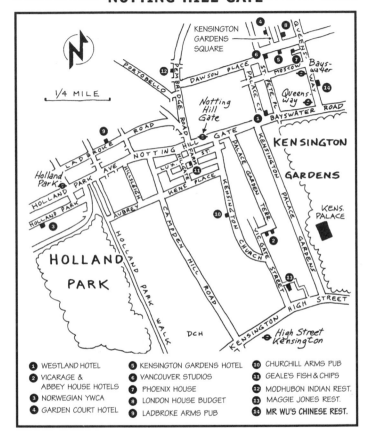

❶ WESTLAND HOTEL	❺ KENSINGTON GARDENS HOTEL	❿ CHURCHILL ARMS PUB
❷ VICARAGE & ABBEY HOUSE HOTELS	❻ VANCOUVER STUDIOS	⓫ GEALE'S FISH & CHIPS
❸ NORWEGIAN YWCA	❼ PHOENIX HOUSE	⓬ MODHUBON INDIAN REST.
❹ GARDEN COURT HOTEL	❽ LONDON HOUSE BUDGET	⓭ MAGGIE JONES REST.
	❾ LADBROKE ARMS PUB	⓮ MR WU'S CHINESE REST.

with a fine lounge, an impersonal staff, and spacious 1970s-style rooms (Sb-£80, Db-£95, cavernous deluxe Db-£110, sprawling Tb-£120, gargantuan Qb-£135, 10 percent discount with this book through 2000, CC:VMA, elevator, free garage, between Notting Hill Gate and Queensway tube stations, 154 Bayswater Road, W2 4HP, tel. 020/7229-9191, fax 020/7727-1054, e-mail: 106411.3060@compuserve.com).

Vicarage Private Hotel, understandably popular, is family run and elegantly British in a quiet, classy neighborhood. It has 19 rooms furnished with taste and quality, a TV lounge, and facilities on each floor. Mandy, Richard, and Tere maintain a homey and caring atmosphere. Reserve long in advance. There's no better room for the price (S-£43, D-£68, T-£87, Q-£92, a six-minute walk from the Notting Hill Gate and High Street Kensington tube stations, near Kensington Palace at 10 Vicarage Gate, Kensington, W8 4AG, tel. 020/7229-4030, fax 020/7792-5989, www.londonvicaragehotel.com).

Another fine value, **Abbey House Hotel**, next door, is similar but has no lounge and is less cozy (16 rooms, S-£43, D-£68, T-£85, Q-£95, Quint-£105, 11 Vicarage Gate, Kensington, W8 4AG, tel. 020/7727-2594, Rodrigo).

Norwegian YWCA (Norsk K.F.U.K.) is for women under 30 only (and men with Norwegian passports). Located on a quiet, stately street, it offers nonsmoking rooms, a study, TV room, piano lounge, and an open-face Norwegian ambience. They have mostly quads, so those willing to share with strangers are most likely to get a place (Jul–Aug: Ss-£27, bed in shared double-£25, shared triple-£21 apiece, shared quad-£18 apiece, with breakfast; Sept–Jun same prices include dinner; CC:VM, 52 Holland Park, W11 3R5, tel. & fax 020/7727-9897). With each visit I wonder which is easier—getting a sex change or a Norwegian passport?

Sleeping on Kensington Gardens

Several big old hotels line the quiet Victorian Kensington Gardens, a block off the bustling Queensway shopping street near the Bayswater tube station. Popular with young travelers from around the world, Queensway is a multicultural festival of commerce and lively eateries (such as Mr. Wu's Chinese buffet, which stuffs locals for £4.50—see Eating chapter). These hotels come with the least traffic noise of all my downtown recommendations. Brookford Wash & Dry is at Queensway and Bishop's Bridge Road (daily 7:00–19:30, service from 9:00–17:30, all coins accepted).

Garden Court rents 34 large and comfortable rooms and is one of London's best accommodations values. The breakfast room is sticky and the public bathrooms are a bit unkempt, but it's friendly and includes a great lounge and super prices (S-£34, Sb-£48, D-£52, Db-£76, T-£72, Tb-£86, Q-£78, Qb-£92, CC:VM, 30 Kensington Gardens Square, W2 4BG, tel. 020/7229-2553, fax 020/7727-2749, e-mail: gardencourthotel@londonw24bg.freeserve.co.uk).

Kensington Gardens Hotel laces 17 fine, fresh rooms together in a tall, skinny place with lots of stairs (S-£50, Sb-£55, Db-£75, 9 Kensington Gardens Square, W2 4BH, tel. 020/7221-7790, fax 020/7792-8612, www.kensingtongardenshotel.co.uk).

Vancouver Studios is a different concept, giving you a fully equipped kitchenette (plates, stove, microwave, and fridge) rather than breakfast (Sb-£55–72, Db-£85–100, Tb-£123, CC:VMA, homey lounge and private garden, rooms with all the modern comforts, 30 Prince's Square, W2 4NJ, tel. 020/7243-1270, fax 020/7221-8678, e-mail: hotels@vienna-group.co.uk).

The Phoenix Hotel, a Best Western modernization of a 130-room hotel, offers American business-class comforts, plush public spaces, and big, fresh, and modern-feeling rooms (Sb-£72, Db-£92, Tb-£120, CC:VMA, nonsmoking rooms, elevator, 8 Kensington Gardens Square, W2 4BH, tel. 020/7229-2494, fax 020/7727-1419, U.S. tel. 800/528-1234, www.phoenixhotel.co.uk).

London House Budget Hotel is a threadbare, nose-ringed slumbermill renting 220 beds in 76 stark but sleep-worthy rooms (S-£40, twin-£54, dorm bed-£20, includes continental breakfast, CC:VMA, lots of school groups, 81 Kensington Gardens Square, W2 4DJ, tel. 020/7727-0696, fax 020/7243-8626, e-mail: hotels @vienna-group.co.uk).

Sleeping in Other Neighborhoods

Euston Station: Methodist International Centre is a youthful Christian residence. Its lower floors are filled with international students while its top floor is open to travelers. Rooms are modern, simple, and comfortable, with fine bathrooms, phones, and desks. The atmosphere is friendly, safe, clean, and controlled. There's a spacious lounge and game room (Sb-£38, Db-£58, Tb-£70, includes breakfast, three-course buffet dinner-£11, CC:VM, nonsmoking rooms, elevator, on a quiet street a block southwest of Euston Station, 81-103 Euston Street, not Euston Road, W1 2EZ, tube: Euston Square, tel. 020/7380-0001, fax 020/7387-5300, e-mail: sales@micentre.com).

Cottage Hotel is tucked away a block off the west exit of Euston Station. It was established in 1950 and, because it's a bit tired, cramped, and smoky, it feels like 1950. But it's cheap, quiet, and has a fine breakfast room (40 rooms, S-£35, Sb-£45, D-£45, Db-£55, 67 Euston Street, tel. 020/7387-6785, fax 020/7383-0859).

Bloomsbury, near the British Museum: The Cambria House, a fine value, is run by the Salvation Army (a plus when it comes to cheap big-city hotels). This smoke-free old building with a narrow maze of halls is all newly painted and super clean, if institutional. The rooms are large and perfectly good. You'll find ample showers and toilets on each floor, a TV lounge, and a warm welcome (S-£29, D-£46, Db-£57, T-£70, CC:VM, north of Russell Square, 37 Hunter Street, WC1N 1BJ, tel. 020/7837-1654, fax 020/7837-1229).

Downtown near Baker Street: For a less hotelesque alternative in the center, consider renting one of 18 stark, hardwood, comfortable rooms in **22 York Street B&B** (Db-£94, Tb-£141, CC:VMA, strictly smoke-free, inviting lounge, social breakfast, from

Baker Street tube station walk two blocks down Baker Street and take right, 22 York Street, tel. 020/7224-3990, fax 020/7224-1990, e-mail: mc@22yorkstreet.prestel.co.uk, energetically run by Liz and Michael).

Near St. Paul's: The **City of London Youth Hostel** is clean, modern, friendly, and well run. You'll pay about £24 for a bed in three- to five-bed rooms, £26 in a single (youth hostel membership required, 200 beds, CC:VM, cheap meals, 36 Carter Lane, EC4V 5AD, tube: St. Paul's, tel. 020/7236-4965, fax 020/7236-7681).

South of London: Caroline Cunningham's humble guest house is on a quiet street in a well-worn neighborhood south of Victoria near Clapham Common (three rooms, S-£15, D-£30 with English breakfast, 98 Hambalt Road, Clapham Common, London SW4 9EJ, tel. 020/8673-1077). It's 15 minutes by tube to Clapham Common, then a bus ride or a 12-minute walk—exit left down Clapham South Road, left on Elms, right on Abbeville Road, left on Hambalt. Rooms in Caroline's brother's house are an equally good value. A good, cheap Thai restaurant (The Pepper Tree) is near the tube station.

Sleeping in Hampstead, the Small-Town Alternative

If you must "do" London but wish it were a small town, make Hampstead your home base-on-the-hill. Just 15 to 25 minutes north of the center by tube (to Hampstead on the sometimes-tardy Northern Line) and you're in the former resort of wealthy Londoners—drawn by spas in the 1700s and the brilliant views of London from the popular Hampstead Heath, an 800-acre park.

Hampstead today glows with Georgian-village elegance—narrow cobblestone lanes, gas lamps (now electrified), and blue plaques noting where Keats, Freud, and other famous locals lived. Even McDonald's has a mock-Tudor facade.

The tube station marks the center of the town (note that in tube terms, Hampstead is in Zone 2, covered by day passes but not carnet tickets). From the station, busy High Street cuts downhill though the center. Following it downhill takes you into a cheery business district of side streets flickering with gaslit charm. The B&B is a brisk 10-minute walk downhill. The hotel is a three-minute walk uphill.

Make a point to explore the back lanes where you can pop into churches and peek into windows—drapes are left open so their elegant interiors can be envied.

Hampstead Village Guesthouse is run in a laissez-faire style by Anne Marie van der Meer, who rents eight rooms and raised her family in this Victorian house. The homey rooms, most of which were named after her children, don't have locks, but the house is secure. All rooms come with a phone, miniature fridge, TV, and even a hot-water bottle (small S-£40, S-£45, Sb-£55, D-£60, Db-£70, price varies for studio/kitchenette for one to five people-£100 for two, breakfast-£6, CC:VMA only for reservation deposit, payment in cash, nonsmoking, extremely quiet, book well in advance, walk 10 minutes from tube downhill on High Street, left at Lloyds Bank on Pilgrims Lane to 2 Kemplay Road, Hampstead, NW3 1SY, tel. 020/7435-8679, fax 020/7794-0254, e-mail: hvguesthouse@dial.pipex.com).

La Gaffe Hotel is a sweet Italian-run hotel and restaurant right on Heath Street. Its 14 rooms are small and worn but floral, comfy, and quiet (Sb-£60–75, Db-£85–120, four-poster room priciest, includes breakfast, CC:VM, TV, phones, nonsmoking, walk uphill from tube station three minutes to 107 Heath Street, Hampstead, NW3 6SS, tel. 020/7435-8965, fax 020/7794-7592, e-mail: la-gaffe@msn.com).

Sleeping near Gatwick and Heathrow Airports

Near Gatwick Airport: These two B&Bs are both in the peaceful countryside, have tennis courts and small swimming pools, and are within walking distance of a good pub. **Barn Cottage**, a converted 17th-century barn, has two wood-beamed rooms, antique furniture, and a large garden that makes you forget Gatwick is 10 minutes away (S-£35, D-£50, can drive you to airport or train station for £5–6, taxi costs £10, Leigh, Reigate, Surrey, RH2 8RF, tel. 01306/611-347, warmly run by Pat and Mike Comer). The idyllic **Crutchfield Farm B&B** offers three comfortable rooms, a great sitting room, and an elegant dining room in a 600-year-old renovated farmhouse surrounded by lots of greenery and a pond. The owner, Gillian Blok, includes a ride to the airport and its train station, whether you're leaving Britain or day-tripping to London (Sb-£45, Db-£75, Tb-£85, Qb-£95, two miles from Gatwick Airport—£5 by taxi, 30 min by train from London, at Hookwood, Surrey, RH6 OHT, tel. 01293/863-110, fax 01293/863-233, e-mail: TonyBlok@compuserve.com).

Near Heathrow Airport: It's so easy to get to Heathrow from central London, I see no reason to sleep there. But for budget beds near the airport, consider the **Heathrow Ibis** (Db-£60, breakfast extra, CC:VMA, shuttle bus to terminals, 112 Bath Road, tel. 020/8759-4888, fax 020/8564-7894).

EATING IN
LONDON

If you want to dine (as opposed to eat), check out the extensive listings in the weekly entertainment guides sold at London newsstands (or catch a train for Paris). The thought of a £30 meal in Britain generally ruins my appetite, so my London dining is limited mostly to easygoing, fun, but inexpensive alternatives. I've listed places by neighborhood—handy to your sightseeing or hotel.

Your £6 budget choices are pub grub, a café, fish and chips, pizza, ethnic, or picnic. Pub grub is the most atmospheric budget option. Many of London's 7,000 pubs serve fresh, tasty buffets under ancient timbers, with hearty lunches and dinners priced from £6 to £8. Ethnic restaurants from all over the world add spice to England's lackluster cuisine scene. Eating Indian or Chinese is "going local" in London. It's also going cheap (cheaper if you take out). Most large museums (and many churches) have inexpensive, cheery cafeterias. Sandwich shops are a hit with local workers eating on the run. Of course, picnicking is the fastest and cheapest way to go. Good grocery stores and sandwich shops, fine park benches, and polite pigeons abound in Britain's most expensive city.

Eating near Trafalgar Square

For a tasty meal on a monk's budget sitting on somebody's tomb in an ancient crypt, descend into the **St. Martin-in-the-Fields Café in the Crypt** (Mon–Sat 10:00–20:00, Sun noon–20:30, £5–7 cafeteria plates, cheaper sandwich bar, profits go to the church; underneath St. Martin-in-the-Fields on Trafalgar Square, tel. 020/7839-4342).

Chandos Bar's Opera Room floats amazingly apart from the tacky crush of tourism around Trafalgar Square. Look for the pub opposite the National Portrait Gallery (corner of William Street and St. Martin's Lane) and climb the stairs to the Opera

Room. They serve £6 pub lunches and dinners (last orders at 19:00, 18:00 on weekends, tel. 020/7836-1401). This is a fine Tragalfar rendezvous point—smoky, but wonderfully local.

Gordon's Wine Bar is ripe with atmosphere. A simple steep staircase leads into a 14th-century cellar filled with candle light, dusty old wine bottles, faded British memorabilia, and local nine-to-fivers (hot meals only for lunch, fine cheese-and-salad buffet all day until 21:00—one plate of each feeds two for £7). While it's crowded, you can normally corral two chairs and grab the corner of a table (Mon–Sat 11:00–23:00, closed Sun, two blocks from Trafalgar Square, bottom of Villiars Street at #47, near Embankment tube station, tel. 020/7930-1408).

Down Whitehall (toward Big Ben), a block from Trafalgar Square, you'll find the touristy but atmospheric **Clarence Pub** (decent grub) and several cheaper cafeterias and pizza joints.

For a classy lunch in the National Gallery, treat your palate to the pricier **Brasserie** (hot meals £8–10, open daily, 1st floor of Sainsbury Wing).

Simpson's in the Strand serves a stuffy, aristocratic, old-time carvery dinner—where the chef slices your favorite red meat from a fancy trolley at your table—in their elegant and smoky dining room (£20, Mon–Sat 12:15–14:30, 17:30–23:00, tel. 020/7836-9112).

Eating near Piccadilly

Hungry and broke in the theater district? Head for Panton Street (off Haymarket, two blocks southeast of Picadilly Circus) for a line of decent eateries. **Stockpot** is a mushy-peas-kind-of-place, famous and rightly popular for its edible, cheap meals (Mon–Sat 8:00–23:00, Sun 8:00–22:00, 40 Panton Street). The **West End Kitchen** (across the street at #5, same hours and menu) is a direct competitor and just as good. The original **Stockpot**, a few blocks away, has better atmosphere (daily noon–23:00, a block north of Shaftesbury near Cambridge Circus at 18 Old Compton Street).

The palatial **Criterion Brasserie** serves a £15 two-course "Anglo-French" menu under gilded tiles and chandeliers in a dreamy Byzantine church setting from 1880. It's right on Piccadilly Circus but a world away from the punk junk (noon–14:30, 18:00–18:30, pricier later, tel. 020/7930-0488).

Luigi Malone's, just off Leicester Square, serves fine £6 salads and pasta (12 Irving Street, tel. 020/7925-0457).

Near Covent Garden, the area around Neal's Yard is busy with fun eateries. One of the best is **Food for Thought** (serving until 20:15, closed Sun, very good £4 vegetarian meals, nonsmoking, 2 blocks north of tube: Covent Garden, 31 Neal Street, tel. 020/7836-0239). Neal's Yard itself is a food circus of trendy, healthy eateries.

Eating near St. Paul's

Ye Olde Cheshire Cheese Pub, rebuilt a year after the great fire of 1666, is a creaky half-timbered tangle of eateries (explained on a chart outside the door). Characteristic restaurants are upstairs while fast, cheap pub meals are served in the rustic cellar bar (Mon–Fri 11:30–23:00, 145 Fleet Street, tel. 020/7353-6170). There's also a good restaurant and café in St. Paul's crypt.

The "Food Is Fun" Dinner Crawl: From Covent Garden to Soho

London has a trendy, generation X scene that most Beefeater-seekers miss entirely. For a multicultural moveable feast and a chance to sample some of London's most popular eateries, consider sampling these. Start around 18:00 to avoid lines, get in on early specials, and find waiters willing to let you split a meal. Prices, while reasonable by London standards, add up. Servings are large enough to share. All restaurants are open nightly.

Suggested nibbler's dinner crawl for two: Arrive before 18:00 at Belgo and split the early-bird dinner special: a kilo of mussels, fries, and dark Belgian beer. At Yo! Sushi, have beer or sake and a few dishes. Slurp your last course at Wagamama. For dessert, people watch at Leicester Square where the serf's always up.

Belgo Centraal is a space-station world overrun with Trappist monks serving hearty Belgian specialties. The classy restaurant section requires reservations but just grabbing a bench in the boisterous beer hall is more fun. Belgians claim they eat as well as the French and as hearty as the Germans. Specialties include mussels, great fries, and a stunning array of dark, blond, and fruity Belgian beers. Belgo actually makes things Belgian trendy—a formidable feat (£12 meals; open daily till very late; "beat the clock" meal specials Mon–Fri 17:00–18:30 cost only the time— £5–£6.30—and you get mussels, fries, and beer; no meal-splitting after 18:30; £5 lunch special noon–17:00; one block north of Covent Garden tube station at intersection of Neal and Shelton Streets, 50 Earlham Street, tel. 020/7813-2233).

Soho Spice Indian is where modern Britain meets Indian tradition—fine Indian cuisine in a trendy jewel-tone ambience. The £15 "Tandoori selections" meal is the best "variety" dish and big enough for two (daily noon–24:00, nonsmoking section, 5 blocks due north of Piccadilly Circus at 124 Wardour Street, tel. 020/7434-0808).

Yo! Sushi is a futuristic Japanese food extravaganza experience. With thumping rock, Japanese cable TV, a 60-meter-long conveyor-belt sushi bar (the world's longest), automated sushi machines, and a robotic drink trolley, just sipping a sake on a bar

—— COVENT GARDEN/SOHO EATERIES ——

SOHO

100 YDS.

= TUBE STN.

Tottenham Court Road

GREAT MARL.

SOHO SQ.

CHINA TOWN

Piccadilly Circus

EROS

Leicester Square

COVENT GARDEN

THEATRE MUSEUM

Covent Garden

TRANSPORT MUSEUM

BRITISH VISITOR CENTRE

NAT'L GALLERY

TRAFALGAR SQUARE

Charing Cross

NEAL'S YARD

- ❶ CHANDO'S BAR
- ❷ GORDON'S WINE BAR
- ❸ CRITERION BRASSERIE
- ❹ NEAL'S YARD
- ❺ BELGO CENTRAAL
- ❻ SOHO SPICE INDIAN
- ❼ YO! SUSHI
- ❽ WAGAMAMA NOODLE BAR
- ❾ SOHO SOHO BISTRO
- ❿ ANDREW EDMUNDS REST.

stool here is a trip. For £1 you get unlimited tea (on request), water (from spigot at bar, with or without gas), or miso soup. Grab dishes as they rattle by (priced by color of dish; see chart) and snag drinks off the trash-talking robot (daily noon–24:00, 2 blocks south of Oxford Street, where Lexington Street becomes Poland Street, 52 Poland Street, tel. 020/7287-0443). For more serious drinking on tatami mats, go downstairs into "Yo Below."

Wagamama Noodle Bar is a noisy, pan-Asian slurpathon. As you enter, check out the kitchen and listen to the roar of the basement where benches rock with happy eaters. Everything's organic—stand against the wall to feel the energy of all this "positive eating" (daily noon–23:00, crowded after 20:00, just past the porno and prostitution core of Soho but entirely smoke-free, 10A Lexington Street, tel. 020/7292-0990).

Soho Soho French Bistro-Rotisserie is a chance to go

French in a Matisse-esque setting. The ground floor is a trendy wine bar. Upstairs is an oasis of peace serving £17, three-course French "pre-theater specials"—order from 18:00 to 19:30 (near Cambridge Circus, two blocks east of Charing Cross Road at 11 Frith Street, tel. 020/7494-3491).

Andrew Edmunds Restaurant is a tiny, candlelit place where you'll want to hide your camera and guidebook and act as local as possible. The modern European cooking is worth the splurge (three courses for £20, 12:30–15:00, 18:00–23:00, 46 Lexington Street in Soho, reservations are smart, tel. 020/7437-5708).

Eating near Recommended Victoria Station Accommodations

Here are places a couple of blocks southwest of Victoria Station where I've enjoyed eating:

Jenny Lo's Tea House is a simple, for-the-joy-of-good-food kind of place serving up £5 Chinese-style meals to locals in the know (Mon–Sat noon–15:00, 18:00–22:00, 14 Eccleston Street, tel. 020/7259-0399).

For pub grub with good local atmosphere, consider the **Plumbers Arms** (filling £5 hot meals and cheaper sandwiches Mon–Fri only, indoor/outdoor seating, 14 Lower Belgrave Street, tel. 020/7730-4067—ask about the murdered nanny).

Next door, the small but classy **La Campagnola** is Belgravia's favorite budget Italian restaurant (£12–15 meals, closed Sun, 10 Lower Belgrave Street, tel. 020/7730-2057).

Across the street, the **Maestro Bar** is the closest thing to an English tapas bar I've seen with salads, sandwiches, and 10 bar stools (very cheap, closed Sat).

The **Ebury Wine Bar** offers a French, candlelit ambience and pricey but delicious meals (£15, daily noon–15:00, 18:00–22:30, 139 Ebury Street, at intersection with Elizabeth Street, near bus station, tel. 020/7730-5447). Several cheap places are around the corner on Elizabeth Street (#23 for take-out or eat-in fish and chips).

The **Duke of Wellington** pub is good, if smoky, for dinner (£5 meals, Mon–Sat noon–15:00, 18:00–21:30, Sun noon–15:00, 63 Eaton Terrace). **Peter's Restaurant** is the cabbie's hangout for cheap food, smoke, and chatter (closed Sun, end of Ebury, at intersection with Pimlico).

The Country Pub in London lives up to its name and serves good £6 to £12 meals (noon–15:00, 19:00–21:30, corner of Warwick and Cambridge Streets, tel. 020/7834-5281).

The late-hours **Whistle Stop** grocery at the station has decent sandwiches and a fine salad bar. The **Marche** is an easy cafeteria a couple of blocks north of Victoria Station at Bressenden

Place. If you miss America, there's a mall-type food circus at **Victoria Place**, upstairs in Victoria Station. **Cafe Rouge** is probably the best food there.

Eating near Recommended Notting Hill Gate B&Bs and Bayswater Hotels

The exuberantly rustic and very English **Maggie Jones** serves my favorite £20 London dinner. You'll get solid English cuisine with huge plates of crunchy vegetables by candlelight (daily 18:30–23:00, CC:VMA, 6 Old Court Place, just east of Kensington Church Street, near High Street Kensington tube stop, reservations recommended, tel. 020/7937-6462). If you eat well once in London, eat here (and do it quick, before it burns down).

The **Churchill Arms** pub is a local hangout with good beer and old-English ambience in front and hearty £5 Thai plates in an enclosed patio in the back (you can bring the Thai food into the more atmospheric pub section, Mon–Sat noon–15:00, 18:00–21:30, 119 Kensington Church Street, tel. 020/7792-1246).

The friendly **Ladbroke Arms Pub** serves country-style meals that are one step above pub grub in quality and price (£8 meals, daily noon–14:30, 19:00–22:00, great indoor/outdoor ambience, 54 Ladbroke Road, behind Holland Park tube station, tel. 020/7727-6648).

For fish and chips, the almost-too-popular **Geale's** has long been considered one of London's best (£8 meals, Mon–Sat noon–15:00, 18:00–23:00, closed Sun, 2 Farmer Street, just off Notting Hill Gate behind Gate Cinema, tel. 020/7727-7528). Get there early for a place to sit (they take no reservations) and the best selection of fish.

The **Modhubon** Indian restaurant is not too spicy, "vedy vedy nice," and has cheap lunch specials (Sun–Fri noon–15:00, 18:00–24:00, Sat noon–24:00, 29 Pembridge Road, tel. 020/7727-3399). Next door is a cheap Chinese take-out (daily 17:30–24:00, 19 Pembridge Road) and the tiny **Organic Restaurant**, which keeps both yuppie vegetarians and carnivores happy (£10 meals, 100 percent organic, Mon–Fri 17:30–23:00, Sat–Sun 10:30–23:00, 35 Pembridge Road, tel. 020/7727-9620).

Café Diana is a healthy little sandwich shop decorated with photos of Princess Diana (daily 8:00–22:30, 5 Wellington Terrace, on Bayswater Road, opposite Kensington Palace Garden Gates, tel. 020/7792-9606).

Mr Wu's Chinese Restaurant serves a tasty 10-course buffet in a bright and cheery little place. Just grab a plate and help yourself (£4.50, daily noon–23:00, across from Bayswater tube station, 54 Queensway, tel. 020/7243-1017). Queensway is lined with lively and inexpensive eateries.

Eating near Recommended Accommodations in South Kensington

Popular eateries line Old Brompton Road and Thurloe Street (tube: South Kensington).

Luigi Malone's, an Italian-food chain restaurant, serves good £6 salads and pasta (73 Old Brompton Road, tel. 020/7584-4323). Its twin brother is just off Leicester Square at 12 Irving Street.

Daquise, an authentic-feeling Polish place, is ideal if you're in the mood for kielbasa and kraut. It's fast, cheap, faded, family run, and a part of the neighborhood (£8 meals, daily until 23:00, nonsmoking, 20 Thurloe Street, tel. 020/7589-6117).

For Indian food, the **Khyber Pass Tandoori Restaurant** is a nondescript but handy place serving good £8 dinners nightly (noon–15:00, 18:00–24:00, 21 Bute Street, tel. 020/7589-7311).

La Bouchee Bistro Café is a classy hole-in-the-wall touch of France serving three-course £11 meals before 19:30 and plats du jour for £8 all jour (daily noon–23:00, CC:VM, 56 Old Brompton Road, tel. 020/7589-1929).

La Brasserie fills a big plain room with a Parisian ambience and good French-style food at reasonable prices (two-course £14 "regional menu," £12 bottle of house wine, CC:VMA, nightly until midnight, 272 Brompton Road, tel. 020/7581-3089).

PJ's Bar and Grill is popular with the yuppie Chelsea crowd for good reason. Traditional "New York Brasserie"–style yet trendy, it serves modern Mediterranean cuisine (£15 meals, nightly until 23:30, 52 Fulham Road, tel. 020/7581-0025).

Eating near Recommended Accommodations in Hampstead

Even if you aren't staying in Hampstead, consider a visit. Hampstead has a small-town feel with easy tube access to London (15 to 30 minutes away; tube stop: Hampstead, on the Northern Line, in Zone 2). Enjoy the gaslit elegance and cobblestone lanes of this former resort. The Freemason's Arms pub (best for dinner) is a 10-minute walk downhill from the tube stop; the other pubs and restaurants are within five minutes of the tube station. Everything's near the park.

Freemason's Arms is the place for classy pub grub. If the lighting doesn't make your partner look delicious, the Czech lager will. Set on the edge of the heath with a spacious interior and sprawling beer garden for summer outdoor seating, the Freemason's Arms serves great English food (£9 meals, Mon–Sat

11:00–23:00, Sun noon–23:00, CC:VM, skittles downstairs on Thu and Sat night—private but peeking permitted; down High Street, left on Downshire Hill Road to #32, tel. 020/7433-6811).

Down High Street from the tube stop you'll find Hampstead swinging at **The House on Rosslyn Hill**. Serving international cuisine, this trendy, modern brasserie attracts a young crowd wearing black, gray, and white (meals start at £10, daily 11:00–24:00, CC:VM, 34 Rosslyn Hill, tel. 020/7435-8037).

French Hampstead cooks a block below the tube station. For a quick bite, **Maison Blanc** on Hampstead High Street not only has the best croissants in town, but also makes great savories like Roquefort and walnut *fougasse* (focaccia pockets) and *tarte Provençal* (tomato, zucchini, and Gruyère miniquiche)—all this, plus strong French coffee, for £3 to £4. **Cafe des Arts** serves French food in a rustic and candlelit English setting (daily noon–23:30, CC:VMA, 82 Hampstead High Street), but just around the corner, a little crepe cart in search of Paris is more popular (on Perrins Lane, a few steps off High Street).

For village atmosphere, shop at the **Hampstead Foodhall** on Fitzjohn Avenue (within a block of tube stop, cross High Street to the only level street). There's no better place for a dinner picnic with a view than Hampstead Heath (a 10-minute hike away, go up Heath Street).

For a laid-back crowd, visit the **Holly Bush** pub (daily noon–23:30, serves sandwiches noon–15:00 except Sun, hidden on a quiet lane uphill from tube, from Heath Street turn left on Holly Bush Steps). For a livelier spit-and-sawdust pub, toss your darts with the locals at **The Flask** (on Flask Walk, two blocks below the tube station).

LONDON WITH CHILDREN

The key to a successful family trip to London is making everyone happy, including the parents. My family-tested recommendations have this objective in mind.

Consider these tips:

• Take advantage of the local newsstand guides. *Time Out*'s family monthly is called *Kids Out*. *Time Out* and *What's On* also have handy kids' calenders listing activities and shows.

• Ask at London TIs about kids' events. Call Kidsline (Mon–Fri 9:00–18:00 or, when school is in session, Mon–Fri 16:00–18:00, tel. 020/7222-8070). The London TI's Children's Line, with recorded information is a pricey toll call (24 hrs/day, tel. 0839-123-404).

• London's big-budget chain hotels allow two kids for free into their already inexpensive rooms (see Sleeping chapter).

• Eat dinner early (around 18:00) to miss the romantic crowd. Skip the famous places. Look instead for relaxed cafés, pubs (kids are welcome), or even fast-food restaurants where kids can move around. Picnic lunches and dinners work well.

• Public WCs can be hard to find: Try department stores, museums, and restaurants, particularly fast-food restaurants.

• Follow this book's crowd-beating tips. Kids don't like standing in a line for a museum. At each sight, ask about a kids' guide or flier.

• Hamleys is the biggest toy store in Britain (Mon–Sat 10:00–20:00, Sun noon–18:00, 188 Regent Street, tube: Oxford Circus, tel. 020/7494-2000.

TOP KIDS' SIGHTS

In East London
Tower of London—The crown jewels are awesome, and the Beefeater tour plays off kids in a memorable and fun way (£10.50,

cheaper for kids, Mon–Sat 9:00–18:00, Sun 10:00–18:00, last entry at 17:00, tube: Tower Hill, tel. 020/7709-0765). ✪ For Tower of London Tour, see page 122.

Museum of London—A very kid-friendly presentation takes you from the Romans to the blitz. Parents will learn something, too (£5, free after 16:30, Mon–Sat 10:00–18:00, Sun noon–18:00, tube: Barbican or St. Paul's, tel. 020/7600-3699).

In Central London

Covent Garden—A great neighborhood for people watching and candy licking. Kids like the Cabaret Mechanical Theater and the London Transport Museum. For details, see page 32.

Trafalgar Square—The grand square is great fun for kids: feed the pigeons and climb the lions. After that, munch lunch in a crypt and tour the National Gallery (below).

St. Martin-in-the-Fields—This church on Trafalgar Square has a brass rubbing center that's fun for kids who'd like a souvenir to show for their efforts. The affordable Café in the Crypt has just the right spooky tables-on-tombstones ambience (Mon–Sat 10:00–20:00, Sun noon–20:30).

National Gallery—Start your visit in the Micro Gallery computer room. Your child can list his or her interests (cats, naval battles, and so on) and print out a tailor-made tour map (free, daily 10:00–18:00, Wed until 21:00, on Trafalgar Square, tube: Charing Cross or Leicester Square, tel. 020/7747-2885). Ask about their "Kids Trail." ✪ See National Gallery Tour on page 71.

Millennium Ferris Wheel—The London Eye Observation Wheel is a delight for the entire family (on the South Bank near Westminster Bridge). For details, see page 39 in the Sights chapter.

Changing of the Guards—Kids enjoy the bands and pageantry of the Buckingham Palace Changing of the Guard, but little ones get a better view at the prechanging inspection: 11:00 at Wellington Barracks (see page 34 in Sights chapter). Horse lovers enjoy the Horse Guards' colorful dismounting ceremony daily at 16:00 (on Whitehall, between Trafalgar Square and #10 Downing Street, tube: Westminster); for details, see page 29.

Piccadilly Circus—This titillating district has lots of "Planet Hollywood"–type amusements, such as Segaworld, Rock Circus, and Guinness Hall of World Records. Be careful of fast-fingered riffraff. For details on the district, see page 31. Hamleys Toy Store is just two blocks up Regent Street.

In West London

Natural History Museum—This wonderful world of dinosaurs, volcanoes, meteors, and creepy-crawlies offers creative interactive displays (£6.50, under 16 free, free after 16:30 and after 17:00 on weekends, Mon–Sat 10:00–18:00, Sun 11:00–18:00, long tunnel leads from South Kensington tube station to the museum, tel. 020/7938-9123, www.nhm.ac.uk). For details, see page 35.

In North London

Madame Tussaud's Waxworks—Popular with kids (in spite of the lines) for its gory stuff, pop and movie stars, everyone's favorite royals, etc. (£11, kids £7, under 5 free, daily 9:00–18:00, closes at 17:00 in winter, Marylebone Road, tube: Baker Street, tel. 020/7935-6861; combined ticket with Planetarium is £13 for adults, £8.50 for kids). For details, see page 33.

London Zoo—This venerable zoo, with more than 8,000 animals, is one of the best in the world (£8.50, cheaper for kids, family-£26, daily 10:00–17:30, Nov–Apr 10:00–16:00, in Regent's Park, tube: Camden Town, then bus 274, tel. 020/7722-3333). Call for feeding and event times.

FUN TRANSPORTATION

Thames Cruise—Young sailors delight in boats. Westminster Pier (near Big Ben) offers the most action, with boats to the Tower of London, Greenwich, and Kew Gardens. See page 25.

Hop-on Hop-off London Bus Tours—These two-hour double-decker bus tours, which drive by all the biggies, are fun for kids and stress free for parents. You can stay on the bus the entire time, or "hop on and hop off" at any of the 20-plus stops and catch a later bus (6/hrly in summer, 3/hrly in winter). To find out how to get a special price with this book, see page 25. The Original London Sightseeing Tour's language bus (marked with lots of flags or a green triangle) has a kids' track on the earphones, but then you miss the live guide.

DAY TRIP

Legoland Windsor—If you have a Lego maniac in the family, consider a quick side trip to Legoland Windsor (£17, £14 for kids, under three free, mid-Mar–Oct daily 10:00–18:00, until 20:00 in summer, train from Paddington station to Windsor Central, tel. 0990-040-404). Combine with a look at Windsor Castle.

WHAT TO AVOID

The **London Dungeon**'s popularity with teenagers makes it one of London's most visited sights. I enjoy gore and torture as much as the next boy, but I do not like this sight and would not waste the time or money on it with my child.

SHOPPING
IN LONDON

Consider five ways to shop in London:
1) If all you need are souvenirs, a surgical strike at any souvenir shop will do.
2) Large department stores offer relatively painless one-stop shopping. Consider the down-to-earth Marks & Spencer (Mon–Fri 9:00–20:00, Sat 9:00–21:00, Sun noon–18:00, 173 Oxford Street, tube: Oxford Circus; another at 458 Oxford Street, tube: Bond Street or Marble Arch).
3) Connect small shops with a pleasant walk (see Oxford Circus to Piccadilly Walk, below).
4) For flea market fun, try one of the many street markets.
5) Gawkers or serious bidders can attend auctions.

Most stores are open Monday through Saturday from roughly 10:00 to 18:00, with a late night (until 19:00 or 20:00) on Wednesday or Thursday, depending on the neighborhood. On Sunday, when many stores are closed, shoppers hit the street markets.

Fancy Department Stores in East London

Harrods—Filled with wonderful displays, Harrods is London's most famous and touristy department store. Big yet classy, Harrods has everything from elephants to toothbrushes. The food halls are sights to savor (Mon–Sat 10:00–18:00, Wed–Fri until 19:00, closed Sun, on Brompton Road, tube: Knightsbridge, tel. 020/7730-1234). Many readers report that Harrods is now overpriced (its £1 toilets are the most expensive in Europe), snooty, and teeming with American and Japanese tourists. Still, it's the palace of department stores. The nearby Beauchamp Place is lined with classy and fascinating shops.

Harvey Nichols—Princess Diana's favorite, this is the department store *du jour* (Mon–Sat 10:00–19:00, Wed–Fri until 20:00, Sun noon–18:00, near Harrods, 109 Knightsbridge, tube:

Knightsbridge). Its fifth floor is a veritable food fest with a fancy restaurant and a Yo! Sushi bar. Consider a take-away tray of sushi to eat on a bench in the Hyde Park rose garden two blocks away.

Oxford Circus to Piccadilly Walk

For this walk from Oxford Circus to Piccadilly Street, allow three-quarters of a mile (and only you know how much money and time). If you'd like to stop for high tea (15:00–17:15), take this walk after lunch. Skip this walk on Sunday, when most stores are closed.

Starting from the Oxford Circus tube stop, Regent Street leads past a diverse array of places to shop, all on the left-hand (east) side of the street. You'll find: **Laura Ashley**; **Liberty**, a big, stately, locals'-favorite department store (Mon–Sat 10:00–18:30, closed Sun, 214 Regent Street); the once-upon-a-decade pop **Carnaby Street** a block away; **Hamleys,** the biggest toy store in Britain (Mon–Sat 10:00–20:00, Sun noon–18:00, 118 Regent Street, tel. 020/7494-2000); **Warner Brothers Studio Store** (at #178); **Beatles Shop** (a block behind Warner Brothers, 8 Kingly Street, tel. 020/7434-0464); **Waterford Wedgewood**; **British Air Travel Shops**, with accessories, guidebooks, travel agents, travelers' clinic, shots, WC, and theater ticket agency (Mon–Fri 9:30–18:00, Sat 10:00–16:00); **Disney Store** (at #144); **The Scotch House** (knits, sweaters, woolens); **Starbucks**; and **Piccadilly Circus**.

Sotheby's main gallery for bidders to review items for upcoming auctions is two blocks off Regent Street (down Maddox Street, left on New Bond Street—see description below).

From Piccadilly Circus, turn right and wander down Piccadilly Street. You'll pass Christopher Wren's **St. James Church** (tiny flea market and leafy café) and **Fortnum & Mason**, an extremely classy department store. Consider a traditional tea in its **St. James Restaurant**, on the fourth floor (£13.50, Mon–Sat 15:00–17:15, closed Sun, 181 Piccadilly, tel. 020/7734-8040 ext. 241). As you relax to piano music in plush seats under the elegant tearoom's chandeliers, you'll get the standard three-tiered silver tea tray: finger sandwiches on the bottom, fresh scones with jam and clotted cream on the first floor, and decadent pastries and "tartlets" on the top floor, with unlimited tea. Consider it dinner.

Just past Fortnum & Mason is the **French Travel Center**, across the street is the delightful **Burlington Arcade**, and a block farther down is the original **Ritz Hotel**, where the tea is much fancier.

Street Markets

Antique buffs, people watchers, and folks who brake for garage sales love London's street markets. There's some good early-morning market activity somewhere any day of the week. The best are Portobello Road and Camden Market. The tourist office has a complete, up-to-date list. If you like to haggle, there are no holds barred in London's street markets. Warning: Markets attract two kinds of people—tourists and pickpockets.

Portobello Road Market—This flea market with 2,000 stalls (open daily but hopping on Saturday) has three sections: antiques at the top, produce in the middle, and clothing and books at the bottom. Antiques are featured on Saturday (until 16:00); clothing takes the stage Friday through Sunday (9:00–16:00). Otherwise, hours are roughly Monday through Saturday 8:00 to 18:00, Thursday 9:00 to 13:00, and Sunday 9:00 to 16:00. (Tube: Notting Hill Gate, near recommended B&Bs.)

Camden Lock Market—This huge, trendy arts-and-crafts festival—London's fourth-most-popular tourist attraction—is held Saturday and Sunday from 10:00 to 18:00. It's also open on Thursday and Friday, but there's less action (tube: Camden Town, tel. 020/8284-2084).

Brick Lane Market—You'll see it all, from frozen food and scrap metal to CDs and furniture (Sun 6:00–13:00, tube: Liverpool Street).

Brixton Market—The food, clothing, hair braiding, and records throb with an Afro-Caribbean beat (Mon–Sat 8:30–17:30, closes at 13:00 on Wed, tube: Brixton).

Petticoat Lane Market—Expect budget clothing, leather, shoes, and crowds (Sun 9:00–14:00, tube: Liverpool Street).

Spitalfields Market—This is best on Sunday and Friday when a lively organic food market (with eateries) joins the crafts and antique market (Mon–Fri 11:00–15:00, Sun 9:30–17:30, closed Sat, tube: Liverpool Street).

Greenwich Market—You'll find homemade crafts, bric-a-brac, antiques, and clothing (Sat–Sun 9:00–17:00, some action on Fri, also a produce market on Sat, more crafts on Sun). See the Day Trips chapter for information on Greenwich's sights and transportation connections.

Famous Auctions

London's famous auctioneers welcome the curious public for viewing and bidding. For schedules, call **Sotheby's** (Mon–Fri 9:00–16:30, 34 New Bond Street, tube: Oxford Circus, tel. 020/ 7293-5000) or **Christie's** (Mon–Fri 9:00–16:30, Tue 9:00–20:00, 8 King Street, tube: Green Park, tel. 020/7839-9060).

ENTERTAINMENT

18

london

London bubbles with top-notch entertainment seven days a week. Everything's listed in the weekly entertainment magazines, available at newsstands. Choose from classical, jazz, rock, and far-out music, Gilbert and Sullivan, dance, comedy, Baha'i meetings, poetry readings, spectator sports, film, and theater.

Music

For easy, cheap, or free concerts in historic churches, check the TI's listings for lunch concerts (especially Wren's St. Bride's Church, tel. 020/7353-1301; St. James at Piccadilly; and St. Martin-in-the-Fields, Mon–Tue and Fri at 13:00, tel. 020/7930-1862). St. Martin-in-the-Fields also hosts fine evening concerts by candlelight (£6–16, Thu–Sat at 19:30, tel. 020/7839-8362).

Even music-loving agnostics could enjoy an evensong. At St. Paul's, evensong is held at 17:00 on weekdays. At Westminster Abbey, it's sung weekdays at 17:00 (but not on Wed), Saturday and Sunday at 15:00. An organ recital is held Sunday at 17:45.

For a fun classical event (Jun–Sept only), attend a "Prom Concert." This is an annual music festival with almost nightly concerts in the Royal Albert Hall at give-a-peasant-some-culture prices (£3 standing-room spots sold at the door, tel. 020/7589-8212).

Walks

Guided walks are offered several times a day. Original London Walks is the most established (tel. 020/7624-3978, www.walks.com). Daytime walks vary: ancient London, museums, Legal London, Dickens, Beatles, Jewish Quarter, Christopher Wren, etc. In the evening, expect a more limited choice: ghosts, Jack the Ripper, pubs, or a literary theme. Get the latest from a TI, fliers, or *Time Out*. Show up at the listed time and place, pay £5, and enjoy the two-hour tour.

Cruises

During the summer, boats sail as late as 21:00 between Westminster Pier (near Big Ben) and the Tower of London. (For details, see end of Orientation chapter.) There are also dinner cruises.

Theater

London's theater rivals Broadway's in quality and beats it in price. Choose from the Royal Shakespeare Company, top musicals, comedy, thrillers, sex farces, and more. Performances are nightly except Sunday, usually with one matinee a week. Matinees, held on Wednesday, Thursday, or Saturday, are cheaper and rarely sell out. Tickets range from about £8 to £35.

Most theaters, marked on tourist maps, are in the Piccadilly/ Trafalgar area. Box offices, hotels, and TIs offer a handy "Theater Guide." To book a seat, simply call the theater box office directly, ask about seats and dates available, and buy one with your credit card. You can call from the United States as easily as from England (photocopy your hometown library's London newspaper theater section or check out www.officiallondontheatre.co.uk). Pick up your ticket 15 minutes before the show.

Ticket agencies are scalpers with an address. Booking through an agency (at most TIs or scattered throughout London) is quick and easy, but prices are inflated by a standard 25 percent fee. If buying from an agency, look at the ticket carefully (your price should be no more than 30 percent over the printed face value; the 17.5 percent VAT tax is already included in the face value) and understand where you're sitting according to the floor plan (if your view is restricted it will state this on ticket). Agencies are worthwhile only if a show you've got to see is sold out at the box office. They scarf up hot tickets, planning to make a killing after the show is sold out. U.S. booking agencies get their tickets from another agency, adding even more to your expense by involving yet another middleman. Many tickets sold on the streets are forgeries. With cheap international phone calls and credit cards, there's no reason not to book direct.

Theater lingo: stalls (ground floor), dress circle (first balony), upper circle (second balcony), balcony (sky-high third balcony).

Cheap theater tricks: Most theaters offer cheap returned tickets, standing room, matinee, and senior or student stand-by deals. These "concessions" are indicated with a "conc" or "s" in the listings. Picking up a late return can get you a great seat at a cheap-seat price. If a show is "sold out," there's usually a way to get a seat. Call the theater box office and ask how. I buy the second-cheapest tickets directly from the theater box office. The famous "half-price booth" in Leicester (pronounced "Lester") Square sells discounted tickets for good seats to shows on the push list the day of the show only

(Mon–Sat noon–18:30). The real half-price booth is a freestanding kiosk at the edge of the garden in Leicester Square. Several dishonest outfits advertise "official half-price tickets" at agencies closer to the tube station. Avoid these. Many theaters are so small that there's hardly a bad seat. After the lights go down, "scooting up" is less than a capital offense. Shakespeare did it.

Royal Shakespeare Company—If you'll ever enjoy Shakespeare, it'll be in Britain. The RSC splits its season between the Royal Shakespeare Theatre in Stratford (Jun–Sept, tel. 01789/403-403) and the Barbican Centre in London (Oct–May, daily 9:00–20:00, credit-card booking tel. 020/7638-8891, recorded information tel. 020/7628-9760). To get a schedule, either request it by phone; write to the Royal Shakespeare Theatre, Stratford-upon-Avon, CV37 6BB Warwickshire; or visit www.rsc.org.uk. Tickets range in price from £10 to £30 (half price for the young and old). Book direct by telephone and credit card and pick up your ticket at the door (Barbican Centre, Silk Street, tube: Barbican).

Shakespeare at the Globe Theater—To see Shakespeare in a replica of the theater for which he wrote his plays, attend a play at the Globe. This thatch-roofed, open-air round theater does the plays as Shakespeare intended (with no amplification). The play's the thing from May through September (usually Tue–Sat 14:00 and 19:30, Sun at either 13:00 and 18:30 or at 16:00 only, no plays on Mon). You'll pay £5 to stand and £10 to £25 to sit (usually on a backless bench; only a few rows and the pricier Gentlemen's Rooms have seats with backs). The £5 "groundling" tickets—while the only ones open to rain—are most fun. You're a crude peasant. You can walk around, munch a picnic dinner, lean your elbows on the stage, and even interact with the actors. I've never enjoyed Shakespeare as much as here, performed as it was meant to be in the "wooden O." The theater is on the South Bank directly across the Thames over Southwark Bridge from St. Paul's (tube: Mansion House, or consider walking across the new Millennium Bridge from St. Paul's, tel. 020/7902-1500, box office 020/7401-9919 to book a ticket with your credit card). Plays are long. Many groundlings leave before the end. If you like, hang out an hour before the finish and beg or buy a ticket from someone leaving early (groundlings are allowed to come and go). The Globe is far from public transport, but the courtesy phone in the lobby gets a minicab in minutes.

Fringe Theatre—London's rougher evening-entertainment scene is thriving, filling pages in *Time Out*. Choose from a wide range of fringe theater and comedy acts (generally £5).

TRANSPORTATION
CONNECTIONS
⑲

Flying into London's Heathrow Airport

Heathrow Airport is the world's busiest. Think about it: 60 million passengers a year on 425,000 flights from 200 destinations riding 90 airlines... some kind of global Maypole dance. While many complain about it, I like it. It's user friendly. Read signs, ask questions. For Heathrow's airport, flight, and transfers information, call 020/8759-4321. The airport has four terminals: T-1 (mostly domestic flights), T-2 (mostly European flights), T-3 (mostly flights from the United States), and T-4 (British Air transatlantic flights).

Each terminal has: an airport information desk, car rental agencies, exchange bureaus and ATMs, a pharmacy, a VAT refund desk (VAT info tel. 020/8745-4216, you must present the VAT claim form from the retailer here to get your 17.5 percent tax rebate on items purchased in Britain), and a £3.50-per-day baggage-check desk (open 5:30–23:00). There's a post office in T-2 and T-4. The best-value eating at T-3 and T-4 is the cheap and cheery Granary self-service cafeteria. The American Express desk (with rates no better than the exchange bureaus) is in the tube station at Terminal 4.

Heathrow's TI gives you all the help that London's Victoria Station does, with none of the crowds (daily 8:30–18:00, a five-minute walk from Terminal 3 in the tube station, follow signs to "underground"). If you're riding the Airbus into London, have your partner stay with the bags at the terminal. At the TI, get a free map and brochures, and if you're taking the tube (subway) into London, buy a Travel Card day pass to cover the ride (see below).

Transportation to London from Heathrow Airport

By Tube (Subway): For £3.40, the tube takes you 14 miles to Victoria Station in 45 minutes (6/hrly, one change). Even better, buy a £4.50 Travel Card that covers your trip into London and all your tube travel for the day (starting at 9:30).

By Airbus: The A2 airbus serves the Notting Hill Gate and Kensington Gardens/Queensway neighborhoods—see recommended hotels, above (departs from each terminal, £6, 4/hrly, 5:15–22:00, buy ticket from the driver, tel. 020/8400-6655 or 020/7222-1234). The tube works fine, but with baggage I prefer the airbus—there are no connections underground and a lovely view from the top of the double-decker bus. Ask the driver to remind you when to get off. If you're going to the airport, exact pick-up times are clearly posted at each bus stop.

By Taxi: Taxis from the airport cost about £35. Especially for four people traveling together this can be a deal. Hotels can often line up a cab back to the airport for £30. For the cheapest taxi to the airport don't order one from your hotel. Simply flag down a few and ask them for their best "off-meter" rate (I managed a ride for £25).

By Heathrow Express Train: This new train service zips air travelers between Heathrow Airport and London's Paddington Station; at Paddington you're in the thick of the tube system, with easy access to any of my recommended neighborhoods—Notting Hill Gate is just two tube stops away (£10 but ask about discount promos at Heathrow ticket desk, children under 16 ride free if you buy tickets before boarding, 4/hrly, 5:10–23:00, 15 minutes to downtown from Terminals 1, 2, 3; 20 minutes from Terminal 4; works as a free transfer between terminals, tel. 0845/600-1515). For one person going to the airport, the tube or a taxi to Paddington and the Express to Heathrow is as fast and half the cost of a cab to the airport.

Buses from Heathrow to Destinations beyond London

The National Express Central Bus Station offers handy direct bus connections to **Cambridge** (hrly, 3.5 hrs, £17), **Gatwick Airport** (2/hrly, 1 hr, £12), and **Bath** (10/day, at 8:40, 10:10, 11:40, 13:10, 14:40, 16:40, 18:10, 19:10, 20:10, 21:40, 2.5 hrs, £19.50, direct, tel. 0990-808-080). Or try the slick 2.5-hour Heathrow–Bath bus/train connection via Reading. You can either use your BritRail pass or buy the £26 ticket at the desk in the terminal (credit cards accepted), then catch the twice-hourly RailAir Link shuttle bus to Reading (RED-ding) to hop on the hourly express train to Bath. Most Heathrow buses depart from the single bus stop that serves Terminals 1, 2, and 3, though some depart from Terminal 4 (bus information tel. 0990-747-777).

Flying into London's Gatwick Airport
More and more flights, especially charters, land at Gatwick Airport, halfway between London and the southern coast. Trains—clearly the best way into London from here—shuttle conveniently between Gatwick and London's Victoria Station (4/hrly, 30 min, £9).

Trains and Buses
London, Britain's major transportation hub, has a different train station for each region. Waterloo handles the Eurostar to Paris. King's Cross covers northeast England and Scotland (tel. 08457/225-225). Paddington covers west and southwest England (Bath) and South Wales (tel. 08457/000-125). For the others, call 0345-484-950. Also see the BritRail map in this chapter.

National Express's excellent bus service is considerably cheaper than trains. (For a busy signal, call 0990-808-080; or visit www.nationalexpress.co.uk or the bus station a block southwest of Victoria Station.)

To Bath: Trains leave London's Paddington Station every hour (at a quarter after) for the £32.50, 75-minute ride to Bath. As an alternative, consider taking a guided bus tour from London to Stonehenge and Bath, and abandoning the tour in Bath. Both Evan Evans (tel. 020/7950-1777) and Travelline (tel. 020/8668-7261) offer Stonehenge/Bath day trips from London. Evan Evans' tours come fully guided with admissions for £46 or with just the bus transportation (free time at Stonehenge and then in Bath) for £25.

To points north: Trains run hourly from London's King's Cross Station and stop in York (2 hrs), Durham (3 hrs), and Edinburgh (5 hrs).

To Dublin, Ireland: The boat/rail journey takes 10 hours, all day or all night (£40–60). Consider a cheap 70-minute Ryanair or British Midland flight instead (see below).

Discounted Flights from London
British Midland, the local discount airline, can often get you to your destination cheaper than the train. You can fly domestically (as little as £60 for a round-trip London–Edinburgh ticket if you stay over Saturday), to Ireland (as little as £70 return to Dublin if you stay over Saturday), and to Paris, Amsterdam, or Frankfurt (round-trip over a Saturday for around £110). For the latest, call 0870-607-0555 or, in the United States, 800/788-0555.

Virgin Air is a Belgian company with incredible rates (no advance-purchase deals, one way is half the round-trip, book by phone with credit card and pick up at the airport an hour before your flight, tel. 020/7744-0004, www.virgin-express.com). Virgin Air flies from London's Stansted and Gatwick to Shannon, Ireland

BRITRAIL ROUTES

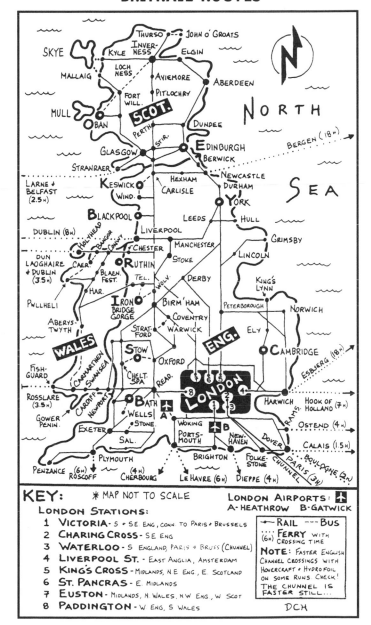

KEY: ✳ MAP NOT TO SCALE

LONDON AIRPORTS: ✈
A- HEATHROW   B- GATWICK

LONDON STATIONS:

1 **VICTORIA** - S & SE ENG, CONN. TO PARIS & BRUSSELS
2 **CHARING CROSS** - SE ENG
3 **WATERLOO** - S ENGLAND, PARIS & BRUSS (CHUNNEL)
4 **LIVERPOOL ST.** - EAST ANGLIA, AMSTERDAM
5 **KING'S CROSS** - MIDLANDS, N E ENG, E. SCOTLAND
6 **ST. PANCRAS** - E. MIDLANDS
7 **EUSTON** - MIDLANDS, N. WALES, N W ENG, W SCOT
8 **PADDINGTON** - W. ENG, S WALES

— RAIL --- BUS
⋯⋯ FERRY WITH
(6H) CROSSING TIME
NOTE: FASTER ENGLISH
CHANNEL CROSSINGS WITH
HOVERCRAFT & HYDROFOIL
ON SOME RUNS CHECK!
THE CHUNNEL IS
FASTER STILL...

DCH

(£47), and Brussels (£30 from Stansted, £40 from Gatwick). From its hub in Brussels you can connect cheaply to Barcelona, Madrid, Nice, Copenhagen, Rome, or Milan (e.g., London–Milan, £50).

Ryanair is a creative Irish airline with more complicated but potentially even cheaper fares. They fly mostly from London's Stansted airport to Dublin, Glasgow, Frankfurt, Lyon, Stockholm, Oslo, Venice, and Turin. Sample fares: London–Dublin—£80 round-trip or £30 one way if purchased a week in advance, Frankfurt—£70 round-trip or £30 with three-day advance purchase. They tend to book up a couple of weeks in advance (tel. 0541/569-569, www.ryanair.ie).

Crossing the English Channel

By Eurostar Train: The fastest and most convenient way to get from Big Ben to the Eiffel Tower is by rail. In London, advertisements claim "more businessmen travel from London to Paris on the Eurostar than on all airlines combined." Eurostar, a speedy passenger train, zips you (and up to 800 others in 18 sleek cars) from downtown London to downtown Paris (12/day, 3 hrs) or Brussels (6/day, 3 hrs) faster and easier than flying. The train goes 80 miles per hour in England and 190 miles per hour on the Continent. (When the English segment gets up to speed the journey time will shrink to two hours.) The actual tunnel crossing is a 20-minute black, silent, 100-mile-per-hour nonevent. Your ears won't even pop. You can change at Lille to catch a TGV directly to Paris' Charles de Gaulle airport or Disneyland Paris. Yes!

Channel fares (essentially the same to Paris or Brussels) are reasonable but complicated. For the latest, call 800/EUROSTAR in the United States (www.eurostar.com). These are prices for 2000: The "Leisure Ticket" is cheap (one way: $119 second class, $199 first class, 50 percent refundable up to three days before departure). The "Full Fare" first class costs $239 one way including a meal (a dinner departure nets you more grub than breakfast); second class (or "standard") costs $159 (both are fully refundable even after departure).

Eurostar discounts for either first- or second-class travel are available to railpass holders ($84 off "Full Fare"), youths under 26 ($80 off second-class "Full Fare"), and children under 12 (about half the fare of your ticket). Cheaper seats can sell out. Book from home if you're ready to commit to a date and time; call your travel agent or call direct (800/EUROSTAR). Prices do not include Fed Ex delivery. Note: Britain's time zone is one hour earlier than the Continent's. Times listed on tickets are local times.

Buying your Eurostar ticket in London is also easy. Here are some sample London–Paris standard—that's second-class—fares

(London–Brussels fares are up to £20 less). Avoid the basic standard fare: £145 one way, £249 round-trip. Here are your budget options: Those with a railpass pay £50 one way, any day. Without a railpass, a same-day round-trip on a Saturday or Sunday costs £99. Those staying at least three nights pay £130 round-trip. Excursion fares (round-trip over a Saturday) are cheaper: £100. "Saturday Night Away" tickets (round-trip, purchased a week in advance and staying over a Saturday) are the best deal: £90 standard, £160 first class. One-way tickets for departures after 14:00 Friday or anytime Saturday or Sunday cost £90. Youth tickets (for those under 26) are £80 to Paris, £65 to Brussels (round-trip any time and changeable). First-class and business-class fares are substantially higher. The only seven-day-advance deal is the Saturday Night Away. Remember, round-trip tickets over a Saturday are much cheaper than the basic one-way fare . . . you know the trick.

In Europe, get your Eurostar ticket at any major train station (in any country) or at any travel agency that handles train tickets (expect a booking fee). In Britain you can book and pay for tickets over the phone with a credit card by calling 0990-186-186. Pick up your tickets at London's Waterloo station an hour before the Eurostar departure.

By Bus and Boat or Train and Boat: The old-fashioned way of crossing the Channel is cheaper than Eurostar; it's also twice as romantic, complicated, and time-consuming. You'll get better prices arranging your trip in London than you would in the United States. Taking the bus is cheapest, and round-trips are a bargain. By bus to Paris or Amsterdam from Victoria Coach Station: £40 one way, £50 round-trip, 10 hrs, day or overnight, on Eurolines (tel. 0990-143-219) or Hoverspeed (tel. 0990-240-241). By train and ship: £42 one way overnight, £59 by day, 7 hrs.

By Plane: Typical fares are £110 regular, less for student standby. Call in London for the latest fares. Consider British Midland and other airlines (see "Discounted Flights," above) for their cheap round-trip fares.

APPENDIX

What's So Great about Britain?

Regardless of the revolution we had 200 years ago, many American travelers feel that they "go home" to Britain. This most popular tourist destination has a strange influence and power over us.

As long as Britain has been important, London has been its capital. With London at the helm, Britain was created by force and held together by force. The city and the country are a product of the 19th century—the Victorian Age—when the British Empire was at its peak.

Generally, the nice and bad stories are not true and the boring ones are. To best understand the many fascinating guides you'll encounter in your London travels, get a handle on the sweeping story of this land.

Britain is small—about the size of Uganda (or Idaho)— 600 miles long and 300 miles at its widest. Its highest mountain is 4,400 feet, a foothill by our standards. The population is a quarter of the United States'. Politically and economically, Great Britain is closing out the 20th century only a weak shadow of the days when it boasted, "The sun never sets on the British Empire."

At one time Britain owned one-fifth of the world and accounted for more than half of the planet's industrial output. Today the Empire is down to token and troublesome scraps such as the Falklands and Northern Ireland. Great Britain's industrial production is now about 5 percent of the world's total, and Italy has a higher per-capita income. Still, Britain is a world leader. Her heritage, her culture, and her people cannot be measured in traditional units of power.

The United Kingdom is a union of four countries: England, Wales, Scotland, and Northern Ireland. Cynics call it an English Empire ruled by London, and there is some tension between the dominant Anglo-Saxon English (46 million) and their Celtic brothers and sisters (10 million). In the Dark Ages, the Angles moved into this region from Europe, pushing the Celtic inhabitants to the undesirable fringe of the islands. The Angles settled in Angle-land (England), while the Celts made do in Wales, Scotland, and Ireland.

Just like the United States Congress is dominated by the Democrat and Republican Parties, two parties dominate the British Parliament: Labor and Conservative. (Ronald Reagan would fit the Conservative Party and Bill Clinton the Labor Party like political gloves.) Today Britain's Labor Party, currently in charge, is shoring up a social-service system undercut by years of Conservative rule (Thatcher, Major). While in charge, the Conservatives, who consider themselves proponents of Victorian values (community, family, hard work, thrift, and trickle-down economics), took a Reagan-esque approach to Britain's serious problems.

This led to a huge Labor victory and the election of Tony Blair as prime minister. He's the most popular PM in memory and his party rules parliament with a vast majority. Blair's Labor Party is "New Labor." Akin to Clinton's "New" Democrats, it's fiscally conservative but with a keen sense for the needs of the people. The Conservative Party's fears of old-fashioned big-spending liberalism have proven unfounded. The economy is booming with very low inflation, unemployment, and interest rates. Social programs such as health, education, and the minimum wage are being bolstered, but in ways more measured than Conservatives predicted. Britain's liberal parliament is also more open to integration with Europe. It looks like Britain is in for a long period of Labor rule.

London Timeline

A.D. 43 Romans invade Britain and establish a small port on the Thames River near today's London Bridge. They call it Londinium.

200 City walls are built. Their shadow survives, arcing out from the Thames in today's street plan.

450 As Rome falls, the Roman Emperor sends a letter to Britain saying, "You're on your own." Angles and Saxons overrun England and set up their kingdoms.

1050 Saxons unite England and their King Edward builds his palace and a church in what becomes the city of Westminster. The church becomes Westminster Abbey and the palace becomes the houses of Parliament.

1066 Normans, led by William the Conqueror, invade from France. William becomes the king of England (and builds the Tower of London).

1500   Henry VIII is king and London is a city of over 50,000.

1600   This is the age of Queen Elizabeth and Shakespeare.

1650   London is now a world capital with 500,000 people. England is torn by civil war. Cromwell and Parliament oppose the divine power of the king and nobility. King Charles I is beheaded.

1660   The monarchy is restored as Charles II is crowned.

1665   Thousands die as the Great Plague ravages London.

1666   Thousands more lose homes as 80 percent of medieval London burns down.

1670s   London is rebuilt. Christopher Wren ornaments the city with 50 churches, including St. Paul's.

1800s   The sun never sets on the British Empire as London becomes the world's biggest city with over a million people.

1847   British Museum opens.

1914–1918   London bombed during World War I.

1939–40   London survives blitz bombing.

1944–45   London survives blitz bombing.

1953   Queen Elizabeth crowned.

1981   Prince Charles and Lady Diana are married in St. Paul's Cathedral.

1990s   Royal scandals, death of Princess Diana, Channel Tunnel opens.

London's History Is Britain's History

When Julius Caesar landed on the misty and mysterious isle of Britain in 55 B.C., England entered the history books. The primitive Celtic tribes he conquered were themselves invaders who had earlier conquered the even more mysterious people who built Stonehenge. The Romans built towns and roads and established their capital at "Londinium." The Celtic natives, consisting of Gaels, Picts, and Scots, were not subdued so easily in Scotland and Wales. The Romans built Hadrian's Wall near the Scottish border to consolidate their rule in the troublesome north. Even today, the Celtic language and influence are strongest in these far reaches of Britain.

As Rome fell, so fell Roman Britain, a victim of invaders and internal troubles. Barbarian tribes from Germany and Denmark, called Angles and Saxons, swept through the southern part of the island, establishing Angle-land. These were the days of the real King Arthur, possibly a Christianized Roman general fighting valiantly, but in vain, against invading barbarians. The island was plunged into five hundred years of Dark Ages—wars, plagues, and poverty—lit only by the dim candle of a few learned Christian monks and missionaries trying to convert the barbarians. The sightseer sees little from this Saxon period.

Modern England began with yet another invasion. William the Conqueror and his Norman troops crossed the English Channel from France in 1066. William crowned himself king in Westminster Abbey (where all subsequent coronations would take place) and began building the Tower of London. French-speaking Norman kings ruled the country for two centuries. Then followed two centuries of civil wars, with various noble families vying for the crown. In one of the most bitter feuds, the York and Lancaster families fought the War of the Roses, so-called because of the white and red flowers the combatants chose as their symbols. Battles, intrigues, kings, nobles, and ladies imprisoned and executed in the Tower—it's a wonder the country survived its rulers.

England was finally united by the "third-party" Tudor family. Henry VIII, a Tudor, was England's Renaissance king. He was handsome, athletic, highly sexed, a poet, a scholar, and a musician. He was also arrogant, cruel, gluttonous, and paranoid. He went through six wives in 40 years, divorcing, imprisoning, or beheading them when they no longer suited his needs.

Henry also "divorced" England from the Catholic Church, establishing the Protestant Church of England (the Anglican Church) and setting in motion years of religious squabbles. He also "dissolved" the monasteries (around 1540), leaving just the shells of many formerly glorious abbeys dotting the countryside and pocketing their land and wealth for the Crown.

Henry's daughter, Queen Elizabeth I, who reigned for 45 years, made England a great trading and naval power (defeating the Spanish Armada) and presided over the Elizabethan era of great writers (such as Shakespeare) and scientists (Francis Bacon).

The long-standing quarrel between England's "divine right" kings and nobles in Parliament finally erupted into a civil war (1643). Parliament forces under the Protestant Puritan farmer Oliver Cromwell defeated—and beheaded—King Charles I. This civil war left its mark on much of what you'll see in England. Eventually, Parliament invited Charles' son to take the throne. This "restoration of the monarchy" was accompanied by a great colonial expansion and the rebuilding of London (including Christopher Wren's St. Paul's Cathedral), which had been devastated by the Great Fire of 1666.

Britain grew as a naval superpower, colonizing and trading with all parts of the globe. Her naval superiority ("Britannia rules the waves") was secured by Admiral Nelson's victory over Napoleon's fleet at the Battle of Trafalgar in 1805, while Lord Wellington stomped Napoleon on land at Waterloo. Nelson and

Wellington—both buried in London's St. Paul's—are memorialized by many arches, columns, and squares throughout England.

Economically, Britain led the world into the industrial age with her mills, factories, coal mines, and trains. By the time of Queen Victoria's reign (1837–1901), Britain was at the zenith of power with a colonial empire that covered one-fifth of the world.

The 20th century has not been kind to Britain. Two world wars devastated the population. The Nazi blitzkrieg reduced much of London to rubble. The colonial empire has dwindled to almost nothing, and Britain is no longer an economic superpower. The "Irish Troubles" are constant as the Catholic inhabitants of British-ruled Northern Ireland fight for the independence their southern neighbors won decades ago. The war over the Falkland Islands in 1982 showed how little of the British Empire is left, but also how determined the British are to hang on to what remains.

But the tradition (if not the substance) of greatness continues, presided over by Queen Elizabeth II, her husband Prince Philip, and Prince Charles. With economic problems, the turmoil of Charles and the late Princess Diana, the Fergie fiasco, and a relentless popular press, the royal family is having a tough time. But the queen has stayed above it all and most British people still jump at an opportunity to see royalty. With the death of Princess Diana and the historic outpouring of grief, it's clear that the concept of royalty is alive and well as Britain enters the third millennium.

Britain's Royal Families

802–1066	Saxon and Danish kings
1066–1154	Norman invasion, Norman kings (William the Conqueror)
1154–1399	Plantagenet
1399–1461	Lancaster
1462–1485	York
1485–1603	Tudor (Henry VIII, Elizabeth I)
1603–1649	Stuart (with civil war and beheading of Charles I)
1649–1659	Commonwealth, Cromwell, no royal head of state
1660–1714	Stuart restoration of monarchy
1714–1901	Hanover (four Georges, Victoria)
1901–1910	Edward VII
1910–present	Windsor (George V, Edward VII, George VI, Elizabeth II)

British TV

British television is so good—and so British—that it deserves a mention as a sight-seeing treat. After a long day of museum-going, watch the telly over a pot of tea in your room.

England has five channels. BBC-1 and BBC-2 are government regulated, commercial free, and traditionally highbrow. Channels 3, 4, and 5 are private, a little more Yankee, and they have commercials—but those commercials are clever and sophisticated and provide a fun look at England. Broadcasting is funded by an £80-per-year-per-household tax. Hmmm, 35 cents per day to escape commercials and public-television pledge drives.

Britian is about to leap into the digital age ahead of the rest of the TV-watching world. Ultimately every house will enjoy literally hundreds of high-definition channels with no need for cable or satellites.

Whereas California "accents" fill our airwaves 24 hours a day, homogenizing the way our country speaks, England protects and promotes its regional accents by its choice of TV and radio announcers. Commercial-free British TV is looser than it used to be but still careful about what it airs and when.

American shows (such as *Frasier* and *ER*) are very popular. Be sure to tune your TV to a few typical English shows, including the top-notch BBC evening news and a dose of English situation and political comedy fun. Quiz shows are taken very seriously here. Michael Parkinson is the Johnny Carson of Britain for late-night talk. For a tear-filled slice-of-life taste of British soap dealing in all the controversial issues, see the popular *Brookside*, *Coronation Street*, or *Eastenders*.

Benny Hill comedy has become politically incorrect but is rumored to be coming back. And if you like Monty Python–type comedy, you've come to the right place.

Let's Talk Telephones

Here's a primer on making direct calls. For information specific to London and Britain, see "Telephones" in the Introduction.

Dialing Direct

Calling between Countries: First dial the international access code, then the country code, the area code (if it starts with zero, drop the zero), and the local number.

Calling Long Distance within a Country: First dial the area code (including its zero), then the local number.

Europe's Exceptions: France, Italy, Spain, Portugal, Norway, and Denmark have dispensed with area codes entirely. To make an international call to these countries, dial the international access code (usually 00), the country code (see chart below), and then the local number in its entirety (OK, so there's one exception: for France, drop the initial zero of the local number). To make long-distance calls within any of these countries, simply dial the local number.

International Access Codes

When dialing direct, first dial the international access code of the country you're calling from. For the United States and Canada, it's 011. Virtually all European countries use "00" as their international access code; the only major exception is Finland (990).

Country Codes

After you've dialed the international access code, dial the code of the country you're calling.

Austria: 43	Finland: 358	Norway: 47
Belgium: 32	France: 33	Portugal: 351
Britain: 44	Germany: 49	Spain: 34
Canada:1	Greece: 30	Sweden: 46
Czech Republic: 420	Ireland: 353	Switzerland: 41
Denmark: 45	Italy: 39	United States: 1
Estonia: 372	Netherlands: 31	

Telephone Directory

Understand the various prefixes: 0891 numbers are telephone sex–type expensive. Prefixes 0345 and 0845 are local calls nationwide. And 0800 numbers are toll free. If you have questions about a prefix, call 100 for free help.

Useful Numbers in Britain

- Emergency Services (police or ambulance): 999
- Operator Services: 100
- Directory Assistance: 192 (free from phone booth, otherwise expensive)
- International Directory Information: 153 (80p); Assistance: 155
- Embassies: U.S.—020/7499-9000, Canadian—020/7258-6600

Emergencies and Medical Problems

- Ambulance: 999
- Hospital With 24-Hour Service: Royal Free Hospital, Pond Street, tube: Belsize Park, tel. 020/7794-0500.
- Nonemergency Medical Services: Great Chapel Street Medical Centre, 13 Great Chapel Street, tube: Tottenham Court Road, tel. 020/7437-9360.
- Dental Emergencies: Referral service, Mon–Fri 8:45–13:00, 14:00–15:30, tel. 020/7955-2186.

Train Information

- Train info for anywhere within Britain: 0345-484-950.
- Eurostar (Chunnel Info): 0990-186-186
- Train and Boats to Europe Info: 0990-848-848

London's Airports and Airlines
Heathrow
- General Information: 020/8759-4321 (transfers to airport, arrivals, airline phone numbers, etc.)
- Air Canada: 020/8745-6584, 0990-247-226
- American: 0345-789-789, 020/8750-1048
- British Air: 0345-222-111, 020/8759-5511, automated departure info: 0990-444-000
- British Midlands: 0870-607-0555, 020/8745-7321, 01332/854-000
- SAS: 020/8750-7675, 0845-607-2772
- United Airlines: 0845-844-4777, 0800-888-555
- Air Lingus: 0845-307-7777

Gatwick
General Information: 01293/535-353 for all airlines except British Airways (0990-444-000).

Stansted
Ryanair (cheap fares): 0541/569-569

Car Rental Agencies (at Heathrow)
Avis: 020/8899-1000
Budget: 020/8759-2216
Europcar: 020/8897-0811
Hertz: 020/8897-2072
National: 020/8897-3232

Climate
The chart below gives average daytime temperatures and average number of days with more than a trickle of rain.

	J	F	M	A	M	J	J	A	S	O	N	D
London												
	43	44	50	56	62	69	71	71	66	58	51	45
	15	13	11	12	11	11	12	11	13	14	15	15
Edinburgh												
	42	43	46	51	56	62	65	64	60	54	48	44
	17	15	15	14	14	15	17	16	16	17	17	18

Numbers and Stumblers
- Europeans write a few of their numbers differently than we do. 1 = 1 , 4 = 4 , 7 = 7 . Learn the difference or miss your train.
- In Europe, dates appear as day/month/year, so Christmas is 25-12-00.

- Commas are decimal points and decimals commas. A dollar and a half is 1,50 and there are 5.280 feet in a mile.
- When pointing, use your whole hand, palm downward.
- When counting with fingers, start with your thumb. If you hold up your first finger to request one item, you'll probably get two.
- What we Americans call the second floor of a building is the first floor in Europe.
- Europeans keep the left "lane" open for passing on escalators and moving sidewalks. Keep to the right.
- And please… don't call your waist pack a "fanny pack."

Weights and Measures (approximate)

1 British pint = 1.2 U.S. pints
1 imperial gallon = 1.2 U.S. gallons or about 5 liters
1 stone = 14 pounds (a 168-pound person weighs 12 stone)
28 degrees Centigrade = 82 degrees Fahrenheit
Shoe sizes = about .5 to 1.5 sizes smaller than in United States

British-Yankee Vocabulary

advert advertisement

afters dessert

anticlockwise counterclock-wise

aubergine eggplant

Balloons Belgians

banger sausage

bangers and mash sausage and mashed potatoes

bank holiday legal holiday

bap hamburger-type bun

ben Scottish for mountain

billion ten of our billions (a million million)

biro ballpoint pen

biscuit cookie

black pudding sausage made from dried blood

bloke man, guy

bobby policeman ("copper" is more common)

Bob's your uncle there you go (with a shoulder shrug), naturally

bomb success

bonnet car hood

boot car trunk

BR British Rail

braces suspenders

bridle way path for walkers, bikers, and horse riders

BTA British Tourist Authority

bubble and squeak cold meat fried with cabbage and potatoes

bum bottom or "backside"

candy floss cotton candy

car boot sale temporary flea market with car trunk displays

caravan trailer

cat's eyes reflectors on the road

cheap and nasty cheap and bad quality (pay monkeys, get peanuts)

cheeky (or saucy) smart alecky

cheerio goodbye

cheers thanks (also, a toast)

chemist pharmacist

chips French fries

chock-a-block jam-packed

cider alcoholic apple cider

clearway road where you can't stop

coach long-distance bus
concession discounted admission
courgette zucchini
courier tour escort or guide
crisps potato chips
cuppa cup of tea
dear expensive
digestives round graham crackers
dinner lunch or dinner
diversion detour
draughts checkers
drawing pin thumbtack
dual carriageway divided highway (four lanes)
face flannel washcloth
fag cigarette
fagged exhausted
faggot meatball
fanny vagina
fell mountain, hill, or high plain
first floor second floor
flat apartment
football soccer
force waterfall (lake district)
fortnight two weeks
Frogs French people
Full Monty The whole shabang. Everything.
gallery balcony
gallon 1.2 American gallons
gangway aisle
gaol jail (same pronunciation)
garden yard
give way yield
glen narrow valley
goods wagon freight truck
grammar school high school
half eight 8:30 (not 7:30)
heath open land without trees
holiday vacation
homely likeable or cozy
hoover vacuum cleaner

hundredweight 112 pounds
ice lolly popsicle
ironmonger hardware store
jelly Jell-O
Joe Bloggs John Doe
jumble sale, rummage sale
jumper sweater
keep your pecker up be brave
kiosk booth
kipper smoked herring
knackered exhausted
knickers ladies' panties
knocking shop brothel
knock up wake up or visit
let rent
loo toilet or bathroom
lorry truck
mac macintosh coat, raincoat
mate buddy, friend
mean stingy
mews courtyard stables, often used as cottages
minced meat hamburger meat
nappy diaper
natter talk and talk
neat a straight drink
nosh food or eat
nought zero
off license liquor store or a place selling take-away liquor
take away to go
pasty crusted savory (usually meat) pie
pavement sidewalk
petrol gas
pissed (rude), paralytic, bevvied, sloshed, wellied, popped up, ratted, "pissed as a newt" drunk
pillar box postbox
pitch playing field
plaster Band-Aid
poppers (or press studs) snaps
pram baby carriage

public convenience public toilets

put a sock in it shut up

queue line

queue jump crowd in line

queue up line up

quid pound (money, worth about $1.70)

randy horny

redundant, made fired or laid off

return ticket round-trip

ring up call (telephone)

rubber eraser

sanitary towel sanitary napkin/pad

sausage roll sausage wrapped in a flaky pastry

Scotch egg hard-boiled egg wrapped in sausage meat

self-catering accommodation with kitchen facilities, rented by the week

sellotape Scotch tape

serviette napkin

single ticket one-way ticket

smalls underwear

snogging kissing and cuddling

solicitor lawyer

stone 14 pounds (weight)

subway underground pedestrian passageway

suss out figure out

swede rutabaga

sweet dessert

sweets candy

ta thank you

taxi rank taxi stand

tea towel dish towel

telly TV

theater live stage

tick a check mark

tight as a fish's bum cheapskate (watertight)

tipper lorry dump truck

tin can

to let for rent

top hole first rate

topping excellent

top up refill a drink

torch flashlight

towpath path along a river or canal

tube subway

twee quaint, cute

underground subway

VAT value added tax

verge grassy edge of road

wellingtons, wellies rubber boots

wee urinate

whacked exhausted

witter on gab and gab

yob hooligan

zebra crossing crosswalk

zed the letter "z"

THE BEST OF GREAT BRITAIN IN 22 DAYS

Day 1: Arrive in London

Day 2: London

Day 3: London

Day 4: Stonehenge, Bath

Day 5: Bath

Day 6: Glastonbury, Wells

Day 7: South Wales, Folk Museum

Day 8: Cotswold villages, Blenheim

Day 9: Stratford, Warwick Castle, Coventry

Day 10: Industrial Revolution Museum

Day 11: North Wales, Snowdonia, Caernarfon Castle, Medieval Banquet

Day 12: Blackpool

Day 13: Lake District

Day 14: Lake District

Day 15: Scottish West Coast

Day 16: Highlands, Loch Ness

Day 17: Edinburgh

Day 18: Edinburgh

Day 19: Hadrian's Wall, Durham Cathedral, Beamish Folk Museum

Day 20: Moors, York

Day 21: York

Day 22: Cambridge, back to London

For all the specifics, see *Rick Steves' Great Britain & Ireland 2000.*

Road Scholar Feedback for London

We're all in the same travelers' school of hard knocks. Your feedback helps us improve this guidebook for future travelers. Please fill this out (or use the on-line version at www.ricksteves.com/feedback), include more info or any tips/favorite discoveries if you like, and send it to us. As thanks for your help, we'll send you our quarterly travel newsletter free for one year. Thanks! **Rick**

Of the recommended accommodations/restaurants used, which was:

Best _____

      Why? _____

Worst _____

      Why? _____

Of the sights/experiences/destinations recommended by this book, which was:

Most overrated _____

      Why? _____

Most underrated _____

      Why? _____

Best ways to improve this book:

_____

I'd like a free newsletter subscription:

_____ Yes _____ No _____ Already on list

_____
Name

_____
Address

_____
City, State, Zip

_____
E-mail Address

Please send to: ETBD, Box 2009, Edmonds, WA 98020

Jubilee 2000—Let's Celebrate the Millennium by Forgiving Third World Debt

Let's ring in the millennium by convincing our government to forgive the debt owed to us by the world's poorest countries. Imagine spending over half your income on interest payments alone. You and I are creditors and poor countries owe us more than they can pay.

Jubilee 2000 is a worldwide movement of concerned people and groups—religious and secular—working to cancel the international debts of the poorest countries by the year 2000.

Debt ruins people: In the poorest countries, money needed for health care, education, and other vital services is diverted to interest payments.

Mozambique, with a per capita income of $90 and life expectancy of 40, spends over half its national income on interest. This poverty brings social unrest, civil war, and often costly humanitarian intervention by the U.S.A. To chase export dollars, desperate countries ruin their environment. As deserts grow and rain forests shrink, the world suffers. Of course, the real suffering is among local people born long after some dictator borrowed (and squandered) that money. As interest is paid, entire populations go hungry.

Who owes what and why? Mozambique is one of 41 countries defined by the World Bank as "Heavily Indebted Poor Countries." In total, they owe $200 billion. Because these debts are unlikely to be paid, their market value is only a tenth of the face value (about $20 billion). The U.S.A.'s share is under $2 billion.

How can debt be canceled? This debt is owed mostly to the U.S.A., Japan, Germany, Britain, and France either directly or through the World Bank. We can forgive the debt owed directly to us and pay the market value (usually 10 percent) of the debts owed to the World Bank. We have the resources. (Norway, another wealthy creditor nation, just unilaterally forgave its Third World debt.) All America needs is the political will . . . people power.

While many of these poor nations are now democratic, corruption is still a concern. A key to Jubilee 2000 is making certain that debt relief reduces poverty in a way that benefits ordinary people: women, farmers, children, and so on.

Let's celebrate the new millennium by giving poor countries a break. For the sake of peace, fragile young democracies, the environment, and countless real people, forgiving this debt is the right thing for us in the rich world to do.

Tell Washington, D.C.: If our government knows this is what we want, it can happen. Learn more, write letters, lobby legislators, or even start a local Jubilee 2000 campaign. For details, contact Jubilee 2000 (tel. 202/783-3566, www.j2000usa.org). For information on lobbying Congress on J2000, contact Bread for the World (tel. 800/82-BREAD, www.bread.org).

Faxing Your Hotel Reservation

Faxing is more accurate and cheaper than telephoning. Use this handy form for your fax (or find it on-line at www.ricksteves.com /reservation). Photocopy and fax away.

One-Page Fax

To: _____ @ _____
            hotel   **fax**

From: _____ @ _____
            name   **fax**

Today's date: ____ /_____ /_____
                    day   **month**   **year**

Dear Hotel _____,

Please make this reservation for me:

Name: _____

Total # of people: _____   # of rooms: _____   # of nights: _____

Arriving: ____ /_____ /_____   My time of arrival (24-hr clock): _____
              day   **month**   **year**   (I will telephone if I will be late)

Departing: ____ /_____ /_____
                day   **month**   **year**

Room(s): Single___ Double___ Twin___ Triple___ Quad___

With: Toilet___ Shower___ Bath___ Sink only___

Special needs: View___ Quiet___ Cheapest Room___

Credit card: Visa___ MasterCard___ American Express___

Card #: _____

Expiration Date:_____

Name on card: _____

You may charge me for the first night as a deposit. Please fax or mail me confirmation of my reservation, along with the type of room reserved, the price, and whether the price includes breakfast. Thank you.

_____
Signature

_____
Name

_____
Address

_____
City   **State**   **Zip Code**   **Country**

_____
E-mail Address

INDEX

Rick Steves' Postcards from Europe

25 Years of Travel Tales from America's Favorite Guidebook Writer

1978   1998

TRAVEL GURU RICK STEVES has been exploring Europe through the Back Door for 25 years, sharing his tricks and discoveries in guidebooks and on TV. Now, in *Rick Steves' Postcards from Europe*, Rick shares stories—ranging from goofy to inspirational—of his favorite moments and his off-beat European friends.

Postcards takes you on the fantasy trip of a lifetime, and it gives you a close-up look at contemporary Europeans.

You'll meet Marie-Alice, the Parisian restaurateur who sniffs a whiff of moldy cheese and says, "It smells like zee feet of angels." In an Alpine village, meet Olle, the schoolteacher who lets Rick pet his edelweiss, and Walter, who schemes with Rick to create a fake Swiss tradition. In Italy, cruise with Piero through his "alternative Venice" and learn why all Venetian men are mama's boys.

Postcards also tracks Rick's passion for wandering—from his first "Europe-through-the-gutter" trips, through his rocky early tours, to his career as a travel writer and host of a public television series.

These 240 pages of travel tales are told in that funny, down-to-earth style that makes Rick his Mom's favorite guidebook writer.

Rick Steves' Postcards from Europe is available at your local bookstore. To get Rick's free travel newsletter, call (425) 771-8303 or visit www.ricksteves.com. For a free catalog or to order any John Muir Publications book, call (800) 888-7504.